CAMBRAI

CAMBRAI

The First Great Tank Battle
1917

by
A.J. Smithers

LEO COOPER

LONDON

First published in Great Britain in 1992 by
LEO COOPER
190 Shaftesbury Avenue, London WC2H 8JL
an imprint of
Pen & Sword Books Ltd.,
47 Church Street, Barnsley, S. Yorks S70 2AS

Copyright © A. J. Smithers, 1992

ISBN 085052 268 4

A CIP catalogue record for this book is available
from the British Library

Typeset by Yorkshire Web, Barnsley, South Yorkshire
in Plantin Roman 10 point

Printed in Great Britain by
The Redwood Press
Melksham, Wiltshire

CONTENTS

ACKNOWLEDGEMENTS

For anyone minded to write about the Battle of Cambrai there is only one possible point of departure. The Library of the Tank Musem at Bovington Camp has the privilege of owning great quantities of manuscript material, all of it authoritive and, for the most part, written by those who fought there and before memories began to fade. My gratitude to David Fletcher, Librarian and author, transcends all the rest. Not only did he produce far more documents than a single volume can digest but, of his kindness, he found time to read the typescript and discover errors. That, I emphasize, saddles him with no responsibility for the now contents. The Imperial War Musem, the Public Record Office and the Liddell Hart Centre for Military Archives at King's College, London – custodians of the papers of Sir James Edmonds and Sir Launcelot Kiggell – have all been laid under contribution and have been generous with help above the call of duty. The Museums of the Intelligence Corps at Ashford, of the Royal Artillery at the Rotunda, Woolwich, and the Royal Engineers at Chatham all furnished necessary ingredients. In particular, the Corps Library RE, personified by Mrs Magnuson, went to much trouble in disinterring for me all that remains to be known about that early surface-to-surface missile the Livens Projector. The Estate of the late Major-General Sir Edward Spears permitted me to quote from *Prelude to Victory* and *Two Men Who Saved France;* this I much appreciate, for the General was in a class of his own as both actor and chronicler. Lastly, my thanks to faithful friends. To Major Derek Poulsen for reading more than one draft typescript and criticizing all of them; and to Philippa Arnott for once again transmuting heaps of what appeared nothing beyond erasures and corrections into typescript that is a pleasure to read. I would include M. Le Patron of the Hotel de la Paix in Albert were it not for his cook, whom I cannot congratulate.

AUTHOR'S NOTE

Throughout the 1930s the Army organized many Battlefield Tours, in which senior men who had participated could pass on their experiences to the next generation. Brigadier P.C.S. Hobart (in later years Major-General Sir Percy) led one of Tanks Corps officers to Cambrai in 1935. A number of those attending, at Hobart's request, wrote down accounts of what they best remembered; as all of them were still serving they were necessarily anonymous. These, together with much else, were put together under the title *A Narrative Of Cambrai* and ended up in the Library of the Tank Museum at Bovington, by whose kind permission I have drawn upon it. In some instances identification of the memorialists has been possible, but others remain unclaimed. In the following pages various unattributed recollections appear. All these come from Hobart's unfinished book.

In a letter to Sir Basil Liddell Hart written in 1953 Hobart calls it 'this pile of dusty pleas from the dead years. And very little response did they evoke'. Any other possible reader of this book may agree that Brigadier Hobart deserved better fortune, here as in other ways.

'Children of to-day, when reading the great stories of the past, will not thrill to them the less when they remember that deeds as wonderful were performed in their own lifetime by their fathers and their fathers' friends.'

John Buchan
Days to Remember 1922

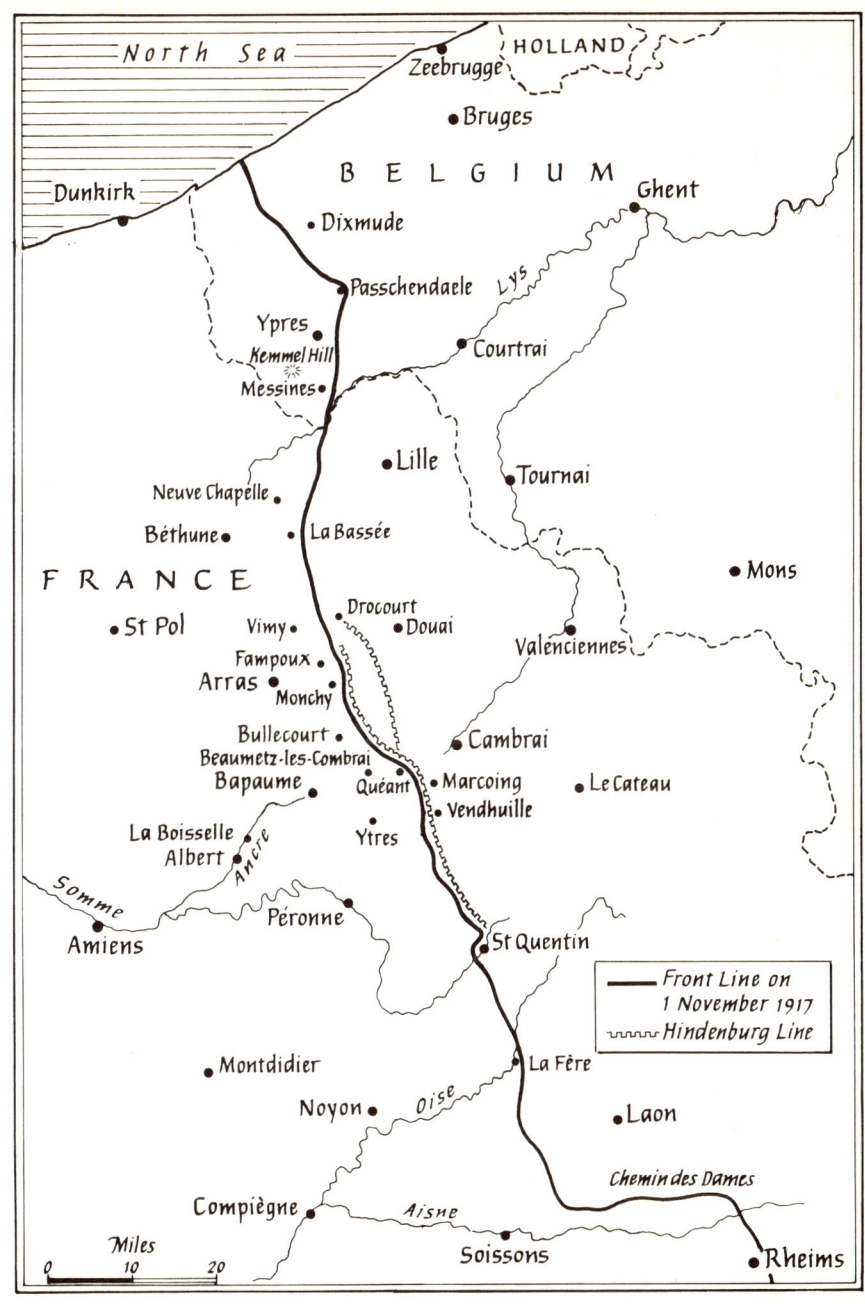

Miles

0 10 20

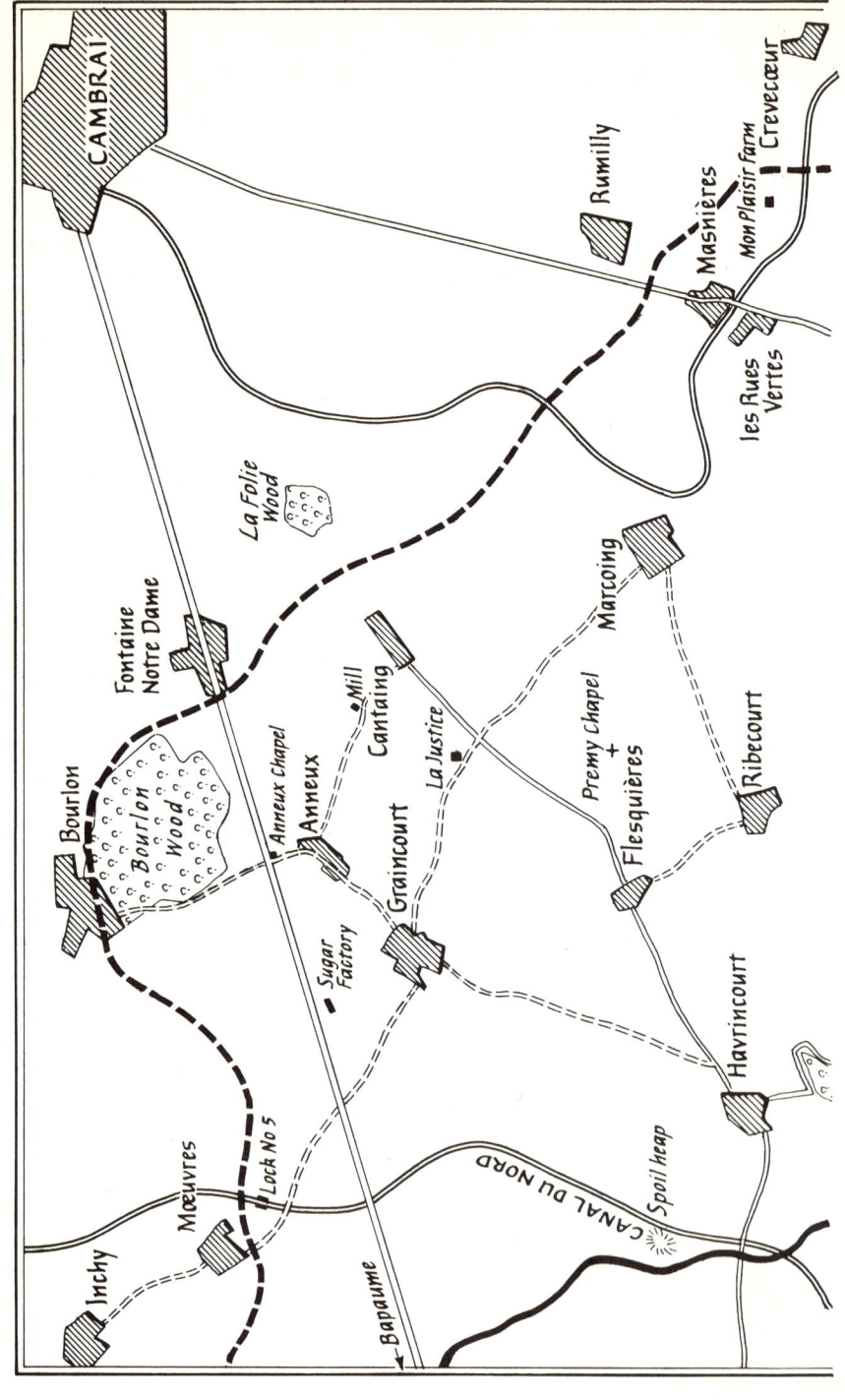

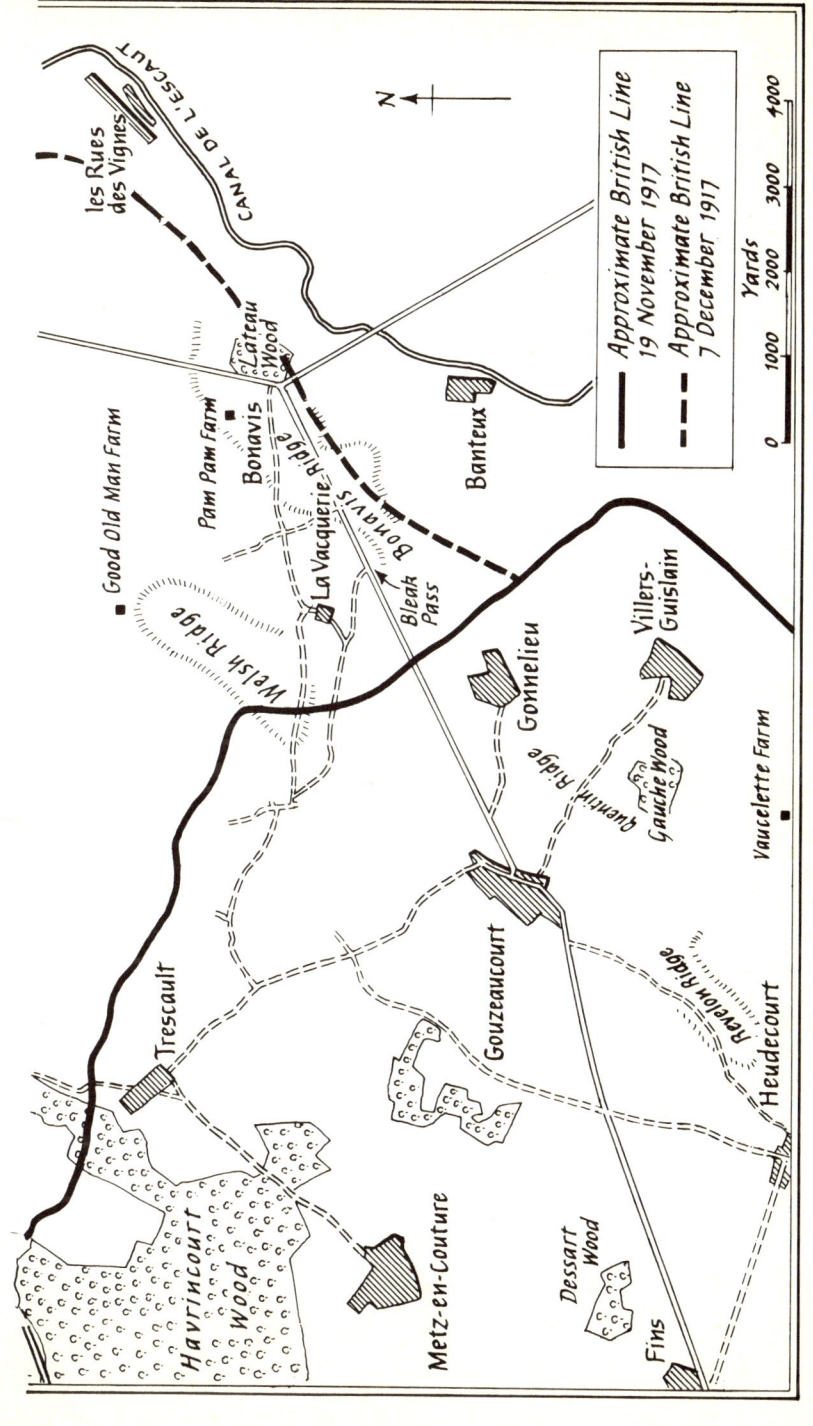

les Rues des Vignes

CANAL DE L'ESCAULT

Good Old Man Farm

Pam Pam Farm

Bonavis

Lateau Wood

Banteux

La Vacquerie Ridge

Bleak Pass

Bonavis Ridge

Welsh Ridge

Gonnelieu

Villers-Guislain

Quentin Ridge

Gauche Wood

Vaucelette Farm

Trescault

Gouzeaucourt

Revelon Ridge

Heudecourt

Havrincourt Wood

Metz-en-Couture

Dessart Wood

Fins

N

Approximate British Line
19 November 1917

Approximate British Line
7 December 1917

Yards

0   1000   2000   3000   4000

INTRODUCTION

By THE SUMMER OF 1914 armies seemed to have come a long way forward since Napoleon and the Duke; it was, in reality, only a matter of degree. The Americans in their Civil War had introduced repeating rifles and a serviceable machine gun. On the fringes there were new things, motor lorries and ambulances all with solid tyres; overhead flew, slowly and uncertainly, those machines that General Foch had marked down as good sport but no good for war. Armies remained, as they had been for a long time, the triumvirate of horse, foot and guns. The greatest of these was the horse. It was the shock arm, carrying everything before it by speed and weight; it hauled backward-pointing guns to battle and it carried all officers of all arms save the most junior infantry subalterns. The horse was the army; lacking it, there would be nothing. The panache had been pulled about a little in South Africa. A sapper officer, who could not be expected to have a proper appreciation of such things, had ended a long guerrilla by herding the enemy between little corrugated iron affairs called blockhouses and great quantities of barbed wire. This, one hoped, would never be repeated.

When the word was given, armies walked and rode towards the battle at an easy pace. They encountered each other, the machine guns raised their voices and all disappeared into the earth. The Germans, who had started it, occupied substantial parts of France from which they would have to be expelled. For the next three years the best men of their generation went to their death or suffered cruel wounds for that end. It slowly dawned upon those at the head of affairs that something new was needed if the war was not to go on for ever and destroy Christian civilization in its entirety.

The new thing came, the machine that would, mercifully, put an end to the use of the warhorse and demonstrate how a few men with a superior science could overcome multitudes without it. That bald statement is accurate enough, but it tells only a part of the tale. Old military qualities, the qualities that put so many battle honours on regimental colours, were still needed as much as ever. In addition there came a call for skills not to be found in the armies led by officers commissioned by Queen Victoria. This is an attempt to tell how they were, after much grief, combined together to bring about victory in the west. If one may speak of a theatre of war, then this battle – Cambrai – was the dress rehearsal. All subsequent productions, even to the Gulf, have taken their tone from it.

I have made no attempt to describe every action of every formation, unit and sub-unit. There can be few people now who would seek information about the doings of high-numbered battalions that have all gone the way of the Saxon fyrd and Elizabethan trained bands. And '*tout expliquer, c'est tout ennuyer*'. The Official Historian, true to his office, recounts it all, both friend and foe alike. There is a place for both the miniature and the mural.

A NOTE ON ABBREVIATIONS

THE BRITISH ARMY STAFF has always been a triumvirate. The side dealing with plans and operations is necessarily predominant, even if said to be only *primus inter pares*. This is the General Staff, 'G'. The Adjutant-General — 'A' — is responsible for men; finding them, training them, organizing them, disciplining them, promoting and posting them. The Quartermaster-General — 'Q' — for the last 100 years has been reduced to a mere purveyor of everything an army needs. 'I' — Intelligence — is a fairly recent creation forming a part of 'G' but not under its orders. Its function is, first, to get and distribute all possible information about the enemy, his strength, identity and his intentions; second, it must watch over the state of our own troops and keep their commanders informed about their plight or condition. 'G', 'A' and 'Q' are represented by officers, decreasing in rank with every step down, from the War Office to Divisions. In Brigades 'A' and 'Q' are amalgamated.

CHAPTER ONE

'Another year! — Another deadly blow!
Another mighty Empire overthrown!
And we are left, or shall be left, alone.'

William Wordsworth

1917 WAS, BEYOND DOUBT, the worst year of the war for the allies; in particular it was the worst for the British Empire. It witnessed the beginning of the break-up of nations, for the war had got out of hand and was taking on a life of its own. The numbered years that had just gone seemed each to have had its own personality. 1914 had been Rupert Brooke's, beginning with the flower of a generation queueing up at the recruiting offices and ending with the scar across the face of Europe running from Alps to North Sea. Still seen only dimly was the brutal truth that this country might have bitten off more than it could chew. But the retreats were over and Germany's victims were still in the field. Techniques for the attack on entrenched positions, seemingly the only way of winning, were now moving away from those taught in the little red and brown manuals so recently published in Aldershot. Major-General Sir Edward Spears , who saw it all, made the first battles sound Napoleonic; he tells of General Franchet d'Esperey, riding in red and blue at the head of his Staff, watching his regiments as, with Colours flying and bands thumping out *La Marseillaise*, they marched straight at the Germans. '*Eh bien, M. le Professeur à l'Ecole de Guerre, que pensez-vous de cette mouvement ça?*', he called out to the lugubrious General Pétain. The answer might well have been 'I am witnessing ancient history. Never again shall such things be'.

On our own sector the attacks launched in 1915, from Aubers Ridge in March to Loos in September, had all gone to show that the BEF, though it could hold its positions, was nowhere near capable of defeating the German army by the then method of making war. In spite of that there was ground for hope; we were learning fairly quickly, our weapons were becoming better and more plentiful and 1916 would bring the great victory to end it all.

There was no mystery about how the business had to be done. It was all a matter of guns. Bring in as many guns as could be found, the bigger the better, smash down the enemy's defences and the infantry would be able to walk forward and take the bayonet to him. In order to achieve this, big guns were borrowed from both the Navy and the defended ports, mounted on traction-engine wheels and dragged, for the most part by animals, into position. The Royal Flying Corps, still a part of the Army, would direct their fire as best it could by wireless and other means. Thus the very latest advanced technology would be applied to war and the battle would be fought scientifically. When it began on 1 July, 1916, the result was not what had been predicted. The guns would not remove the wire nor were they yet powerful enough to make well-constructed trench systems untenable. This was a tough generation, capable of taking casualties even on a fearful scale without whimpering or becoming hysterical. Nevertheless, *The Times List of Fallen Officers* – 'all Second Lieutenants unless otherwise stated' – made agonizing reading. No country could go on destroying the best of its young men in such a fashion. Both amongst the fighting men, who had a freemasonry of their own, those whose business it was to furnish them with better weapons and the remainder who were helpless bystanders the cry went up. There must be a better way than this. Men should never be obliged to march across the open, quite unprotected, and offer their chests to the barbed wire, the machine gun and the shrapnel shell. A kind of armoured tractor, tentatively called a tank, had certainly put in an appearance on the Somme but its numbers had been small, the experience of its crews slight, its reliability uncertain and its future equally so. Hardly anybody knew anything about it for it had been produced by civilians mostly camouflaged as sailors.

The months following the Somme were those in which war-weariness flourished. The bitter winter, one of the coldest and longest on record, made peace on any sort of reasonable terms seem a consummation devoutly to be wished. The first move came from the Kaiser in December, 1916, but it amounted to something much like a demand for surrender and was very properly rejected. Lord Lansdowne, the young Emperor Karl, successor to Francis Joseph, President Wilson and the Pope all tried their best to bring an end to the slaughter on honourable terms. The war, which seemed almost a living thing, was too strong for them. In February, 1917, the German Government took two serious decisions. The first, undoubtedly sensible, was to withdraw from the large and dangerous salient between Arras and Soissons to a prepared fortified line on which work had been concentrated for some time. Once there, in an inexpugnable position, battered formations could be rested and low-grade ones employed to free the others for offensives somewhere else. The second decision, to begin unrestricted submarine warfare, was more of a gamble. It would probably bring the United States into the war but that need not be too alarming. By the time America had raised, trained and equipped an army worth having Britain might have been starved into surrender and the armies in France would be monstrous irrelevances. The gamble nearly succeeded. Germany's submarine fleet had multiplied fivefold during the past year. The loss of British merchant ships during the last months of 1916 had averaged 300,000 tons. In February, 1917, it rose to 468,000 and in April, surely the most frightening month of the war, it rocketed to 875,000. There remained exactly six weeks' supply of corn in the Kingdom. The same month witnessed the entry of the USA into the war, not as an ally but as an Associate Power. The first intimation of this came, most effectively, at sea. It was the extra destroyers under the Stars and Stripes that made possible the convoy system. By September the sinkings had come down to less than 200,000 tons. In addition to making up and protecting convoys the Lords of the Admiralty decided that the time had come for the soldiers to smoke out the pirates' lairs along the Flanders coast. It was something that needed doing but it came near to breaking the British army.

Much was to happen, however, before that operation could even reach the planning stage. At the end of 1916 and the beginning of 1917 the French army, its prestige more than restored by Verdun, remained senior partner in the West. The actual battlefront had shifted north, into the bailiwick of Sir John French's successor, Sir Douglas Haig. Whatever criticism may be made of the first of the Somme battles, the last ones were very different. The BEF was more professional now and looked like being able to acquire local mastery of the field. This was not generally understood, least of all at home, and civilian enthusiasm for war was not whipped up by the coldest, wettest, darkest and windiest winter that anyone could remember. Twenty-seven continuous days of frost, from 19 January to 17 February, did nothing to lift the spirits of a tired and hungry population. For soldiers in or near the line this was only a beginning. March and April added heavy snow to the burdens of trench life, but at least they were the same for both sides. It still brought no end to the battles. General Gough's offensive on the Ancre in January turned the frozen ground to advantage and his Fifth Army advanced four miles with only light casualties. This was the deciding factor that compelled General Ludendorff to accelerate his plans for a move back to the still incomplete fortifications known to the British as the Hindenburg Line.

March had been the time of the beginning of revolution in Russia. It had not worried the Allies in the West nearly as much as it should have done, for Kerensky was reckoned sound in carrying on the war and nobody had much time for Tsar Nicholas. Revolution or no, an Eastern Front still existed and would keep many German divisions occupied for a long time to come. Worrying reports were seeping out of Italy but, in April, only a few realized quite how badly matters were going there.

In the air things were very serious indeed. The Royal Flying Corps, in the early years, had one task only, and that one of tremendous importance. In country where the Army was without any heights of land from which its gunners could observe the fall of their shells the airmen were the artillery's eyes. Every other activity was subordinate to spotting and photographing. In the nature of things, aeroplanes thus engaged were vulnerable and unable to protect themselves against those of the enemy. The business of the machine-gun-armed aircraft was to fight off these intruders and, inevitably, success depended in large part upon the quality of the equipment provided by Governments. In 1915 advantage had passed to Germany. The Fokker Scout, with the great benefit of an interrupter gear enabling its gun to fire forwards without blasting the propellor, was better than anything the British or French could muster. Until the Constantinescu gear became available the RFC was restricted to 'pusher' aircraft such as the FE2b or such slightly better machines as could be got from France. By the time of the Somme battles in 1916 the RFC was once more on top, but the omens were not good. On 17 September new German equipment appeared, a formation of Albatrosses under command of Oswald Boelcke. Fourteen British 2-seaters were on their way to attack the railway station at Marcoing. Eight were shot down. By the end of October the RFC had lost eighty-eight aircraft against the German twelve. By January, 1917, affairs had reached such a pitch that General Trenchard was writing to the Director of Air Organization that 'You are asking me to fight the battles this year with the same machines as I fought it last year. We shall be hopelessly outclassed and something must be done.' It was a state of affairs with which British armies were to become well acquainted. The RFC owned a motley collection of about 750 aircraft of one kind and other; the German Imperial Air Service mustered about one-third of that number but of far better quality. The RFC never fought more like heroes than in the spring days of 1917 when 18-year-olds with a dozen or so flying hours behind them took off daily in their wretched machines with full knowledge that they would probably never see the Mess again. During the Arras battle, when the Canadians moved through the snow to take Vimy Ridge, the RFC never failed in its army co-operation work; it was made possible by the same tactics as were to be used by the next generation. As four or five British tanks were then to be needed to take on a single German, so did the RFC swamp the sky with everything flyable, forming aerial laagers around the spotters. The pendulum would swing again in a few months. For Boelcke and Richtofen (and for Herman Goering, then a decent-enough young flying officer before he went slumming) the RFC was about to field Ball and Bishop and the Albatros and Halberstadt were going to be taken on by the Bristol Fighter and the SE 5. In the late spring and early summer of 1917 this seemed like a dream.

The Imperial German Air Service seemed in England to be having things far too much its own way. The great Zeppelin raid of 13 October, 1915, when Breithaupt appeared to be quite deliberately bombing the Lyceum, Strand and − worst of all − the Gaiety theatres, killing 71 and wounding 128 in the process, seemed long ago. There had been other Zeppelin raids since but they had fallen off and were unalarming. Then, on a bright summer's day on 13 June, 1917, the citizens of London were outraged by the sight of twenty-odd huge aircraft with black crosses on their wings flying in formation over London and bombing the City at their ease. The *Manchester Guardian* correspondent, Francis Perrot, spoke for all civilians: 'Everyone's instinctive feeling was that with this magnificent target our airmen and anti-aircraft guns combined could hardly fail to destroy some of the raiders over London. But they persisted in their course and flew away. The feeling is unanimous that the steady flight of an air-fleet over London is a thing which should have been prevented and ought never to be allowed to happen again.' It did happen again, on 7 July. The combined casualty list amounted to 192 killed and 672 wounded.

Such was the state of affairs when the general line to be adopted for the battles of 1917 came up for discussion. Lord Kitchener, alone amongst men, had predicted that the war would last for three years and that by 1917 the British Army should be at the peak of its strength, whereas that of France would be on the downgrade. He was perfectly right on all counts.

There was no shortage of despondency. Everybody knew that, as Sir Henry Rawlinson put it, 'the Boche was up to something'. In a vague way it was supposed that he was busy straightening out an untidy line; by no means everybody grasped the magnitude of what was going on and hardly anybody suspected the abomination of desolation Germany was painstakingly making out of abandoned French land. The Somme had by no means put paid to the British Army's aggressiveness and some new attack, probably in concert with the French, was generally expected before the summer. Mr Lloyd George, now Prime Minister, found himself captivated by the achievements and personality of General Robert Nivelle to a greater degree than anybody save only the General himself. Against all military advice he did his best to contrive that the King's Army and its experienced Commander-in-Chief should be degraded to the status of a subordinate formation under the orders of a junior foreign General answerable only to the Cabinet of another country. Had Madame Nivelle, the General's mother, not been an Englishwoman who had taught him to speak her language as she did herself this would probably never have happened. Mr Lloyd George was no polyglot. The mutual contempt and loathing between him and Sir Douglas Haig were hardly secrets but those at the head of military affairs still could not fathom the Prime Minister's reasons. Major-General Sir Edward Spears, then liaison officer attached to the French Sixth and Tenth Armies, explained it long afterwards. 'After the war I consulted Sir William Robertson (CIGS in 1917) on this point, and he told me that the Prime Minister was very alarmed at the time by the progress of pacifist tendencies in England whether the country would hold out.' *'Pourvu que les civils tiennent,'* as the famous cartoon put it, was not that funny in England. The Army, though increasingly made up of conscripts, was of sterner stuff than its political leaders. Of the new pressed men Captain Charles Carrington of the Royal Warwicks remarked that the first batch were much like the others, young men who would probably have volunteered anyway as soon as their birthdays came round.

By early 1917 the French Army with 101 active divisions still remained by far the biggest of the allied forces in the West. Much of it was deployed along the quiet parts of the line, in Alsace and thereabouts, where nothing much was expected to happen nor ever did. In Joffre's time there had been an unspoken recognition of the facts of life; the junior partner must conform to the wishes of the senior. As he and Sir Douglas had worked on much the same lines and had genuine respect for each other this had presented no insuperable difficulties. The arrival of Nivelle, however, put paid to all that. In an effort to build up the size of the BEF the call went out for more troops for France. Six new Divisions arrived in January and February. The 42nd, from Egypt, was the best of them. In 1914 it had been the East Lancashire Territorial Division and escaped being shunted off to India by being caught up in the Dardanelles campaign.

The other Divisions, 57th (West Lancashire), 58th (London), 59th (West Midlands), 62nd (2nd West Riding) and 66th (2nd East Lancashire) were second-line Territorials made up originally of men who had not volunteered for overseas service. All had been used for draft-finding, the 59th had been in Ireland putting down the rebellion there, and their best friends would not have called them crack troops. When their time came they performed unexpectedly well, but that time was not yet. In April, 1917, their presence brought the BEF up to the respectable total of 64 Divisions. According to GHQ Intelligence on 28 June, 1917, the Kaiser disposed of 157 Divisions in the West plus 66 more in Russia.*

The Division of all arms was Wellington's creation to meet the needs of his Peninsular campaign and its composition had hardly altered since then. In general terms it was made up of three infantry brigades each of four

* There were nine more on the Danube and two in Macedonia.

battalions with four brigades (they call them regiments now) of field artillery, a cavalry squadron for reconnaisance and errands, a couple of Field Companies RE and their usual ancillaries. The first eight of them were all Regular, including reservists, as were the cavalry divisions. For reasons not relevant to this story the 27th, 28th and 29th, notwithstanding their numbers, were Regular also, with some contribution from the Territorial Force. The New Army, or Kitchener, Divisions, being technically regulars enlisted for the duration, began their numbers with 9 and ended with 41. Then came the Territorials which before the war had not carried numbers. From 42 to 56 were the first-line, men who had volunteered to serve anywhere. Three of them, to their disgust, were sent early to India to relieve Regular troops. The second-line, numbered from 57 to 75 (save for 63, provided by the Royal Navy from its surplus sailors and marines) mostly saw overseas service somewhere before the war ended.

Lastly, and claiming pre-eminence over all save the cavalry and left to the end because it was not formed until August, 1915, came the Guards Division. Envied, but not the subject of jealousy because the Army acknowledged this to be the best of them all.

The Divisions, nearly every one with its distinguishing sign, soon became a focus of loyalty almost on a par with that owed to a regiment or corps. Obviously some were better than others; equally, nearly all of them had up and down periods, but every one had a lasting *esprit de corps*. Since the Duke of Wellington's time, however, the Army had acquired new, extra-divisional units. Heavy artillery, gas projectors, tunnelling companies (surely the most dreadful work of all) and all manner of technical troops made up a substantial part of the ration strength but owed allegiance only to higher authority, being sent where they were needed from time to time. All this had been foreseen by Edward Gibbon. After treating of 'military engines' in his exegesis of the Roman Army, he added a footnote. 'We may observe that the use of them in the field gradually became more prevalent, in proportion as personal valour and military skill declined. When men were no longer found, their place was supplied by machines.' Gibbon's theories held water until after the Somme. When battalions went over the bags on 1 July it was standard practice to halt and pick up the dressing before moving forward at the 'High Port'. Why this imbecile practice continued is unclear. Captain Carrington, already quoted and to be quoted again, was one of those who had to endure it. Long ago he remarked to the present writer that he had been taught fire and movement in his school OTC years before having it repeated to him in the 23rd Division under the general direction of Sir Archibald Hunter. Somebody in France knew better. By 1917, belatedly, it had come to be accepted that Captain Gibbon of the Hampshire Grenadiers may have been right once but was now outdated. Artillery and machine guns killed men and men must find better ways of avoiding mass immolation than had so far been discovered.

Artillery had been tried on the Somme and had failed. The great proportion of 'dud' shells, mostly furnished by manufacturers in the USA, and the absence of a fuse that would be effective to burst a shell where needed had combined to leave the defending Germans too active for the infantry to get near them. An armed and armoured agricultural tractor called a tank had been given a trial; it had had local successes but won few converts from the old ways. The gunners must try and do better next time.

The early months of 1917 were dominated on the side of the Allies by the appointment of General Nivelle to supreme command of the French armies. The departure of the under-appreciated General Joffre, to be Marshal of France but with no specific duties, was the handiwork of M. Briand and General Lyautey; the choice of Nivelle was Joffre's own. Spears has his own explanation. Nivelle, a cavalryman, had made himself some sort of a name by carrying out successful operations at Verdun which had caught the imagination of politicians. Joffre had picked him during the brief period when he himself was titular Commander-in-Chief, believing him to be a loyal subordinate and one who would accept the advice of his senior. Seldom had the old Marshal made a greater mistake. Nivelle had allowed his limited and small-scale successes to turn his head. Whatever he might have been before his translation, he now became a man driven by self-satisfaction compounded by the knowledge, slowly growing, of his inadequacy. His idea of the *attaque brusquée* was hardly original; few people attack gently. That apart, he had no contribution to make to advancing the science of war. Joffre, with less than five weeks to go before oblivion claimed him, had agreed with Sir Douglas Haig that the heavy end of the next offensive should be carried by the British Army. This was only fair. The losses of the Somme, mostly infantry, had been made up, the Army was in peak condition, and the French were still bled white by the Verdun slaughter. The German Army too had been badly hammered and was not anxious to be attacked any more in its present positions. It demanded moral courage to pull back into the fortress of the Hindenburg Line but the decision was a wise one. The weather was neutral; frozen ground had made Gough's advances possible but sub-zero February temperatures put paid to anything more ambitious.

The long and unpleasing story of the Nivelle offensive is fascinating but has no place here. Suffice it that the part given to Sir Douglas was 'breaking the enemy's front on the greatest possible width and pushing at once all your reserves beyond the breach in his line in order to gain the Cambrai region'. This appears in Nivelle's directive of 6 March. Whatever Haig and Joffre might have agreed about the distribution of duties it was France that now gave orders. In accordance with that nation's custom the plans were carefully explained to wives and mistresses over hotel dinner tables. Thus assisted, the Germans made plans of their own. The less sociable English kept them guessing harder about the Arras attack, even though a Canadian prisoner had blurted it all out at the end of March.

Under General Allenby the gun, once *ultima ratio regis*, would again be master of the field. The Royal Artillery was in far better shape than ever before. The Somme losses had borne most heavily upon the infantry and the gunners had learned much. The late General Sir James Marshall-Cornwall in an address at the Imperial War Museum in September, 1977, spoke with authority: 'It breaks my heart as a gunner to say this but the fact is that on the Somme the artillery let the infantry down.' The Royal Regiment should not be blamed, any more than the Duke should be censured for not having put a section of Maxims into La Haye Sainte. Never again, however, would there be room for even implied criticism. By the time the ball was due to open for the Arras battle there were 963 pieces of heavy artillery in place, one for every 25 yards of front.* Even more helpful was the arrival of the 106 fuse; HE shells would now burst on graze, cut wire better and kill more men.

Quite apart from the guns themselves, their servants had advanced greatly in the techniques. Those who had watched the Somme failures had in the months that followed come up with new devices that consigned 1 July, 1916, to an earlier age. On that awful day and on those that followed it the curtain of fire dropped by the guns ahead of the advancing infantry had followed an unalterable time-table worked out in intricate detail. If the bayonets could not keep up with it they must face the consequences. Should it result in their marching on to uncut wire that too would be their misfortune. The gun was master, and they were its servants. On no account could the programme be altered, no matter how desperate the straits of the advancing battalions. The unsuccess of all this had been understood by some senior artillery officers and a better method would take over next time. The novelty was French in origin. The barrage henceforth would creep, a terrific avalanche of shells, large and small, moving ahead as if it were a skirmishing line 50 yards or so in front of the attackers. Much skill was needed to perfect this. The infantry must maintain uniform progress, the gunners must shoot with the greatest precision and the shells would have to burst exactly where they were wanted. Creeping barrages were not things to be swiftly improvised but, once perfected, they were the foot soldier's best friend, so far.

The spring of 1917 produced a further improvement in the arts of the gunner with the arrival of the first sound-ranging equipment. By its use the

---

* The full panoply of guns and howitzers numbered 2,817 serving the 14 Divisions of First and Third Armies.

operators could calculate not only the range of the enemy gun to be targetted but also its exact position on the map. From that moment onwards counter-battery fire became a science rather than empirical business. The ranges of artillery pieces in 1917 were in the order of three miles for a field gun, seven or eight for a medium and, of course, far more for the huge railway-mounted affairs.

A further torment to the enemy, one that he deserved, was added by courtesy of the Royal Engineers. When the German gas from IG Farben was first set loose at Ypres in 1915 Lord Kitchener had given an assurance that they would get it back 'with some extra spice in it'. William Howard Livens, of Oundle and Christ's College, Cambridge, had enlisted in August, 1914, at the age of 25 and was soon given one of the first Special Reserve commissions in the Corps. After a spell at Chatham he was posted to Flanders with that famous sub-unit the 171st Tunnelling Company, whose business it was to make a start on the great mines that were, long afterwards, to lift the Messines Ridge skywards. His company commander, Captain Brian Frayling, spoke of him as 'a benevolent, soft-spoken undergraduate who wore glasses. At the front I found him peddling a new mortar he had invented, the Livens projector, which could drop on the enemy anything one liked, explosive, coal tar, canned sewage, the lot.' For the purposes of the Arras battle his invention was limited to hurling great canisters of poison gas for distances of some hundreds of yards. Livens, who ended the war with both DSO and MC, had other brainchildren, of which more later, but was never completely allowed his head. His Large Flammenwerfer had been used on the Somme with success; the form of flame attack called by the inventor Boiling Oil was left in abeyance. Our fathers still preserved some degree of fastidiousness even in warfare.

For any attack to be rated a success it was quite essential for the enemy's gun line to be carried. Turning infantry out of front-line trenches would seldom be reckoned worth the candle. Thus it was that attacking infantry, having driven their adversaries from their battered forward defended positions, found that their troubles were only beginning. This would be the moment when machine guns that had lurked underground throughout the bombardment would surface and other parties would emerge from dugouts and open fire from behind. It would also be the time when their own guns had reached the limits of their effective ranges and must themselves be moved forward. The contribution made by the bombing aeroplane was, so far, nowhere near to being a substitute for regular shellfire. The RFC's greatest assistance to the destruction of Kronprinz Rupprecht's army was carried out by men of remarkable sang-froid in the wicker baskets depending from captive balloons. Naturally enough they were the target of every German airman, led at this moment by the red noses of von Richtofen and his circus. There was, beyond doubt, some degree of chivalry amongst airmen although only a master fool would risk his own life for a gesture. The RFC plodded on and the guns were fed with all the data they needed.

It was used to good effect. During the last week of Lent, at 4.30 pm on 4 April, the artillery fire reached its climax. For the previous three weeks a systematic bombardment had been going on, cutting the German wire, searching the rear areas, smashing up his trenches and killing or wounding his soldiers. The enemy medium and heavy artillery had been pounded on the day before. All the guns and howitzers of Allenby's Third Army of a calibre of 6″ or more had concentrated their whole fire power on each of the villages within range for a period of 10 minutes. The ploy succeeded. Great numbers of German siege guns, existence suspected but not confirmed, opened up in their turn and about half of them were overwhelmed. The last bombardment was delivered with equal ingenuity. While never ceasing until the moment on Easter Sunday when the infantry went over the top through the snow, the barrage was not consistent. There were moments almost piano and others decidedly forte, the object being to delude the German into believing that the English would be upon him at any moment. Each gun fired out 5½ tons of metal and explosive every day; the figure for the Somme, reckoned to be the heaviest bombardment so far, had been 3 ¾. Captain Livens chipped in with 1500 of his drums of gas, fired electrically from his projectors in batches of 100; they could now manage a range of some 1200 yards and when the battle was over it was learned that they had killed 460 men in the Blangy area alone.

It is an ancient truism that all battles are won by the goodwill of the private soldier. The British and Canadian infantry had never been in higher feather than in the hours before the Battle of Arras opened. They had felt the earth shuddering under the punishment inflicted upon it, they had seen the fine new guns under their nets waiting to be moved into position and the great roadside dumps of shells. Spears, who saw it all, and had vast recent experience upon which to draw, remarked that the infantry always had a kind of premonition of whether an attack was going to be a success or not. This time they were quite certain of their ability to capture the positions assigned to them. The chance of achieving some degree of surprise by the ingenious use of caves and sewers under Arras as both forming-up places for reserves and covered ways leading well towards the enemy positions was critical; the Canadians, given the task of storming Vimy Ridge − something that the French had never been able to do − were dead set on making 9 April, 1917, a day that would be remembered for ever and not only in Canada.

Easter Sunday, 9 April, brought rewards beyond expectations. The snow fell heavily but the airmen maintained contact and the creeping barrage worked like a charm. Canada took and held Vimy, something which called for deep thanks during the March Retreat of the following year, and the 4th Division seized Fampoux, a little more than three miles ahead of the start line. Two days later, after a deal of hard fighting, the German reserves thickened up from behind and the battle petered out in some of the worst snowstorms of a dreadful spring. The cold, assisted by a cut in rations to enable more shells to be brought up, had killed great numbers of draught horses and mules. The cavalry fared even worse; in the 5th Cavalry Brigade 130 horses died of exhaustion and exposure as against 347 killed and wounded in action.

The battle of the foot and guns had followed a developing pattern that started with the coming of gunpowder. The Somme and Arras, like the earlier attacking battles on the western front, were Waterloo and Gettysburg with modern additions. Wellington, Lee, Meade or Grant could have picked up the command of either side at a moment's notice and would probably have done much the same as Allenby and Rupprecht. The other arm, the horse, was not quite in the same case. The assault of Monchy-le-Preux, the village on a hill that they attempted to take at the charge, was surely final proof that animals with men on their backs no longer had any place in this kind of battle.

Since the time when the horse had first become domesticated somewhere in the Middle East the social divide had always been between the man who rode and the man who walked. Even in matters of dress the distinction persisted. No raiment is more becoming than a lady's habit or a gentleman's breeches and boots; few are less so than trousers and puttees. Nowhere was the gap wider than in armies. The foot soldier had, over many centuries, been promoted from a flint axe to a short Lee Enfield. Apart from the medieval invention of the stirrup the cavalry remained, complete with horse-furniture, much as it had been under Tiglath-Pileser. It retained theatrical qualities. 'It was a magnificent sight to see the perfectly aligned squadrons swing over the hill at full gallop through a heavy barrage of artillery and machine-gun fire,' wrote Spears. There are judges of high standing who hold that Monchy would probably not have been taken without them, at any rate on 11 April, since the infantry was utterly exhausted. Brigadier-General Bulkeley-Johnson, who died as he would have wished sword in hand, may be reckoned the last of the knights.

The English passion for the horse went deep. Mr Kipling had explained it. 'Four things greater than all things are — Women and Horses and Power and War'. The first commodity was temporarily hardly relevant but the last three clung together. The Memoirs of every General gave far more space to the horses in his life than to anything else. Cavalry still played in some rival theatres. Allenby's Desert Mounted Corps, in which the Australian Light

Horse was calling loudly for swords, was the supreme example. It can not be unkind to remark that the Desert Mounted Corps was never attacked by Richtofen's circus. The patron saint of cavalry in Europe ought to have been Sir Horace Smith-Dorrien. It had been this infantryman who, in South Africa, had compelled reluctant regiments of horse to dismount and learn to shoot. No other cavalry could touch the British in point of marksmanship. It may be worth mentioning here, although the time for telling of the new arm is not yet, that nearly all the senior commanders in the Heavy Section MGC, in due course the Tank Corps, were cavalry colonels of impeccable credentials.

Despite that, it would hardly have been a matter for surprise if, in mid-April, 1917, there were few people who saw in the tank the future of the army. It had had some flashes of success during the late September battles on the Somme; it had done well enough, at any rate in the opinion of the majority, at Arras, though many breakdowns had reduced its effectiveness. Deliberately, no plan had been made which relied upon it. There was much worse to come. In the bitter cold of the morning of 10 April a force of eleven tanks, some, unaccountably, not armoured but covered only in boiler plating, were supposed to lead the 4th Australian Division into the attack on the Drocourt-Queant Switch, a formidable segment of the Hindenburg Line. They did not arrive. General Gough ordered them all to try again next day. As the few that turned up lumbered conspicuously across the snow in the dawn light they either broke down or were ripped to pieces by German fire. The Australians continued to advance regardless of the fact that they were walking into uncut wire. In a world of confusion caused partly by the tank failure and helped by some undistinguished staff work at most levels the first wave actually fought its way into the Hindeburg Line unaided. It could not stay there in the face of German fire power. The Division lost more than 3,000 all ranks. Of these 1,000 were prisoners, the only large bag of Australians of which the German army was ever able to boast. The reputations of the tank and General Gough plummetted to zero. No Australian wanted anything more to do with either of them ever again.

Sir Douglas Haig's contribution to the April battles was, of course, that of junior partner — almost of subordinate — to General Nivelle. When all efforts by senior soldiers and assorted politicians had failed to kill it off, the French attack went in on the 16th. The Germans, having captured a sufficiency of documents to tell them all they needed to know about it, were waiting. Nivelle, knowing that they knew, sent a quarter of a million Frenchmen to storm the heights of the Chemin des Dames.

Their artillery, forced to hurry by reason of the sudden German withdrawal, had gone on before. Spears watched it. 'Never in all the war had such immense masses of guns and tractors moved at once. They advanced in two columns, each 45 kilometres long, so that a man standing at one point could have watched for two whole days the rattling, jangling, rumbling guns, tractors and munition wagons bumping their immense weight along roads that gave way under the stupendous flood of steel, until their surfaces became uneven and rough like a river bed under torrential waters. The spectacle was terrific. I had never seen and hope never again to see anything like it. Guns of every kind jolted by, enormous mastodons behind creaking tractors which made some of the old-fashioned horse-drawn guns look like medieval toys. It was as if all the guns since artillery was invented were taking part in a gigantic parade. Nothing so colossal or so varied could, one felt, have been the work of a single generation.' Nevertheless this was the style of warfare in 1917. Vast numbers of guns must be dragged over roads barely fit for farm carts, wrecking every form of communication behind them in preparation for wrecking the same things ahead of their own infantry.

The French army, in a hopeless position and knowing it, added yet one more to *toutes les gloires de la France*.' Not least concerned were Mangin's especial pride, the Senegalese troops. There is nothing wrong with the African soldier when decently led; it is not very sensible to take him from his near-equatorial climate and set him down in frost, snow and bitter wind with the expectation that he will perform at his best. Once numbed with cold they abandoned the struggle. The *piou-piou*, the ordinary French soldier of the marching regiments, took his courage in both hands and walked uphill towards the crest line along which ran the Chemin des Dames. He was expected. 'When every unit displayed such magnificent qualities of courage and determination it seems invidious to pick out any divisions as having specially distinguished itself. The result was the same as usual. Deep dugouts disgorged defenders, quite undamaged by shell-fire and well able to fire belt after belt into the backs of such infantry as had passed them.' Thus Spears again.

The fate of the tanks was worse. The French had taken to the idea of an armoured fighting vehicle at much the same time as the British. French engineering, one must remember, was at the top of the world in reputation. The best aircraft possessed by the RFC until the arrival of the SE5 and Bristol Fighter were the Nieuport and the SPAD. French very heavy artillery was probably the best in the business and the 75 already had more than 20 years service behind it. Their motor cars were stylish and excellent. Nevertheless their first tanks were not good. General Estienne, in charge of all things mechanical, and M. Breton, Under-Secretary of State for Inventions, had wanted something small enough to be carried on to the battlefield on the back of a lorry and had asked Louis Renault to produce one. He was working on it, but the day of the Renault FT 17 was not yet.

As something much bigger and heavier was needed for trench-crossing and machine-gun squashing the great armament firms of Schneider and St Chamond were told to produce a bigger machine without loss of a moment. Both obliged, but the result was unsatisfactory. They were ill-balanced, clumsy to handle and unventilated inside. The 16th April, 1917, marked their first and last public appearance. Something like eighty machines arrived by degrees at Juvincourt, several hours late, and moving desperately slowly. Each drew down upon itself what Spears, not a man for the dramatic adjective, called 'a hellish fire'. Soon flame and smoke enveloped each one, helped considerably by the French habit of draping festoons of petrol cans over the outside. A further forty-eight, earmarked to attack towards La Ville-aux-Bois, fared, if possibly, worse. The German air force spotted them, reported back to their gunners and watched as the shells followed them uphill. The bridge by which they were supposed to pass over the first German trench had not been completed. The leading tank tried to cross, became ditched, was hit several times and burst into flames. Those following tried to deploy in a swamp where 'they caught fire and in a few seconds they were red glowing masses of metal, incinerators of their roasted crews'. Thirty-two out of forty-eight were destroyed in this fashion.

The rest of the story of how the Nivelle offensive petered out leaving the French army close to disintegration need not be repeated here. The inevitable result was that the responsibility for most of the land war, in addition to practically the whole of that at sea, passed to the British. Sir Douglas Haig, lately the object of an elaborate plot by Mr Lloyd George and the French to disparage him, now dominated the land forces of the Allies in the west. He had not wanted the Arras battle; it pointed in the wrong direction, away from the Flanders coast where Sir John Jellicoe was insisting that the thunderhead of danger impended. He had lost 150,000 good men, men who would soon be greatly missed. On the other side he had gained the heights of Vimy and his army was still in excellent fettle. Nobody ever thought or spoke of Arras with the horror that must always cling to the Somme and Passchendaele. The French army could not say the same; never again would it fight as it had done in the first years of the Kaiser's war. Many people whose opinions are worth having still hold Nivelle's offensive to have been the root cause of the events of 1940.

The time for driving the Germans from the Belgian coast could not come so long as Nivelle's army was still in straits. In the faint but understandable hope that the French might even now recover themselves, Sir Douglas pressed on with his share in the general offensive on the existing front. The operations that began on 3 May, 1917, operations carried out by men already worn out almost to breaking point, were a dreadful failure. A second battle of Bullecourt lasted for a fortnight, this time without tanks; it was a bloody business and not justified by its results save for those intangibles called pride and morale. The series of battles died down and by the end of the month they were all over. The French army was in no state to do anything; only by good fortune and the exertions of General Pétain did it remain an army in being. The word mutiny was avoided, the secret was somehow kept and Pétain set himself to nurse his poilus back to health. For the British Expeditionary Force, the hastily constructed and still semi-amateur army, it was time for the next series of battles. Their position on the map was certainly to be chosen by Sir Douglas but he had little enough scope for virtuosity.

Sir Herbert Plumer's Battle of Messines was unlike any other. Not merely because it was a demonstrable success but because it was the most perfect example of the use of surprise. This was something that could not be hastily improvised. Plumer's arrangements for a battle lasting a week had taken well over a year and were of a kind unlikely to be repeated. In order to mount a general offensive from the Ypres Salient towards the coast he would need first to secure his right flank. The German front line there lay neatly along the eight miles of a ridge with an average height of about 200 feet and sitting firmly on a sub-soil of clay. It gave to the Germans excellent views of the British positions, enabled them to be taken in enfilade and even, for some distance in the north, to be shot at from the rear. Prince Rupprecht, having learned from the Arras experience that such positions are hard to hold when pounded by a superior artillery, wished to vacate the place before battle commenced. His local commanders, like their British opposite numbers a short walking distance away, would have none of it. To abandon any position, even one as awful as the Ypres Salient, without a fight was unsoldierly. The Prince gave in.

General Plumer certainly intended to swamp the Wytschaete-Messines ridge with shells from the biggest guns he could muster but his plans did not stop with that. Given the conditions that Spears had described for the movement of heavy artillery along poor roads, it might be thought that a surprise attack would be impossible. Sir Herbert had prepared a surprise of an original nature.

The brain behind it all was of a man born out of his time. John Norton Griffiths was a middle-aged civil engineer and Conservative MP for Wednesbury. His first experience of soldiering had been under Major Plumer in the Matabele war of 1896, after which he had had further opportunities of showing his mettle against the Boers with Brabant's Horse. His last appearance in that war had been as Adjutant of Lord Roberts' Bodyguard — sufficient credentials for him to be authorized in August, 1914, to raise that rather distinguished unit the 2nd King Edward's Horse. He did not remain long among the animals but attached himself to the Staff of the

Engineer-in-Chief, BEF, his friend of South African days Sir George Fowke. Once there he was given temporary rank as Lieutenant-Colonel and put to work organizing the Tunnelling Companies RE. Colonel John Charteris, Haig's Chief of Intelligence, certainly accepted that this was the first mind behind the business; his diary entry for 26 June, 1917, says 'We have also had Norton Griffiths again, claiming most of the credit for the Messines mines and, indeed, if it had not been for him we should not have had tunnelling well enough advanced to have prepared the mines 18 months ago. He is a typical buccaneer of the cloak-and-sword age. I would like to see him sent to Russia just now.'

Earlier, on 12 April, he had written 'Norton Griffiths, fresh from his exploits in Rumania, is here, an extraordinarily vital and forceful man. His adventures in Rumania, as he recounted them, would make a real thriller of the Stanley Weyman type. He was out to destroy the oil-fields and wheat of Rumania to prevent them falling into the hands of the Germans, and seems to have accomplished wonders. He was with me for an hour and a half, and I could have listened to him for twice as long if I could have spared the time. When I last saw him he was starting the tunnelling show with the old First Army. I think if it had not been for him it would never have been started, though it is now far bigger than even he dreamed at the time.' The romances (thriller is an inapt word) of Stanley Weyman are, deservedly, still read and enjoyed. It is not, however, the Sieur de Marsac come again that Norton Griffiths personified. He is pure Richard Hannay even though Hankey* calls him 'a clever man in a technical sense but stupid, unpractical and visionary in his ideas'.

Be that as it may, the work began early in 1915 on a small scale. The original galleries were cut only at a depth of about 15 feet until an opinion was obtained from Lieutenant-Colonel Tannatt William Edgworth David, an Australian geologist with a past almost equal to that of Norton Griffiths. David had been Professor of Geology at Sydney University since 1891, had been on geological surveys all over the Pacific and had led the party which reached the south magnetic pole in 1909. On the outbreak of war he had immediately raised the Australian Mining Corps and had taken the shilling himself at the age of 57. Three years later he was Geologist to the British Armies on the Western Front. David and Fowke concluded that the only way in which the Ridge could be undermined was by going much deeper, something like 100 feet, into the subjacent blue clay. By January, 1916, half-a-dozen mines had been started. Within a year there were fourteen more. David was remembered by the shaft names of Sydney, Hobart and Brisbane. At that time there was no distinguishable plan for what was to

* Hankey was jealous: 'I believe the first idea was mine but Norton Griffiths carried it out.'

become the Battle of Messines. Indeed the whole of the mines then existing were nearly touched off in July, 1916, simultaneously with those at La Boisselle in order to cause a distraction from the Somme. Only a fluke saved them; a German aircraft dropped a bomb on the great shell dump at Audruicq and destroyed it with the result that ammonal became a commodity not to be wasted.

Operations of this kind demand unusual skills and few men possessed them. Major Hyland of the Royal Engineers, who had made a speciality of this appalling kind of work, found himself advanced from subaltern to brigadier-general within four years. Few would grudge him such promotion. His 171st Tunnelling Company had been hurriedly put together from men whose civil employment had been among the sewers of Manchester or in the London Underground. They were known in the trade as 'clay kickers', for their weapon was the grafting tool, a small sharpened spade which a man on his back can push with both feet into the clay face. As the clay kickers alone were insufficient for such enormous works reinforcements were called for among experienced coal miners. They came from every pit in the Kingdom. Frayling soon learned their measure. 'In a difficult situation underground one Geordie from Durham was worth two of any other kind.' There was no shortage of difficult situations. The Germans from time to time would detonate charges in the hope that there might be somebody or something that they would injure. Many months of work went into making it all ready. On 20 May the usual preliminaries began. The voices of 2374 guns rose to a deafening bellow, pulverizing Prince Rupprecht's soldiers with the aid of a masterful air service.

Then, at 3.10 am on 7 June, 1917, the mines went up. From a camouflaged OP on Kemmel Hill all the great ones, with Frayling at their side, watched the show. First came a tremor, which travelled over 12 miles. After the violent shaking underfoot there came a long pause before the first, a 'common' mine with a charge calculated as being just enough to lift and drop it back, went up in a glow of orange-red with black smoke. All nineteen exploded, (one had been discovered and abandoned) although some had been waiting for more than a year. Spanbroekmolen went up in a white incandescent light darting high into the air; last to go was Ontario Farm, this time in a shower of red. In case all this had not been enough to discourage resistance, 70 tons of Captain Livens' gas containers and boiling-oil cans were added to thicken things up. The attack, not surprisingly, was a complete success, with infantry advancing so quickly that in many instances the tanks could not keep up with them. Even then, the Battle of Messines claimed 17,000 casualties on the British side. For the first time since 1914 the German losses, reckoned at about 25,000, were the higher. To a stern generation willing to accept that war can mean death and wounds to every family, these were encouraging figures. At something like 1,000 to the Division, on average, they were about a third of those taken on 1 July, 1916.

The dreadful spring and early summer of 1917 seemed to have passed. The seven weeks following Messines were of glorious sunshine and were duly enjoyed. The Germans put them to excellent use, building fine, solid pillboxes and other aids to defence. It seems the natural moment to consider how affairs stood in other places.

CHAPTER TWO

TOUR D'HORIZON

THOUGH MEN DOING the actual fighting could hardly be expected to remember it, there was a world outside the trenches where matters of the highest importance were being transacted. For reasons of vicinage it seems natural first to treat of France. There, in May, 1917, military affairs had to be viewed from two different standpoints, depending upon how much the viewer knew of the state of the post-Nivelle French army. A staff of sixty British officers headed by Sir Henry Wilson was maintained at GHQ almost entirely for the purpose of keeping the British Government's military adviser, the CIGS, informed about its true plight. In this duty it failed utterly. So also did the Military Attaché's office at the Paris Embassy. For Colonel Herman Le Roy-Lewis it is possible to make excuses. A Yeomanry officer of nearly 60 who gives his recreations in *Who's Who* as 'hunting and riding in Tubes' must have his limitations. Sir Henry Wilson, with enough subordinates to form a couple of defence platoons if the worst were to happen, is another matter. He was deliberately kept in the dark because General Pétain did not trust him. On 15 May, the first day of his tenure of the chief command in Nivelle's place, the General sent for Spears, announced that he was off to GQG at Compiègne and that by the time he arrived he expected to find Wilson gone. *'C'est un intriguant.'* Not everybody had taken the length of this strange man's foot so quickly. Very different was Pétain's assessment of Sir Douglas Haig. On 2 June he sent his own Chief of Staff to Montreuil briefed to tell the British general everything that he knew. Or nearly everything. Nobody will ever know what passed between the two soldiers. Debeney asked for a pledge of secrecy and Sir Douglas, having no choice, gave it. Whatever it was he learned from the Frenchman, he told it to nobody, not even to the faithful 'Wully' Robertson, still CIGS in spite of Mr Lloyd George. All that Robertson learned was that the French army was exhausted and discouraged; to keep it as an army at all the British offensive had got to be maintained, cost what it might. The attack promised by Pétain for 10 June would be postponed. Very possibly, though this has to be guesswork, Sir Douglas formed the view that Mr Lloyd George, were he to be told what Debeney had said, would panic and forbid the Battle of Messines even though the preliminary bombardment was already under way.

Spears, well aware that he was trespassing upon the functions of both Embassy and GQG, set himself to work to find out as much of the truth as possible. Rumours of mass disobedience, even of actual mutiny, were floating on every draught. Every French officer, naturally and properly, was doing his best to keep both friend and enemy from learning just how bad it was. In this they were successful, for it was very bad indeed.

It was common knowledge at the time, and it remains so now, that France owed her survival to the qualities of General Philippe Pétain. In all probability nobody else, not even Foch or Franchet d'Esperey, could have won back the goodwill of the private soldier as he did. Some years after the war the Marshal, as he had become, handed Spears a folder containing his account of what had happened and invited him to get it published. For a variety of reasons this was not done; the arrival of Hitler's war and the events of 1940 killed off the idea. The text, nevertheless, remained with Spears and he set it out in extenso at the end of his own book on the subject.

It was during the months of May and June that things were at their worst. During the last and ill-starred offensive by the British army there came the first public indication that something was up. It could hardly have started less violently. The little sewing-girls of Paris − 'midinettes', because they all poured out for luncheon on the clap of noon − went on strike because they could not live on starvation wages. Their procession through the streets was joined by a great number of soldiers on leave who marched cheerfully with them. It all seemed quite fun. The events of a night or two later were not funny in the least. For some tactless reason a number of public buildings were guarded by Tirailleurs Tonkinois; presumably they would be called Vietnamese today. Nobody liked them. The row over a woman that began at a café in the Saint-Ouen district soon flared into a riot. The Tirailleurs ran back to barracks, chased by a mob, and got their rifles. The authorities quickly took the situation by the scruff, the Asiatics were removed from Paris and, inevitably, those whose business it was to stir up trouble promptly gave out that coloured troops had fired on the people. It felt as if something like 1789 had come again. Certainly the likes of Hébert and Marat had their descendants in M. Malvy, the Minister of the Interior, the interesting Bolo Pasha (unquestionably a paid German agent) and M. Almereyda, an anagram of y a la merde, of the subversive newspaper Le Bonnet Rouge and, worst of the lot, M. Caillaux. When Clemenceau assumed power he had Malvy tried for his life. He was probably lucky to receive no worse a sentence than exile. With such men and a good many less important ones death-watch-beetling away in the fabric of France it seems remarkable that nothing more terrible happened.

It was still bad enough. The behaviour of sorely tried troops was not so much that of pirates who had seized the ship as of trade unionists taking industrial action. The most evil influence, civilians apart, was that of the Russian brigades. There were two of these, both in the area of the French Vth Army, and neither was a credit to the Tsar. From the beginning they had not got on with the poilus, who teased them. Well before the Revolution was under way in their homeland they were penetrated by agitators and bolshevised. One of those devoted to the good work was M. Bronstein, alias Trotsky, who was living inconspicuously in Paris at the time. His main task was to edit the paper called *Natchalo* whose message it was that the Russians were mere cannon-fodder sold to the French in exchange for munitions. They had fought well enough and of their own free will under Nivelle; after taking fairly heavy casualties they had turned quasi-political and were by now completely out of hand. The only possible thing to be done was done. The Russian Brigades were quickly entrained for the camp of La Courtine near Limoges. Once there, after they had refused to return to duty, they were decimated in the Roman fashion by French artillery; those who came out alive were shipped to Algeria and not heard of again until after the Armistice. They were, without doubt, soldiers of poor quality; all the same it is hard to withhold any grain of sympathy from them. This is easy to say in 1992; it would have been much harder in 1917. It was only the Russians who went to the length of shooting one of their Colonels. The French mutineers were not over-fastidious in their handling of officers they disliked, but there were no killings. Fortunately for the allies the cavalry was hardly affected and made no bones about policing units of other arms in revolt.

The CIGS, unconscious of Sir Douglas's meeting with General Debeney, had heard many rumours but knew little or nothing about what was happening. To acquaint himself better he travelled to the Officers' Club at Abbeville on 9 June, a week after Haig's secret had been imposed on him, to which place he had summoned Spears. There he expressed heavy displeasure at the uselessness of the British Mission at GQG – 'Wully' Robertson had never had much time for Henry Wilson – and demanded to be told all that Spears had been able to find out about the state of the French army. When he had heard it he packed Spears off again with orders to find out as much more as he could. In particular he was to try and form a judgement as to whether the rot was so deep that the French army was finished or whether it was still capable of salvation. And he was to hold himself ready to come to London at short notice. Spears went back to General Franchet d'Esperey with whom he had worked before. In spite of the great gulf of rank and age these two exceptional officers were on terms of cordiality. Franchet d'Esperey, a man of very different mettle from that of Nivelle, gave his considered opinion. The French soldier was a man of patriotism and intelligence and these qualities would in the long run carry him through. Even the disaffected units had promised to resist attacks though they would take part in none of their own. It can hardly be believed that Franchet d'Esperey really knew the depths that his army was touching. There is Pétain's authority for saying that even whilst this conversation was taking place there had been acts of mutiny all over France. They spread throughout the back areas, from Nantes to Bordeaux and Limoges, though the greater part and the most serious were in the formations in the Aisne area behind the Chemin des Dames. Sixty-eight of the 110 units involved were there, with six more before Monts-de-Champagne. They belonged to fifty-four different divisions, more than half the number the entire army could muster. Trains and railway stations throughout the land were infected by loads of recalcitrant troops, often drunk and with the deplorable habit of singing the *Internationale*. In Pétain's words, 'Such was the storm of madness which for several weeks swept a harassed and distracted France, threatening to blind her both to her objectives and to her duties.' Very few people outside knew it.

The summons to London reached Spears on 13 June. At the War Office he reported himself to Robertson, told him what he had learned and walked with him to Downing Street. Then followed a colloquy of the oddest kind. It was no secret that the Prime Minister and the CIGS thought nothing at all of each other. Each was a man who had risen from the humblest beginnings to the top of his particular tree. Spears was a 30-year-old cavalry officer holding a brevet of Lieutenant-Colonel. Like all regular officers, and many other people, he was wary of politicians in general, of this one in particular. Nothing was to happen that would change this. Mr Lloyd George was unamiable. Spears remembered how Charles à Court Repington had told him that a school of thought in London believed the Prime Minister to be ready to snatch at a separate peace if the army were to collapse. This was unjust to Mr Lloyd George but Spears at that time and place could hardly be so sure. When the blunt question 'Is the French army going to recover?' was thrown at him Spears had to think fast. Like a sensible man he hesitated to answer firmly a question of such tremendous weight. The Prime Minister went for him like a terrier. 'I am sure it will,' said Spears and told of the high qualities of General Pétain. This was not enough. Spears tried to explain something of the character and mystique of the French army. It was no good. In a completely altered tone the Prime Minister put the incredible question: 'Will you give me your word of honour, as an officer and a gentleman, that the French army will recover?' This was too much. Spears, outraged, tore into the Welshman telling him that he 'did not know the meaning of either officer or gentleman and could indeed only have the most imprecise views concerning the meaning, purpose and obligations of giving a word of honour.' All the same, he gave an answer. 'Call Hankey and he can take down what I say. You can have me shot if I am mistaken. I will stake my life on it, but not my word of honour. The French army under Pétain will surely recover.' 'That will do,' said Wully and they walked out of the room.

Though none of those present could have known it, the worst was by then over. Pétain's unpublished book contains a time-table of events, setting out the exact nature of the indiscipline by units and formations. He put the first three days of June as being the culminating point of the mutiny, coinciding exactly with Debeney's mission to Sir Douglas. For these three days there were violent disorders among men of all arms in sixteen divisions, either in action or resting in the same area. Pétain does not spare language; 'intoxicating madness,' 'mutiny conceived in cold blood,' 'appalling danger' are expressions unlikely to have ranked as the small change of conversation with a man so unexcitable. How he set about the pacification of division after division and the recall of hundreds of thousands to their duty is a story worthy of the telling. This, however, is not the place for it. Philippe Pétain, Marshal of France, will for ever be a name to be hissed. 1940 was not all that far away and its consequence was not always justice for everybody. In 1917 Spears was proved right; the French soldiers of the Kaiser's War, like most soldiers of all the western armies, were stouter men than their sons. None of which helps to find out exactly what Debeney said to Haig. The Field-Marshal's diary is laconic. It tells of a meeting with Major Lytton, the officer in charge of foreign newspaper correspondents, who told him of 'a feeling of despondency abroad' and of the *midinettes'* strike. 'Altogether the situation wants careful watching.' Against that, the French, it seemed, were at last beginning to realize that the British army had some hand in this war and not always futilely. 'Some sort of success is wanted to raise the spirits of the French people.' Then came Debeney, with a letter from Pétain: 'The French army was in a bad state of discipline.' As part of the cure he was sending great numbers of men on leave and would not be able to put on the attack promised for 10 June. There followed talk about the French divisions promised to Haig for use by him on the Yser. This was not of immediate concern. Debeney was with the Field-Marshal from 6.30 to 9.30, both pm. Then he returned to Compiègne: 'I thought him straightforward and businesslike.' Quite a compliment, but the diary conveys not the least sense of urgency. To find out Sir Douglas's thoughts it is necessary to look elsewhere.

France, of course, was not his only source of trouble. There were also Russia and Italy. During the early summer of 1917 the affairs of the former did not look hopeless. Kerensky seemed to be captain of the ship, Comrade

Lenin lurked in Finland and his co-adjutor Trotsky, his work in Paris done, was behind bars. The last battle of the Tsar's army, the Brusilov offensive, began on 1 July and soon ran out of steam. The German counter-offensive did not. It was hardly accidental that it coincided with a rising in Petrograd which ended with the *coup-de-grace* for the Eastern front of the Allies. It could now only be a matter of time, and that not a long time, before the excellent German formations facing Russia would have turned about, added themselves to those of Marshal Conrad von Hotzendorf of Austria, and set about either France, Italy or both.

Information out of Russia came almost entirely from diplomatic sources. These were the young Robert Bruce Lockhart in his capacity of Consul-General, the middle-aged Colonel Knox, Military Attaché in Petrograd, and Major-General Hanbury-Williams, chief of a special Mission to the Stavka – Russian GHQ. Knox was a man with a great deal of experience of Russia for he had held his present appointment since 1911. Hanbury-Williams – surely the only man to include in his *Who's Who* entry the fact that his horse had been shot at Tel-el-Kebir – was nearer the throne but more handicapped in getting his intelligence out. All their reports naturally went by way of the Foreign Office to Mr Lloyd George. Sir Douglas had no sources of information that he could call his own. His Intelligence department, under Brigadier-General Charteris, should have been able to tell him that the German army in the West had still been strong enough to entrain four divisions eastwards to help defeat Brusilov; this hardly suggested an army in desperate straits to keep itself in business. It told him nothing. That apart, Russia remained the usual enigma. When hearing of the coming offensive, Knox had written in his diary that 'There will be no success'. Events were to reveal this as meiosis. Colonel Bruchmuller, one of history's greatest artillerymen, routed the Russians and by August von Hutier's army was threatening Riga.

The effects of all this were felt more in Italy than in most other places. The Italian army, direct descendants of the Legions of Imperial Rome, has seldom been fully appreciated. By mid-1917 it had not performed at all badly in the mountains which were its *specialité de la maison*. Ten battles on the Isonzo were not matter for contempt. Martial qualities apart, the Italian army suffered from one serious disadvantage. Its recent, and brief, history under the monarchy had been in Abyssinia and Libya. Neither had demanded much in the way of artillery and hardly anything other than small field-pieces existed. Austria, on the other hand, made some of the biggest and best guns to be had anywhere. In days when Czechoslovakia was not even a name the Skoda works were turning out huge weapons that few others could match. The monstrous pieces, polished to perfection, in the Imperial Army Museum at Vienna are still awesome in the nuclear age. In mountains where even a goat cannot pass without panting it can only be advantageous to own weapons capable of bombarding a distant enemy without fear of retaliation. Very soon after Salandra's holy self-interest had coaxed Italy into the war the cry had gone up that her allies must find heavy guns for her out of their own stores.

'Wully' Robertson worked on the sound dogma that every foreigner is a fiend until proved otherwise. In January, 1917, he had made the journey to Rome: in the train with him were M. Briand ('a delightful fellow traveller and the life and soul of the party'), Marshal Lyautey, a figure something between Lords Kitchener and Lugard, and the generously whiskered Minister for Munitions, Albert Thomas. It was a large Conference. Of all the foreigners present the one the CIGS distrusted the most was a Welshman. The feeling was mutual. Mr Lloyd George was in the grip of an idea for ending the war by a thrust through the mountains that would seize Trieste and, quite soon, Vienna also. Though he reduced all this into writing, in paragraphs 23 and 24 of his memorandum prepared before the Conference, the Prime Minister was at pains to keep them from his professional adviser. 'Wully' would have explained, without excessive consideration for the author's feelings, what amateurish nonsense the whole thing was. All politicians enjoy a brute ignorance of the elements of staff work; Mr Lloyd George enjoyed it more than most. The upshot of the Conference, however, did not meet with his expectations. Robertson agreed to let the Italians have ten newly-raised batteries of 6″ howitzers at once (they were sent as the Arras battle was opening) and another twenty in July. In addition careful planning was put in hand for the swift transfer of six good British divisions from France 'en cas d'urgence'. General Cadorna began his offensive on the Isonzo on 7 May. In three weeks it had petered out, with the Italians having lost 26,000 killed, 90,000 wounded and 27,000 prisoners. The Austrian casualties were much lighter. There was an ominous similarity to the last act of the Nivelle offensive. Most of the prisoners came from the Third Army and Cadorna put its feeble performance down to 'seditious propaganda'. There was no comfort to be had in the south.

Even less was there any nearer to home. The atrocious weather had been depressant enough but with the summer came also the air raids. Since that now remote day in 1914 when Mr Terson, the popular and respected house agent of Dover, had gone into history as the first man to have a bomb fall in his garden, the air attack had been kept up to the limit that skill and knowledge then permitted. First there had come the gas-filled airships, the handiwork of Count Zeppelin and others. They had been a pest but at a price. Since October, 1916, when L31 had been destroyed, not much had been seen of them. The German army took over from the German navy. It had excellent aerodromes around Ghent and had devoted much time and thought in producing aeroplanes that could use them to best advantage. The

Fliegerkorps der Obersten Heeresleitung, created soon after Belgium had been over-run, had had to be put into a non-operational state shortly afterwards as the British Army denied it the use of the area around Calais that had been marked down. As a platform for the bombing of London it would just about have met the needs of the aircraft then in service. Ghistelles, the Zeppelin base near Bruges, would have been a little too far away. A specification for the kind of large bomber needed was drawn up and the factories put to work on it.

By the end of 1916 the Gothaer Wagonfabriek AG had come up with a prototype that looked adequate for the purpose. The GIV — Gotha to the English — was a large, ungainly-looking but powerful affair, bigger by far than anything in regular service with any of the belligerents. The twin 260 h.p. Mercedes engines were not as good as one expects Mercedes engines to be but they had to suffice. The wingspan was 77 feet, the overall length 41 and the flight deck sophisticated for its time. The commander had his place in the bows with a bomb-sight made by the Goerz company; this alone demonstrates how far bombing had advanced from the light-hearted tossings over the side of a couple of years earlier. The crew of three had a machine gun each, electrically heated to prevent freezing by means of a dynamo run from the starboard engine. The bomb load was equally impressive. Each GIV could carry seven bombs of 50 kilograms — about a hundredweight in English — in three racks, worked by release levers in the large cockpit. Fortunately for London neither type of fuse provided, one for a fiftieth of a second's delay and another of one tenth, was always reliable. In order to reach the capital, elude whatever aircraft might be sent up and be out of gun range, the Gotha was planned to fly at 18,000 feet, an altitude that took an hour to reach, and to carry at least 175 gallons of petrol. The fact that the machine had a top speed of about 80 mph, which a headwind could reduce to 50, did not greatly matter. Nothing owned by the RFC and based in England could come near it. The designated targets began with Downing Street and its environs, the Admiralty, the Bank of England and, if all else failed, Fleet Street. Should these prove impracticable there remained such useful subjects as Woolwich Arsenal, Tilbury and the coastal towns. Much store was set, reasonably enough, on the moral effect. When Londoners saw air fleets cruising unmolested over their most sacred places they would surely realize that they could not hope to win against the massive power of the Kaiser's Germany.

The first raid, on Friday, 25 May, did not go quite as planned. The fine summer weather, in which the Gothas had travelled high over Essex impervious to all forms of molestation, broke. London disappeared under a thick layer of cloud and the raiders wheeled south into Kent. A number of villages were hit, a civilian or two slain and an attempt was made to strike the Ashford railway works before the bombers moved on to Hythe. After killing the verger and wounding the vicar and his wife on the church steps, they flew slowly towards Folkestone. On its outskirts lies Sir John Moore's great camp of Shorncliffe, home in peacetime to an entire infantry brigade. In 1917 it had largely been given over to the Canadian Corps as a transit and training centre. As one company was falling in for an evening route march the Gothas arrived. Over the area of St Martin's Plain they dropped six of the 50 kg bombs and twenty-one of the 12½ kg. The bomb-aimers could take their time and make their calculations, for nobody interfered with them. Seventeen Canadian soldiers were killed and ninety-three wounded.

That accomplished, at about 6.30 on a fine sunny evening of early summer twenty-two Gothas cruised slowly over the town. There was no air-raid warning since such things did not exist. Being Friday the housewives of Folkestone were doing their week's shopping, their children looking up pleasedly at the pretty white aeroplanes. Then came the bombs. A lamp-post in Tontine Street still bears, or did recently, a plaque reminding that sixty people, nearly all of them women and young children, died between Mr Gosnold's draper's shop and Stokes brothers the fruiterers. The total, taking in the other bombs on the town, was seventy-two dead and ninety-one seriously injured. The guns of Dover banged uselessly away: Navy pilots based on Dunkirk, with better aircraft than the home squadrons, shot down two and a third crashed from unknown causes.

Inevitably a great rumpus followed. Badly needed squadrons of the new SE5s and Camels were brought back from France and new aerodromes ringed London. The raids continued, in spite of brave efforts by the RNAS pilots to smash up their airfields. It was, inevitably, in the capital where they made the most impression, the raids of 13 June and 7 July being the most destructive and humiliating of them all. Over 200 civilians were killed in these and the damage to property was considerable. Pinpricks, by contrast with the mighty events then taking place in Flanders, but damaging out of all proportion. It would be quite untrue to claim that all Cockneys behaved like Ajax defying the lightning. In 1917 there were two Englands; those who wore the King's uniform and fought his battles for a pittance were poles apart from a lot of others who stayed at home and worked for wages so high as to be hardly credible. Some of these last — 'embusqués' the French called theirs — were not men of virtue. When a few bombs fell they funked, and made much noise about it. Nor were they the only ones affected. 'Wully' Robertson, whom nothing could shake, observed on leaving a meeting of the War Cabinet that one would have thought the world to be coming to an end. On one night, when there was no raid, only about a quarter of the night shift at Woolwich Arsenal clocked in; in the East End of London 300,000 people crammed nightly into the Tube stations long after the raids had ceased.

It had been a good bargain for the Kaiser, at a price of only a few aircraft and their crews. Three first-class squadrons had had to be brought home and that, during the Richtofen days when they were most needed; three more had to be constituted from pilots who would otherwise have been in France. The game could not go on for ever; vile weather, the worst for 50 years, caused the Gothas more trouble than anything else and the last raid took place on the morning of 22 August. Margate, Ramsgate and Dover came under the lash but this time it was no walkover. The guns and the fighters brought down three Gothas into the sea and the German air service reckoned it to be no longer worth the effort. In all they had lost thirty-two aircraft, mostly by stress of weather. The dividend had been a good one. Day bombing, however, had served its purpose. Henceforth, rather than run what had become quite an efficient gauntlet, the Gothas and their new acquisition the 'Riesenflugzeug' or Giant would have to perform their feats by the light of the moon. Full moons, in London, came to be regarded with apprehension.

The soldier and the civilian do not always hold synoptic views of warfare. When the RFC brought down a Zeppelin on the night of 6/7 June, 1917, they saw to it that the crew had Christian burial and caused an inscription to be put upon their grave: 'Who art thou that judgest another man's servant? To his own master he standeth or falleth.' The civilian population, led by politicians, yowled for vengeance. Mr Joynson-Hicks, MP, helpfully demanded in the Commons that 'Everytime the Germans raid London then British airmen must blot out a German town'. The upshot of it all was the creation of General Trenchard's Independent Air Force, to operate from somewhere near Nancy as that would give his bombers the shortest run to appropriate targets. His journey there to make arrangements turned up some useful evidence of the plight of the French. Soldiers and civilians alike, they were streaming southwards along every road in terror of a German attack. In one village his car was held up for six hours, blocked in by a rabble of soldiers and refugees with their belongings. This was the kind of evidence the British government needed. The French army was no longer to be counted on as fit to engage the German. Not only must no plans be based upon its participation. It would have to be protected.

The doings of the Independent Air Force can find no place here. Everything to do with air-raids and counter-strikes was insignificant, mere fly-swatting compared to the tiger that was at England's throat. Old Jackie Fisher, out of office but very much all there, put the only question that mattered in one of his letters to Maurice Hankey. Could the Army win the war before the Navy lost it? As the Canadian Corps was swarming up the heights of Vimy and Mangin's Senegalese were listening to their teeth chattering, the U-boat captains were having such a harvest as never was. The German Admiralty had done careful sums. There existed about 20,000,000 tons of British shipping space; after deducting that needed for military purposes, about 8,500,000 were left for the ordinary requirements of life. Send 600,000 tons to the bottom every month and in half a year something like 40% would be gone for ever. Helpful neutrals would soon be frightened off. Particular attention would be given to Norwegians, who were supplying the vital timber for pit-props; the failure of the US grain harvest in 1916 would mean that ships could not help making targets of themselves by fetching wheat cargoes from such distant ports as those of Australia and Argentina. The U-boat captains were doing even better than they were asked. As there were now something like 120 of them on the loose it was only a matter of quite a short time before a famished England and a starveling army would have to cry 'Enough'. That would happen long before American intervention would have counted for much.

The English have always loved the Royal Navy to an extent almost greater than that of their mild dislike for the Army. Bell-bottomed trousers outrank even kilts any day of the week. And any scribbler with the thesis that all Generals are stupid will acquire an immediate following. Let him suggest, however, that in Admirals there can be any fault or flaw and his windows will be broken. Or as Fisher had put it, in a slightly different context, his wife would be a widow, his children fatherless and his home a dunghill. Risking that, it has to be said that at the British Admiralty in 1917 it was not only hearts that were of oak. The First Lord, Sir Edward Carson, had made a sort of reputation on land; Sir John Jellicoe had kept his fleet in being and, after Jutland, it was hardly apt to call the Kaiser's ships the High Seas Fleet. Neither Carson nor Jellicoe was the man for the task now facing them, when the very existence of the Kingdom was at stake. By the end of July Carson had gone, replaced by the only universal genius since Leibnitz, originally from the railways, Sir Eric Geddes. One of his first actions was to dismiss Jellicoe, and that with some economy of courtesy. His successor, Sir Rosslyn Wemyss, sailored on for long enough to sign the armistice agreement in the railway carriage. Maritime affairs began to improve.

The United States Army had little enough to offer to the cause in 1917. The US Navy was another matter. Had it consisted of nothing more than Admiral Sims and a handful of destroyers it would still have turned the scales. The Admiral reached London early in April and sought out the First Sea Lord. It is fortunate that the imbecile expression 'the public has a right to know' was not then part of ordinary conversation. Sims knew nothing, and what Jellicoe had to tell him made the flesh creep. A quarter of a million tons had already been sent to the bottom in a single month. At that rate, said Jellicoe, it would be impossible to continue with the war for much longer. He had no suggestions to offer. It was the American, a near contemporary of Alfred Thayer Mahan, more than any British admiral who may claim the credit for bringing back the ancient and serviceable system of convoy. It soon demonstrated its continued usefulness but convoy alone was not enough. Shields are valuable but swords and spears kill the foemen. The U-boat bases must be taken, burnt or otherwise destroyed. A reasonable question to follow this would have been, 'Well, where are they?' The truthful answer, 'We think Ostend and Zeebrugge, but we are not quite sure' was never given. Jellicoe had said that there was food enough in the country for no more than three weeks and that there was no point in discussing plans for next year: 'We can not go on.' And so, as Jackie Fisher had said, it was up to the Army to mount a campaign, not to fight its main enemy to the death but to move through the mud and sand of the Flanders plain and coast until it could do the Navy's work for it. Thus matters stood in England around the summer solstice of 1917. The French army was on the ropes, the Russians and Italians looked like joining them, the Greeks seemed about to change sides and certain of the Irish were causing all the trouble they could. The country was tormented by air-raids, extremely hungry and its only hope of survival seemed to be the campaign demanded by the Navy. Sir Douglas Haig, most fortunately, appeared imperturbable. Few men in our long history have carried a burden anything like the one bent upon his soldierly back.

No military situation is ever quite as good or quite as bad as it appears at first glance. The surface ships of the Royal Navy were keeping up an effective blockade of Germany; the sub-surface ships of the Imperial Navy were doing the same thing in reverse. The result depended partly upon what the food producers could do to mitigate things and partly upon what armed forces might be used to break the deadlock. At both Dover and Dunkirk the Navy, soon to be strengthened by the US Northern Bombing Group, maintained strong sea and air equipment but had little to show for it. Admiral Bacon was convinced that his barrage was preventing the U-boats from moving up and down Channel but in this he deceived himself. The arrival of Roger Keyes was to demonstrate that for a long time past there had been a tacit non-aggression pact between Dover and Zeebrugge. Neither had much inclination to set about the other for fear of retaliation. It was an imperfect way of seeking a military decision. The Germans could not bring the blockade of their country to an end by taking Portsmouth, Plymouth, Chatham and Harwich. The Royal Navy could not take Ostend, Zeebrugge, Wilhelmshaven and Cuxhaven. Even accepting that, the army could win a great naval victory by seizing the first two. It would call for fresh thinking, new weapons and new men.

Even with an imperfect knowledge of all this, the Kaiser and his entourage might have been expected to climb up to the topmasts of hope. They did not. In Imperial Germany the Army was the senior service and it did not admire the Navy above half. Admirals might hold forth about their U-boats having the *Englander* by the throat. Generals were not so sure. They had been handled more roughly by the British Army than anybody had expected, sometimes outgunned and often outfought. The fact that three British officers had been killed for every one German did not seem to deter them. The Kaiser was not jubilant. On 17 March he withdrew from life to the castle at Homburg and refused to budge. The new Emperor of Austria, whom everyone knew to desire peace at almost any price, arrived with his Foreign Minister, Count Czernin. The young Emperor told the older one that Austria was done for and could not last out until the end of the year. Czernin told Admiral von Müller that if the war did not end within three months the peoples would end it without reference to their rulers. The blockade was not working only in one way. In Berlin there had been food riots in February and March, followed by a strike of half a million workers during the following month. Herr von Ballin, Germany's biggest shipping magnate, wrote to von Müller on 20 June cursing the Chancellor for weakening on the question of unrestricted U-boat warfare, Admiral Holtzendorff for alienating more and more of the neutrals and the Kaiser 'who was always in Cloud Cuckoo Land'. The great European effort at mass suicide was progressing nicely. Only the refusal by all sides to give in kept the war going. And it had a long way still to go. Everywhere the factories were churning out ever greater quantities of every kind of war material; but the belligerents were running out of young men to use them.

It was not the killed, however grievous the final loss might be, that alone mattered. The brutal accountancy of war makes it more cost-effective to wound than to slay. A dead man needs no more than a hole in the ground and another to take his place. Wounded need to be transported, doctored, nursed, fed, housed, paid, clothed, entertained and pensioned. Every one of these activities demands the services of more people who thus contribute little to success in battle. One point, however, is missed. The dead were, for the most part, young men. The sons and daughters they never had, the children of a nation's finest, were to be sadly missed two or three decades later. The truth was that the war had got out of anyone's control. No statesman of any nationality who was not certifiably insane would have started it had he the least idea of what he was turning loose on the world. By mid-1917 it was pride that kept it going, the entirely praiseworthy and manly feeling that one's nation − more particularly one's regiment − did not give in or admit another to be better men. Nobody, save the United States, had any possible advantage in continuing it until somebody threw in

35

the towel. All that Europe had built up over many centuries was being squandered with little chance of replacement. The war had acquired an identity of its own; and it chose to go on to the end.

CHAPTER THREE

THE COMING OF THE TANK

IT WAS IN THE WEEKS following Messines that the end of western Christendom in its then form began. In the French army less than a third of the infantrymen were now of ages between 20 and 32. The British Government was about to raise the call-up age to 55. The enemy was in no better case, especially the now reluctant Austrian. It was to take two generations before Europe became what we now see, but the ground had been made ready and fertilized.

As the supply of men diminished so it became needful to make each one as efficient a machine of destruction as possible. The weapons of the first couple of years had all been those of the 19th century. Now was the moment to improve on them. Pétain gave his infantrymen a number of 37mm guns (the same ones that were to be put into American tanks in Hitler's war) and Stokes mortars in order to help them in taking on the machine guns. Every section was kitted out with the new grenade-discharger called the VB, more and more light machine guns – Chauchart and Hotchkiss for the most part – appeared from somewhere and the artillery was greatly expanded in proportion to the other arms. The vast increase even in field pieces in the BEF is demonstrated by their shell consumption. From 3,000 shells a month in September, 1914, it had mushroomed to 8,000,000 in the summer of 1917.

Though all Generals were tied to their own national doctrines of war, hammered out over the years in Staff Colleges and mitigated, in the British case, by much Indian and African experience, there were other minds at work. The demands for some new thing came, as it had to come, from those whose profession was other than war. In Germany, the home of abstract thought, it was the scientists who contributed the most. IG Farben, with advantages denied to Boots Cash Chemists, had given the first chance with its introduction of asphyxiating gas two years earlier. Brigadier-General Baker-Carr, who witnessed it, was quite certain that it gave the German army its best opportunity of winning the war. Only stupefaction at its own success held it back. The same learned men, now that chlorine and phosgene had been countered by masks, produced something new; it was called mustard gas. It seldom killed but could cause hideous injury and, more important, it could make large parcels of land unfit for human habitation over quite a long period. The inventors gave their masters fair warning. Mustard gas was not difficult to make and the allies with their superior resources ought to be able to swamp the German army with it inside a twelvemonth. In fact Germany had the field to itself for little more than half that time. The free period was not wasted.

From the allied point of view there was more to it than inventing a new Excalibur. The greatest weakness in the new mass armies was in their systems of communication. The inadequacy of telephone line in shelled territory needed no explaining; wireless telegraphy was still very imperfect and the radio telephone little more than a dream. Sir Douglas had other worries; anything he might wish to do was limited by the physical problem of moving men, guns, ammunition and stores to wherever they were needed; the Nord railway, built long ago by the Rothschilds, was hopelessly inadequate for current purposes and utterly unreliable; roads, never designed for more than farm carts, coaches and *la diligence*, needed constant and massive repair. Had the C-in-C been offered the choice he would pretty certainly have foregone the tank in favour of locomotives, sidings, plank roads, hutments and timber — together with unlimited labour.

Nevertheless good minds had been and still were working on more spectacular aids to victory. If, as somebody once said, victory has a thousand fathers but defeat none at all then the same apophthegm will serve for the tank.

Probably the first fighting vehicle of modern times was the one invented by the Bohemian General Zizka, to whom we are supposed also to owe the word howitzer. This imaginative man put his peasant army into farm carts, formed wagon-laagers and with them ruined his enemies as the Boers under Andries Pretorius were to ruin the Zulus at Blood River. In 1914, especially after the French army had lost something like a third of a million men in the opening battles, everybody had an idea of some sort of armoured locomotive that might walk through small arms fire unscathed. The internal combustion engine had demonstrated its ability to propel a flying machine; only the track was needed. Such a thing certainly existed. As long ago as 1909 'Wully' Robertson, about to become Commandant of the Staff College, went to a demonstration at Aldershot. A Hornsby tractor, closely resembling one of the creations of the late Rowland Emmett, was put through its paces. 'Wully' felt sympathy for the driver who 'experienced all the sensations of acute sea-sickness and looked it', but no business resulted. As it happened, the chief engineer to the makers was a man of some distinction. Mr Howard

Livens, in a sort of partnership with his more famous son, added something to the tally of new-style weapons as will presently be told. No military man showed the slightest interest in smelly, noisy and unreliable substitutes for the horse.

No military man save one. Major Ernest Swinton RE possessed a mind as enquiring as it was well-stocked. After service in South Africa he had devoted much attention to the machine gun, a weapon of little use on the veldt but plainly with possibilities. These were realized during the Russo-Japanese war of 1904 of which Swinton became the British Official Historian. Amongst his qualifications for this were a proper respect for the English language, a keen sense of the ridiculous and the ability to be deadly serious without ever being solemn. Proof of this had already been given.

In 1904, at the age of 36, he had written a book. Under the pseudonym 'Backsight Forethought' and armed with much South African experience he produced the splendid *The Defence of Duffer's Drift*. It tells of a young and green subaltern left to hold a river crossing against probable Boer attacks. He dreams of the various dispositions he has made of his little garrison, each ending with a commando swarming over them; at last he sees how the thing should be done, and does it. *Duffer's Drift* combines amusement and instruction better, probably, than any little red manual from Gale & Polden. It was recently reissued and is still worth reading.

It was the books (other excellent ones followed) that settled Swinton's future and may have accelerated the tank's arrival. Very early in the Kaiser's war it became plain that something had to be done about the reporting of it. The great correspondents, the Bennet Burleighs, W.E. Hentys, Mortimer Mempes and their kind were gone. Most happily wireless and television had not yet come to make military secrecy impossible. Lord Kitchener, though he had had much time for G.W. Steevens, long in his grave at Ladysmith, loathed the whole breed. As he was under the necessity of doing something, the great man sent for his brother Sapper and ordered him to France as a kind of journalist. Under the name of 'Eyewitness' — his peers never addressed him as anything else — Swinton's task was to write monographs on the *faites et gestes* of Sir John French's army and send them back direct to the War Office. His book, bearing the same name, on what happened to him in that capacity remains a delight. He tells in particular, because the subject was near to his heart, of the makeshift weapons forced upon that army for lack of others when trench warfare set in. He met the American Colonel Lewis whose light automatic, once rejected, was now being snapped up by every country that could get it. The Colonel was at GHQ to exhibit 'a rocket gun, a type of trench-mortar designed by himself'. One has to suppose that it got no further than Sir John French since no more is heard of the weapon. Which was a pity but unsurprising.

There were Royal Engineers other than the ingenious Captain Livens who were set to work at making bombs and mortars from scratch. To the Royal Regiment of Artillery such things were impure. No proper gunner would wish to be associated with them. 'Flying Pigs' had moments of glory and hopefulness until one reversed course in full flight and nearly destroyed a covey of general officers. The mortar that survived, the 3″ Stokes (still in service in much of its original form) was the gift of a civilian. Mr (later Sir) Wilfrid Stokes was chairman of the famous company Ransome & Rapier and an experienced civil engineer. His creation was simplicity itself. A steel tube about four feet long held at an acute angle by a bi-pedal frame and with a base plate at the other end had no working parts. At the bottom of the tube a spike was screwed in. The bomb, with tail fins to give it stability and cotton bags of explosive clipped between them, was dropped down the tube. A 12-bore cartridge with a spiked clip over the cap lay in the tail, between the fins. The weight of the 10 lb bomb as the cap hit the spike touched off the cartridge and the rest followed. Range could be adjusted by the number of little cotton bags and screw adjustments for line and elevation were simple. The Stokes mortar was soon to become one of the handful of sovereign weapons thrown up by the war.

It may be appropriate, even though the immediate circumstance is trifling, to introduce a character of first importance to this story. Swinton — and, for that matter, Lord Kitchener — had a brother Sapper named George Montague Harper, then Brigadier-General and 'a sort of fifth wheel in GHQ coach, having no very definite duties and no responsibility'. He was a burly man, well liked by his peers and seemed long since to have adopted a style known in the theatre as 'the heavy' or 'buffo'. The occasion of this meeting was Swinton's arrival in the office of 'Uncle' Harper — he was never called otherwise — wearing black ammunition boots; the damp had swollen his feet and he could get no others. 'Uncle' attached much importance to what was or was not 'done' and the right places at which to buy clothes, especially breeches and boots. He also had the habit, plainly resented by Swinton, of poking fun at his literary efforts. 'Hallo, Eyewitness,' he said, 'your last shocker was pretty poor stuff.' Swinton tactfully agreed. 'Then his critical eye wandered over my uniform, plainly not made by the "right" tailor, and finally stopped at my boots. "What the devil have you got on your feet?" "Boots," said I promptly and accurately. "Yes, but who made them? I never saw such things." "They are the very latest from town," I glibly answered. I knew my interlocutor's weakness. Interest was at once aroused. "Whose are they? Fortnum & Mason's?" ' Swinton, having had other things to do than learn from the magazines that this illustrious firm had indeed gone into the boot trade, thought 'Uncle' to be teasing him. It would not be a battle of equals. ' "Oh no. These aren't Fortnum & Masons. Their boots are quite out of date now." "Then whose are they?" snapped "Uncle", his dignity as arbiter of modes wounded. "Oh, just, just — Justerini & Brooks," said I at a venture, mentioning the name of the first establishment of the same class that occurred to me. "Good Lord. Do you mean to say that they've taken to making boots too?" said "Uncle" in a tone implying that the matter must be investigated without delay. "Well," said I, "I don't see why a — wine merchant should not make boots as well as a — grocer".' 'Uncle', it seems, was persuaded. This facet of his character is mildly amusing but there was a more dangerous side to it.

Colonel (he was promoted Brigadier-General in November 1914) Harper, at just over 50, was not nearly as old as his white hair and black eyebrows suggested. His principal claim to fame, so far, had been in the shadow of Henry Wilson. When that officer had been Commandant of the Staff College in the years before the war Harper had been on the directing staff and the two had become fast friends. Harper's record of service until then had been of a routine kind and it is understandable that he still remained what Fuller called an 1870 soldier. When Wolseley slipped a Division through the Suez Canal and the Household Cavalry charged by moonlight at Kassassin, Gentleman Cadet Harper was a 'snooker' at Woolwich. Six months before Gordon died in Khartoum he had been gazetted and for 16 years his career followed the usual lines. In South Africa he had had the misfortune to contract enteric fever and was sent home. In the words of his DNB entry by Colonel de Watteville, 'He was rewarded with the DSO'. Not every dysentery patient could claim this. Apart from presence as a Captain of Engineers at Spion Kop 'Uncle' had not so far smelt much powder. In the months before August, 1914, when Henry Wilson was DMO at the War Office, Harper had worked under him in preparing the intricate plans for getting an Expeditionary Force to France. His part in this had been carried out admirably but in doing so Colonel Harper had worked himself out of a job. 'Uncle' had not been at Omdurman. When that campaign was in progress he had been Adjutant of the RE Volunteers in Leeds. He knew nothing of machine guns, beyond the customary disapproval common to most regular officers, and when made aware of plans for grafting large numbers of them on to the army he knew and loved 'Uncle' Harper decided that they should die of inanition. In February, 1915, he was to be given a Brigade in General Keir's 6th Division and see a lot of infantry fighting around Hill 60 which taught him better but in the autumn of 1914 he had no time for such new-fangled things.

It came about in this way. Christopher Baker-Carr had been a Rifleman and had witnessed both Omdurman and South Africa. The first had shown him how Sir Hiram Maxim's machine gun was the first weapon of mass destruction and that it would thenceforth be the arbiter of battlefields. As hardly anybody else in the army seemed to share his views he had sent in his papers in 1906. When the war started he was devoid of any military status but by no means uninterested at the age of 36. His first appearance was as one of the volunteer motor drivers raised by the RAC to put themselves and their automobiles at the disposal of GHQ. Chance guides the destinies of men. When Swinton, alias Eyewitness, first arrived in France he was given a fine claret-coloured Mors car with a fork-bearded driver whom he called the Assyrian. When, after some interruption, both Mors and Assyrian disappeared he was furnished with an equally fine Mercedes and its owner-driver, Mr Baker-Carr. They got on very well together. As Baker-Carr, who had learned his business at Hythe, knew more about machine guns than most men it is hardly surprising to learn that he was soon back in the commissioned ranks of the Army.

Though Swinton was by a decade the older man their shared faith in mechanical warfare and an irrepressible sense of the ridiculous kept them on excellent terms. The Maxim gun, soon to be replaced by the rather lighter version known to history as the Vickers-Maxim, was the only automatic weapon then in the British service. It was a marvel of ingenuity, belt-fed, water-cooled and worked by the forces generated by each recoiling cartridge case. This alone had probably led to its neglect. To many infantry COs the thing was a nuisance; it spoilt the look of a parade and the section was usually turned over to the colonel's least regarded subaltern. Baker-Carr knew all about this. 'The reason for the phenomenon is somewhat obscure but may be largely traced to the average Englishman's deep-rooted dislike and distrust of machinery in general.' In no Englishman did the roots go deeper nor the distrust blossom more strongly than in 'Uncle' Harper.

GHQ was at this period of the war settled uncomfortably and largely by accident at St Omer. Baker-Carr, in his capacity of chauffeur to the great, found himself constantly there; it was an opportunity to pick up old army friendships and to make new ones. Among the former was General 'Tommy' Capper, one of the 1914 Army's great names. His 7th Division, having smashed the German attack at First Ypres, now numbered less than a weak battalion. Baker-Carr had qualified at the Small Arms School, Hythe. Capper had not a single trained machine-gunner left. The next step was obvious. Never mind about having resigned his commission. Would Baker-Carr take over training machine-gunners to replace them? After a talk with French's Military Secretary, Colonel Lambton, it was agreed that something more was needed. Baker-Carr should be taken back on the strength and train machine-gunners for the whole BEF. He would only have to 'fix it with Uncle'. This sounded easy enough. His response to Baker-Carr was straightforward enough. 'Go away and do what you like, but don't bother me. I'm busy.' Thus began the formation of that mighty engine of destruction the Machine Gun Corps. At the beginning it consisted of nothing but Baker-Carr himself. He could obviously expect no help at all from Harper. Fortunately there were people who took another view. Very quickly the Machine Gun School began its courses of instruction and the English machine-gunner became, by degrees, at least as competent as his German opposite number.

All of this owed nothing whatever to Brigadier-General Harper. 'I didn't dare to ask "Uncle" for such trifles as cooks, etc. He would in all probability tell me to go to blazes and might even regret having told me to get on with it. It was far safer to keep out of his sight and arrange matters myself.' For months to come, whilst it was training officers and NCOs by the hundred, the School did not, officially, exist. The Sergeant Instructors were temporary, acting, honorary, without pay, allowances or anything else. On paper they were all, until the Hythe men arrived, private soldiers on the strength of the Artists Rifles; Baker-Carr managed to obtain commissions for two of them fairly quickly. Later on the Artists Rifles furnished another dozen educated young men to be trained as instructors. The guns — both of them — came from an Irish regiment that had lost all its machine-gunners at First Ypres and saw little prospect of replacing them. Harper's experience of war had been confined to sapper business in South Africa, the 'last of the Gentlemen's wars' as one of Swinton's co-adjutors would one day call it. Perhaps he should not be too harshly judged for failing to grasp in 1915 that the first of the Players' wars had arrived.

Baker-Carr had no such fine feelings; no man who had seen what Maxim guns could do to massed dervishes should be expected to. At his instigation the *Times*, the *Morning Post*, the *Telegraph*, and the *Mail* all published articles on the need for more machine guns. Baker-Carr had one advantage over his companions. With all the credentials of a Regular officer, he had no career in the Regular Army to worry about. When Mr Asquith arrived in the neighbourhood he was buttonholed and lectured. Hardly surprisingly he took little of it in. Better informed was Lord Kitchener when he paid a visit in September, 1915. He spent several hours with Baker-Carr and obviously approved of him. Thus emboldened, and when sent for by K for a second meeting, Baker-Carr spoke of manpower. 'How many men do you want?' 'About 40,000 to start with, sir.' 'It's going to be a difficult job to find them.' In the end it was, 'Very well, my boy. You shall have your men. Some of the other arms will have to go a bit short, but it can't be helped.'

On 22 October, 1915, the Machine Gun Corps was born and it began to look as if the Olympian disdain with which mechanical toys like the Vickers were viewed was beginning to melt. Only in one quarter was it as entrenched as ever. 'With very considerable hesitation I approached "Uncle", but my very mild and tentative suggestions called forth such a torrent of half-jesting vituperation that I vanished from his presence with the utmost rapidity.' Such was Brigadier, shortly to be Major-General, George Montague Harper. When he reappears, as he will at a highly important phase of a great battle, it may not come amiss to remember what manner of man he was. For the time being let him return to his desk in St Omer. Baker-Carr and his co-adjutors continued the unremitting work of creating a *corps d'élite* from precious little. Their reward was very great indeed. On the day of the Armistice 6,427 officers and 123,835 other ranks wore the crossed Vickers badges of the Machine Gun Corps. Its dead numbered more than the rifle strength of two divisions. The words 'glorious heroes' on the Corps memorial at Hyde Park Corner are not hyperbole.

All this time, when he had any to spare from 'Eyewitnessing', Swinton was busying himself with plans for some armoured object, petrol-driven and caterpillar-mounted, that would squash the nests of German machine guns as boot heels do those of wasps. His heart was in the right place but nothing tangible appeared from his efforts. All that was on offer anywhere for the first year of the war appeared to be the armoured motor-car. This originated in Belgium, home to the excellent Minerva. The Cockerill works at Antwerp furnished steel plates and the result, so long as it stayed on metalled roads, was serviceable. Mr Churchill, then a present Naval Person, approved and ordered a number of similar machines for his Dunkirk Circus. Being designed for the Navy, for whom the best was always good enough, they came from Rolls-Royce.

This was of no immediate relevance to Swinton's problems, but by devious ways they led there. The City of London, in earlier days, contained many young and middle-aged gentlemen ready and willing at their country's call to exchange scrip for sword. Here, less than 20 years before, Sir Howard Vincent had raised the CIV – the City Imperial Volunteers – who had wrought famously in South Africa. Amongst the most important finance houses was that of Stern Brothers and not least of its partners was Albert Gerald, never called other than Bertie. Of his two brothers one was a Major in the South Irish Horse and the other Lieutenant in the Westminster Dragoons. An ankle damaged in some earlier accident kept Bertie from joining them, but he was not to be left out of the fray. Money is not always a thing to be regarded suspiciously. Since the Sterns had plenty of it Bertie decided to expend some for the good cause. It all began with a letter to Mr Churchill in November, 1914, containing an offer to 'provide and equip an armoured car, with crew complete, to be attached to Lieut. Spencer Grey's bombing squadron in Flanders'. The First Lord was not effusively grateful. 'In his opinion,' went the answer, 'an Armoured Car would be of little use to this unit and it would be much better if you were to arrange an interview with Captain Sueter, the Director of the Air Department at the Admiralty, and offer the services of the Car and yourself to the regular Armoured Car section which is being built up and organised under Commander Boothby at Wormwood Scrubs.' Stern, with uncharacteristic meekness, did as he was bidden.

The whole business began at the *Daily Mail* Airship Shed. On arrival there with a commission as Lieutenant RNVR in his pocket, given over the counter by Sueter, Stern found an organized chaos. There was no building but the shed, no accommodation nor any roads. Only mud. In this were forming armoured car squadrons and motor-cycle machine-gun squadrons, all dressed as sailors and with little idea of what was intended for them.

The Mess contained like-minded men, racing motorists, soldiers and others. There was Hetherington, the second-in-command, who had begun life as a Hussar, left the service young to become a pioneer airman and had won prizes as both horseman and pilot. At 28 he had not only all these things behind him but also three years on the shop floor at Coventry. An even older Harrovian had been the only fag of his generation to sport a Crimean medal. Rookes Evelyn Bell Crompton was 70 now but at 11 he had accompanied his naval uncle to that war, as a rather spurious cadet, and returned genuinely entitled to his decoration. His exploits in between, mostly connected with electrical engineering, had been many and far-ranging. You may still see his name on light bulbs. Co-opted were 'Bendor', Duke of Westminster, and Winston Churchill. Regularly, over very good cigars, talk returned to Swinton's theme. Young, or fairly young, men saw visions; the old man dreamed dreams. There were plans for a Big Wheel, like that set up at the White City by Mr Kiralfy for the amusement of the masses; it might, propelled by some yet uninvented engine of vast power, be able to roll across the Rhine. There was the Pedrail, invented by an eccentric man named, almost as eccentrically, Bramah Diplock. This was simply one wide caterpillar track, capable of moving forward or backward but nothing else. Colonel Crompton saw possibilities in it and spent much time and money in producing the basis for a huge land battleship. It was too big, underpowered and soon discarded, much to the Colonel's displeasure. Commodore Murray Sueter came up with something on the same lines: a twin Pedrail machine closely resembling a submarine on tracks, complete with conning tower and various optional extras. That too had no future. Some of the ideas were doomed to failure before they started. Mr Churchill's revival of King Porus' elephants, two side-by-side steam rollers, roared and thrashed but made no forward movement on an inch or so of mud. Yet it was Mr Churchill who, more than any other man, set the business on its feet.

Colonel Crompton was consulting engineer to the Road Board. The Admiralty, under orders from its First Lord, borrowed him so that he might design Landships. Crompton awarded the contract for his Pedrail machine to Fodens of Sandbach in Cheshire. The Admiralty had formed a Landships Committee and had put it in the charge of Mr Eustace Tennyson-d'Eyncourt, Chief of Naval Construction since 1912. Having work to do other than inspecting Pedrails, d'Eyncourt asked Hetherington to find him a secretary with a sufficiency of what was then called 'push and go'. The name of Bertie Stern leapt to the mind and he willingly picked up the burden.

In June, 1915, the Committee delivered a long report to Mr Churchill, the greater part of it telling of trials and errors. The First Lord, with only days left of his tenure, took it very seriously. He himself had already written memoranda on the *Variants Of The Offensive*, the first bearing the date 6 December, 1914, and having been delivered to Sir John French. The most important item in Stern's document was an account of the discovery of the Bullock Creeping Grip caterpillar track, made by a firm in Chicago. It was not something revolutionary. In July, 1914, Swinton had been told by Mr Marriott, a mining engineer whom he had known in South Africa, that there was to be found in Antwerp an example of the Holt Caterpillar Tractor, also American, that had great powers of crossing rough ground. Swinton brought it to the notice of Lieutenant-Colonel Maurice Hankey, Secretary to the Committee of Imperial Defence and to the Director of Artillery and Transport at the War Office. 'These officials were mildly interested; and there the thing remained.' Why, with all this knowledge in Whitehall, none of the Committee had ever heard of the Holt Tractor remains a mystery. It was in service before long in both British and French armies for towing heavy artillery pieces. On the whole this may not have been entirely unfortunate. No Holt tracks would have been made available to crackpot civilians. Enquiries showed a tractor with the Bullock Creeping Grip to be at work in the marshes at Greenhithe. Strictly speaking it was a half-track with the Bullock device pushing from behind and a pair of wheels steering it like a car. The experts hurried to Greenhithe and were captivated by what they saw. Lieutenant (strictly temporary) Field was packed off to Chicago with a cheque-book.

With the caterpillar apparently available, the next thing was to marry it to an engine. This proved surprisingly easy. Admiral Bacon was a sailor with ideas ahead of his time. They were not always successful. When Roger Keyes took over the Dover Patrol from him early in 1918 he found the German navy to be treating Bacon's anti-submarine barrage as a huge joke. He had, however, his better ideas. Bacon had left the Navy during the internecine struggles of the Fisher era and taken a civilian post with the Coventry Ordnance works. In 1914 he became its Managing Director. Bacon had no intention of remaining a civilian and demanded to be taken back under the White Ensign. A compromise was reached. His company had the necessary rights over the Daimler 150 hp petrol engine, probably the biggest thing of its kind in England. Using this, the Coventry works could and did turn out half-a-dozen huge-wheeled tractors fit to tow anything. Bacon was given a new commission as Colonel of Marines and allowed to take to France his tractors and the Coventry-made howitzers they were to pull. The tractors were of no use to Stern's people but the engine was just what they needed. Armour plate, at this stage of the war, was not a great difficulty. So long as only flat sheets were required the Admiralty could purvey them. One thing remained: the machine lacked a transmission system.

Here again fortune smiled. Swinton had remarked that the Artists Rifles could probably, if needed, find him a deep-sea diver or a Hooghly pilot. The Royal Navy, as expanded, was no less versatile. In its ranks, wearing the two wavy rings of Lieutenant RNVR, was one of this century's most remarkable engineers. Walter Gordon Wilson had more right to his rings than most for he was an old Britannia cadet; the Navy, however, had not detained him long and he had turned to mechanical engineering. With Otto Lilienthal and Percy Pilcher he had been one of the pioneers of flying; the motor-car he and Pilcher built in 1904 still stands treasured by the Tank Museum at Bovington. In 1914, at the age of 40, he had left the firm of Armstrong Whitworth for the duration and had turned his skill to the design and building of armoured cars. As he was the first authority in the country on transmissions, clutches and gear-boxes he was soon drafted on to the Landships Committee. Stern first met him in June, 1915, at the Burton-on-Trent experimental ground that the Committee had hired. Of all the men concerned it was Wilson alone who was irreplaceable. Happily the need did not arise. He was still designing tank transmissions at the beginning of Hitler's war.

By July, 1915, the characters had assembled, the props had arrived and the play was about to begin. Swinton, in his capacity not of Eyewitness but as a member of the futile Inventions Board, went to see Lord Kitchener. As to a brother Sapper, Swinton held forth about machine-gun destroyers. Kitchener referred him to d'Eyncourt; d'Eyncourt passed him on to Stern. 'I wrote at once to the latter. This was like lighting the fuse of a mine. He bounced into my room, bubbling over with enthusiasm, and proceeded to explain what his Committee was doing. He was dressed in naval uniform but was obviously no sailor, and I could not at first fathom his position *dans cette galère*. To learn, after tactful enquiry, that he was a banker made things "curiouser and curiouser". We both burst out laughing —an auspicious beginning of an association which was to last for over a year.'

Mechanized warfare as the twentieth century understands it was invented in August, 1915, at the White Hart Hotel, Lincoln. There the two genuine experts, Mr Tritton of Fosters and Wilson, sat up night after night sketching, planning and calculating. Stern, the all-purpose goader, visited them from time to time with messages. On the 26th he brought the latest requirements of the War Office, a body dragged into the tank business by Swinton on Mr Churchill's leaving the Admiralty. The demand was for a machine capable of crossing a five-foot trench with a four-foot-six high parapet. Tritton dealt with tracks; the Bullock system needed much modification before it could be considered reliable enough. Wilson did much of the designing and attended to the transmission. D'Eyncourt, with his warship experience, designed the sponsons — metal boxes bolted to the sides and carrying the guns like panniers on a donkey. The first-born, called 'Little Willie', was a motorised iron potting shed on tracks, swiftly abandoned as not worth further effort. The second was altogether more serious. Swinton was taken to see it at Foster's works on Sunday 19 September — 48 hours before the Battle of Loos was to open — and was suitably impressed. After watching Little Willie's unexciting performance, carried out in front of an audience of Lincoln citizenry, he was taken behind closed doors. There he was shown a wooden mock-up of a lozenge-shaped contraption with an upturned nose and caterpillar tracks running all round it. 'These were the *clou* of the design and the essential and original characteristics of the machine, and had been introduced to enable it to surmount or climb the stipulated vertical height of five feet.' He congratulated the designers heartily on a 'stupendous achievement'. 'Dinner on the train on the return journey to London was a joyous occasion.'

The next day, on Stern's orders, the mock-up was brought by lorry to the Trench Warfare Experimental Ground at Wembley where a large and distinguished audience would inspect and pass judgment. On the Friday 14 British Divisions, two of them freshly arrived in France, were marched into the uncut wire and massed machine-guns. The only good result of the Battle of Loos was the removal of Sir John French from a command that he should never have held. It cost, on this one occasion, some 50,000 casualties.

Stern laid on his exhibition for a week after Loos when all that had happened there was common knowledge. About a score of people, including Swinton, attended. All but one expressed satisfaction. General Sir Stanley von Donop, Master-General of the Ordnance, did not like it. 'He viewed with dismay the fact that the War Office, the Committee of Imperial Defence and the Admiralty were all mixed-up in deciding this question. He was also somewhat annoyed that he should have been asked to provide guns and ammunition when he had not been consulted as to their pattern.' Perhaps it was as well that he had been excluded. 'A 2.95 inch mountain gun was borrowed from Woolwich and proved satisfactory, but it was impossible to get, so in the end the 6-pounder naval gun was adopted, Admiral Singer (Director of Naval Ordnance) having told us that he was ready to release a number of these.'

October, 1915, as has been mentioned, witnessed the arrival in the Army List of the Machine Gun Corps. It needed, as all Corps do, a permanent home or depot. Whether by accident or design this was chosen to be at Grantham, no great distance from Lincoln. In consequence the MGC and the producers of the new machines were close to each other at the beginning. It was in the same month that the thing came to be called a Tank. For obvious security reasons it had had to have a jargon name of some kind; 'water carrier' seemed as good as another. Committees in governmental circles are known by their initials. Stern eyed the WC Committee bleakly; at his suggestion it became 'Tank and Tank Supply'. Inapt the name may have been but in three-quarters of a century nobody has come up with anything better. Practically every known language has engrossed it.

The first tank, variously called Centipede or Mother, was shown off as a finished product ready for the field at Hatfield Park in January, 1916. On that historic spot where, not so very long before, Robert, 3rd Marquess of Salisbury, had been accustomed to take tricycle exercise, frock-coated, with a running footman in attendance to help him over the steeper parts, the shape of things to come was revealed. There is no need here to go into all the details. Many excellent books, along with some others, have set them all out. Suffice it that the tank emerged triumphant and in two forms. The male was equipped with 6-pdr naval guns in its sponsons wherewith to smash up enemy machine-gun positions. The female carried only machine guns, the better to slaughter foemen who might swarm over her consort. The gun chosen was a cut-down model of the cavalry's strip-fed Hotchkiss light automatic.* It was not very accurate but marksmanship from a moving tank was nearer that of Chicago than Bisley. Wilson's hurriedly-contrived transmission was clumsy; the wonder was that it worked at all.

The Mk I tank was, in round figures, 31 feet long, 8 feet high and nearly 14 feet in beam. It weighed, fully laden, some 28 tons. To work and fight it demanded a crew of eight men, distributed in this fashion. Right forward, high up in a kind of conning tower, sat the driver and the commander, the first-named on the right. The top of the tower was raised a foot above the level of the tracks and in front of each man was a window that could be closed from inside by means of a steel flap. Below these the wall sloped downwards to foot level and there it met the upward slope of the floor. The driver, in the first models, was given a steering wheel like that of a car; this worked by cables and pulleys the pair of trailing wheels which were supposed to steer the tank as a rudder steers a boat. They were not a success but lasted for some time. In addition he had a clutch and

---

* For unsatisfactory reasons the Hotchkiss was, for a time, replaced by the less handy Lewis. This was the main armament during the Battle of Cambrai.

gear-lever of the usual kind, with a range of four speeds. In bottom the tank could grind along at ¾ mph; in top it could manage four. The change from bottom to second could be effected by the driver alone but further upward movement called for help. Wilson had come to the conclusion that the 2-speed box made for Little Willie would not be man enough for Mother. He had therefore contrived supplementary gears between the differential and the final drive sprockets, housed in the track frame behind the sponsons. This called for two extra gearsmen, placed inevitably where they could see the driver but he could not see them. To change into 3rd or 4th gear the driver would bang on the engine cover to attract the gearsmen's attention and raise one or two fingers to indicate his requirements. In order to make a full turn the driver would raise a clenched fist and point to one side or the other. The gearsman thus indicated would put his gears into neutral whilst the track on the other side continued as before. The commander, whose responsibilities included the handbrakes, would pull on the appropriate lever and the tank would slew round. In addition to more obvious duties, the commander had to keep on his knee all the maps and aerial photographs needed for the current task and, in order to keep him from idleness, he had a light machine gun of his own, swivel-mounted and facing forwards. The other four of the crew were the gunners and loaders. In males, the 6-pdr gunners knelt on the sponson floor, eyes to the telescopic sight and finger on the trigger, searching around for enemy machine guns or batteries. Whenever they fired, which was often, the noise of the explosion filled the inside of the tank above all other noises; the loading number extracted the empty case, fed in a fresh one and, as the opportunity offered, slung out the empties through a small opening beneath the sponson door. In action, with all guns blazing, the 105 h.p. sleeve-valve Daimler engine roaring away, bullets and shell fragments clanging against the steel walls (and not always being kept out by them) it was an unquiet form of warfare. The temperature inside, even though ventilation was provided by a small fan, commonly averaged 125° and the pipes leading to the exhaust grew red-hot. As the first models lacked silencers the noise, sparks and flames from open exhausts swiftly revealed the presence of a tank to anybody interested. Makeshifts conjured out of old oil drums, wet sacks and mud had to serve until better arrangements could be made. On top of everything was a great curved starting handle that took three men to swing. The petrol tanks, feeding by gravity, were high up by the driver's cab. When they caught fire, as did happen, the whole tank would go up and the crew with it. The petrol, incidentally, was the worst procurable, sometimes little better than kerosene. The Royal Flying Corps had a monopoly of no 1 aviation spirit.

With all her faults, some remediable and others not, Mother was pronounced *bon pour la service*. There were reservations from Colonel

1. Sir Ernest Swinton "possessed a mind as enquiring as it was well stocked" (p.39).
(*Royal Engineers Library*)

2. (*below left*) 'Uncle' Harper "adopted a style known in the theatre as 'the heavy' or 'buffo'" (p.40).
(*Royal Engineers Library*)

3. Brigadier-General Baker-Carr "knew more about machine-guns than most men" (p.40).
(*Tank Museum*)

4. *(left)* Lieutenant-Colonel Albert ('Bertie') Stern (p.44).

5. *(below left)* Colonel F. E. Hotblack "had an encyclopaedic knowledge of the Belgian coast and the German order of battle" (p.70).
(Tank Museum)

6. *(below right)* Brigadier-General Hugh Elles: "Not, perhaps, an intellectual giant but a good man with whom to go tiger-shooting" (p.76)
(Tank Museum)

7. *(left)* Brigadier-General John Hardress Lloyd (p.78).
(Tank Museum)

8. *(below left)* Brigadier-General John Charteris, "like a good nanny, determined to keep up [Haig's] spirits with soothing stories" (p.79).

9. *(below right)* Brigadier-General H. H. Tudor "was the proponent of of the idea of using the guns unregistered and uncalibrated" (p.95).

10. Field-Marshal Haig (*centre*) with (*from left*) Sir Henry Rawlinson, Sir Julian Byng, Sir Henry Horne, Sir Herbert Lawrence and Sir William Birdwood. Cambrai, 11 November, 1918. (*IWM*)

11. Queen Mary inspecting Central Workshops at Erin, 7 June, 1917. The Tank is a hermaphrodite with both 6pdr and Lewis Gun. (*IWM*)

Crompton, still feeling ill-used. He called her the Slug. This was less than kind but the tank was not what the Colonel had envisaged. The machine, unlike his Pedrail, was a fighting vehicle but not a personnel carrier. Crompton's plan had been to carry men, probably a couple of infantry sections at a time, across shell- and bullet-swept ground and to set them down behind enemy positions. Mother could not do that. It may be that Colonel Crompton will have the last laugh. Current doctrine in some authoritative places is on his side. The main Israeli battle-tank, the Merkava, is designed to carry not only a substantial armament but also an infantry section. It is, perhaps, also worth mentioning that the Victoria Crosses and other high decorations in which the Corps prides itself were for the most part won by members of crews driven out of broken tanks fighting as infantry with dismounted Lewis guns in places that no infantryman could have reached.

The other ostensible non-convert, Lord Kitchener, also said cruel things about mechanical toys but only because he was shocked by the lack of security. It took 20 years and the appearance of Mr Lloyd George's memoirs before the world knew Lord K to be a tank enthusiast. Had he lived but a little longer the story of the tank might have been very different. As it was, the Government placed a toe-in-the-water order for 100 Mk I Tanks, half of them 6-pdr armed males, the others females with sponsons modified to take the Vickers machine gun. Tritton, whose firm could not manage this unaided, had to see ¾ of the valuable contract going to the Metropolitan Carriage, Waggon & Finance Company.

Thus the machines. The men were not difficult to find. Under blood-curdling pledges of secrecy they came in to join the Heavy Section of the Machine Gun Corps and were packed off to the remote fastness of Lord Iveagh's estate in Norfolk.

Colonel Swinton now reappears. In early February, during one of his regular visits to the War Office, he had had a chance encounter with General Bird, the Director of Staff Duties. 'To my astonishment he informed me that the Army Council had selected me to raise and command the Tank Detachment, the new unit which was to be formed to man the Tanks. I was to be in charge of it at home, while in France it was to be under the local commanders.' Swinton did not want the job. He was 54 years old now and working quite happily alongside Hankey as secretary to the Dardanelles Commission. It was an order, and he obeyed. To begin with he composed the famous Memorandum which laid down the organization and drills for armies yet to come. Whilst so engaged he bamboozled Mr Driver Jonas, the agent, into giving him immediate possession of the Elveden estate and put Captain Martel, of whom more later, to the task of making it look like a regular battlefield.

In point of manpower Swinton did not have to start from scratch. Early in the war there had come into existence something called the Motor Machinegun Service, dedicated to turning motor-cycles and side-cars into weapons of mass destruction. Though it had proved not to be a good idea, its members, all of high intelligence and, says Swinton, superior education, were transferred bodily to the Heavy Section. One of those who joined, later to be Captain J.K. Wilson, says that many of the new entry who joined at Elveden were coal miners, men supposed to be familiar with machinery, noise and claustrophobic conditions. There could have been no better choice. A Colonel of Blue Marines — Royal Marine Artillery — John Brough, was put in charge of training and five company commanders were appointed, against the day when they would have their twenty-five tanks each. One was a Gunner, three came from the infantry and the last pair were, like Stern, paper sailors. The Navy furnished gunnery instructors. Major Knothe of the ASC, who had been in charge of the Holt tractors used by the artillery, was borrowed to re-assemble Mother and get her to Elveden.

Hankey and Stern were regular visitors and with brains of such excellent quality at work there emerged a doctrine of war a little in advance of its time. Swinton was firmly, and rightly, of the view that the tank's most serious enemy would be some sort of field gun. This would have to be eliminated either by our own artillery or by air bombing. Hankey suggested what he called 'Grasshoppers', aircraft not wanted for any other purpose and fitted with an armoured plate under the pilot's seat, as working partners for the tanks. Swinton held to the same view. When it was put up to General Sir David Henderson of the RFC he came back with a flat 'Can't be done'.

Proudly aware that they were going to make history, the young men of the Heavy Section swarmed all over their ungainly charges for hour after hour, acquainted themselves with the intimate details of their interior economy and drove them almost to the point of destruction. This they did in greasy canvas suits and, in defiance of custom, they talked even in the Mess nothing but shop. Their discipline was real, but it was the discipline of the bomber or submarine rather than of the Brigade. Swinton, sensible man that he was, left it alone. Enthusiasm and skill with machinery mattered more than turn-out or close-order drill. Some visiting senior officers took another view. Though he had, as yet, no reason to know it, Swinton had incurred heavy displeasure by permitting what Sandhurst called 'idleness'. He became a marked man both in Whitehall and at Montreuil where GHQ was comfortably ensconced. Only some spectacular feat of arms by his new model warriors could keep him in a job he neither had sought nor wanted. Failing that, Colonel Swinton could go back to his desk and some proper Aldershot-style soldier would straighten the backs and cut the hair of these sloppy-looking young men.

In this fashion the tank assumed its place in the British Army's order of battle.

CHAPTER FOUR

YOU CAN'T GET AWAY FROM THE GUNS!

R. Kipling

THE YEAR 1916 had opened with an improvement in the fortunes of the allies additional to the debut of Mother. The diminutive, militarily illiterate and foul-tempered Commander-in-Chief of the British Expeditionary Force had been translated to regions where his unsuitability for high command could no longer do much harm. In his chair sat the educated and imperturbable man who, not without failures of his own, would see the business through to its victorious end.

The whole feel of the war was now quite different; the battles fought in support of the French by men wearing flat caps with ear-flaps seemed to belong to an earlier age altogether. In large part this was a matter of the guns. Field-pieces, 18-pdrs and their foreign counterparts, were now quite outranged and outclassed. In war of movement, even at the sluggish pace of the animal transport era, they had been the fists of their armies. Now, though still excellent man-killers with shrapnel shells – the 'long-range grape' of Wellington's day – they found themselves of little use in a war of position. Since the armies had gone to ground it had been of the essence to find any heavy piece of ordnance that would drop a shell on to an earthwork and obliterate it. The British army had done no such thing since it had lain in front of the Redan and the Malakoff in a Crimean winter.

Fortunately the last act of the Balfour government in 1905 had been to order an excellent medium gun, the 60-pdr. Good though it was, it was still no more than medium and not nearly enough of its kind existed. By various devices the range was increased to something over eight miles but it still called for at least half-a-dozen Clydesdales to move it. All that could be procured in the way of heavy weapons were some 6″ howitzers dated 1896 with a range of just over three miles, rather less than the 18-pdr. It took two hours to level the ground and lay the wooden platform on to which their travelling carriages would have to be screwed. The shell weighed just under a hundredweight, the same as that of the other Victorian relic, the Mk VII

6″ gun. The best weapon to be had was the 9.2″ howitzer; it was fairly modern, fired a shell of 290 lbs for about six miles and could be moved around provided that careful preparations were made. The barrel, the carriage, the cradle and the bed each weighed something over four tons and each demanded a special 4-wheeled truck. Probably the worst of these makeshifts was the 6″ gun taken from the fixed defences of various ports, bored out to 8″ and mounted upon a Heath Robinson carriage with enormous traction-engine wheels. Each of these weighed a ton and stood about seven feet high. The gun naturally called for a wooden platform, a crane with which to load the cordite cartridge and the shell, and four enormous wedges to go under the wheels. There was no recoil mechanism. The 9.2″ guns, also stripped out of the harbours, were in the first instance even older, the Mk VI bearing the date 1888. This was the best that a leading industrial nation could do for the first two years of the war. New weapons were needed: mere improvements on those that had survived from the nineteenth century would not do.

The French were in similar straits but were swifter to put things in order. Serré de Rivière's forts at Verdun, like those of Brialmont in Belgium, had been equipped with heavy guns. Joffre, needing all that he could lay his hands on for the attacks in Artois and Champagne, had had them taken out and put on wheels. This very nearly lost his country her hardest battle of the war; as a small consolation it did give her field army a nucleus of what was called *Artillerie de Grande Puissance*. Railway guns seemed to come most naturally to the French; soon they were turning out the biggest specimens yet seen, but they would not be ready for use in 1916.

German taste has always been for the ponderous. So it was in this form of activity. As Brialmont built cupolas that sank like lift shafts and were reckoned indestructible, so did Herr Krupp construct monstrous guns that would prove him wrong. Biggest of all were the 420 mm − over 16″ − mortars. These were the cruise missiles of their day but less mobile. The complicated apparatus was broken down into four separate loads. As no horses ever foaled could have shifted them at all, let alone over the poor roads of 1914, mechanical aids were called for. The Holt tractor not yet having made its mark, the business was done by steam. Each section was hauled by three snorting steam traction-engines of the kind one associates with fairgrounds; regrettably, most of them bore the brass plates of English manufacturers, for traction-engines were a very English thing. Even thus equipped, it took a month to drag the great brutes into position by Liège, mainly because of the necessity of making new roads for them.

These were factors that could not be escaped. Any serious attack had to begin with a lengthy pounding of the enemy's positions by the biggest guns that could be obtained. Making them, getting them into position and feeding them were almost more of a nightmare than the battle itself. There was another consideration. The blocking and tearing-up of roads, not for minutes but for days on end, created a zone of devastation behind the army nearly comparable with the one the guns would make in front of it. And through this must come everything an army needed to sustain life, let alone the essentials of battle. There was no help for it. The bombing aeroplane was coming along nicely but it had a long way to go before it would displace the gun. Until that day should come these great dinosaurs, impossible to conceal, must grope their way across country shouting aloud the intentions of their owners. Surprise had become a word of no meaning.

The distances involved, once the battlefield had been reached, were not great. Even after the German doctrine had changed from holding an unbroken line to defence in considerable depth it was still within the power of the longest-barrelled gun to harass the enemy's back areas. It was, of course, as important to keep his reserves from moving forward as to wreck the front and supporting line trenches. And one can never do very wrong by depriving one's enemy of food and sleep before the battle.

The first of the new-style artillery fights fell upon the French, beginning on the memorable 21 February, 1916. In the woods around Verdun the German High Command had built ten new railway lines to feed and munition the great guns and the 140,000 men who were to kill the French Army. For the first time in history it was not the infantry that mattered most nor was it the only task of other arms to help the bayonets to reach their adversaries. Napoleon's dictum that cannon kill men was to be tried out, this time upon Frenchmen. Whether or not the German infantry would move on and occupy the city of Verdun was not a matter of cardinal importance. The death of a thousand cuts for the French army could probably be achieved by what in the American Civil War had been called 'Artillery Hell'. The Wehrmacht sent out to its furthest-flung outposts in order to gather in every big gun it owned. They raked up thirteen of the great 420 mm mortars, capable of lobbing high explosive shells weighing more than a ton; to help thicken up their fire storm the Austrian Imperial Army contributed seventeen rather smaller but still huge pieces of 320 mm. These were the deliverers of great destruction from short distances and thus were vulnerable to counterblast from ordinary medium artillery. Consequently their days were numbered. It took the French artillerymen, using siege-guns more than 20 years old, until the beginning of April to take the mortars out. They had, by then, served their purpose. The other German weapons, a pair of 15″ naval guns of enormous range and power, the much-feared 5.9 and the long-barrelled 150 mm, could pound away at their ease from safe distances. This was to be, throughout the war, the principal German use for mechanical vehicles; their work was to move and nourish the guns that were slaughtering the

French army. In defence the sovereign weapon would be the Maxim machine gun, mounted on an iron sledge rather than the tripod used in the British service. It provided a more solid base but was harder to move; in attack the British equipment, often using pack mules, was to be preferred. The German infantry was believed to have come a long way since First Ypres, Germany's first day of the Somme. By degrees it would be re-organized, the best being graded as *Stosstruppen*, Storm Troops; their extra equipment would include light trench-mortars and they would be trained to move furtively and carefully in small parties each seeking for the weak spots in a defensive position. This, probably, brought to perfection all the weapons and doctrines of the late nineteenth century. The internal combustion engine, apart from powering the only really new arm flying overhead, should serve as a mechanized horse, riding or draught as the case might be. The bass voice, the voice of the guns, would dominate the choir.

The French government were quick off the mark to find something newer and efficacious in attack. The Schneider-Creusot works had the capability of building almost anything; their first effort at a tank had not been successful. When Swinton took his French opposite number, Colonel Estienne, to see what Tritton's people were turning out he learned that the St Chamond and the Schneider were not as big and powerful as Mother but '*plus souples*'. The Nivelle battles had given *chars d'assaut* a bad name, although the internal combustion engine had already rescued France not once but twice. Gallieni's taxis had done things beyond the powers of the fiacre; Pétains solid-tyred lorries, trundling up and down *La Voie Sacrée* from Bar-le-Duc, saved Verdun.

Then, in June, had begun the long-planned offensive we call the Battle of the Somme. Sir Douglas Haig, though more than willing to fight, had not wanted to fight here. As from the beginning, the chosen battleground for the BEF would have been further north, in Flanders. In that arena an advance of 20 miles would have driven the Germans up against the sea and the Dutch frontier; combined with an amphibious landing this might have proved decisive. Still, as a loyal ally and the junior partner, Sir Douglas conformed. His army was probably the best in spirit that ever took the field. Its equipment seemed awesome by 1916 standards; a year later it would have been reckoned pitiful. This applied most particularly to the artillery arm. The heavy guns and howitzers were what furniture auctioneers call 'a harlequin set' and yachtsmen 'a menagerie class'. In all there were about 455 of them against the 400 of Germany. Mere counting of batteries, however, is deceptive. Guns, with their flat trajectories, made much noise but did little harm to entrenchments. It was the donkey-drops of the howitzers that in the course of five days were reckoned to have killed 20,000 German soldiers. The fact that the British army possessed such weapons at all was due to one man. Read Mr. Lloyd George's *Memoirs* with an uncynical mind and you will believe him never to have been mistaken and always at grips with fools. This oversimplifies, but on one occasion he had the right of it. When, back in 1915, he had proposed a great increase in heavy artillery Lord Kitchener had instantly dismissed the idea. Such guns were not needed and, were that not enough, we could not find the men for them. Mr Lloyd George persisted. Just this once he was right and Lord Kitchener wrong. Orders were placed with the Elswick foundry which not only gave Sir Douglas his heavies but built for the future. Five colossal 18″ howitzers with 60-foot barrels were delivered in 1918; so big, in fact that nobody could find a use for them and they went straight into store. The frenzy of activity designed to produce the biggest guns and the greatest heaps of shells for them produced some unexpected by-products. One of them was the State of Israel.

It was all to do with acetone. This chemical, essential for the production of cordite, was brewed by a process called the destructive distillation of wood. Before the war the exiguous needs of the services had been supplied from waste cordwood by a cottage industry in the Forest of Dean. Vast, though undefined, quantities of wood are needed to turn out each ton of acetone and wood enough for war purposes was not to be had in England. American suppliers, once they had cottoned on to this, found it convenient either to default on their contracts for a higher price or to sell their timber twice over. Once again a benevolent deity took a hand. Mr Lloyd George, as near to his wits' end as an ebullient nature allowed, had a chance meeting with C. P. Scott of the *Manchester Guardian*. Scott, being trustworthy, was told about the acetone and asked to keep an eye open for some chemist of ingenuity. He had an immediate answer. 'There is a very remarkable professor of chemistry in the University of Manchester willing to place his services at the disposal of the state. I must tell you, however, that he was born somewhere near the Vistula and I am not sure on which side. His name is Weizmann.' Scott added that his Manchester genius was not all that concerned about the war save only so far as it might work towards his heart's desire, the return of his people to Zion. To truncate a story not without interest but hardly intelligible save to another chemist, Weizmann did all that was asked of him and more. Within months acetone was being conjured out of maize; within a year a factory at King's Lynn, harmlessly employed on oil-cake, was turning it out in great quantities not only from maize but also, later on, from the humble horse-chestnut, or conker. Such a contribution to victory merited a great reward. Mr Lloyd George, possibly thinking of something in the higher reaches of his new Order of the British Empire, expressed himself willing to recommend the Professor for an honour. Weizmann said bluntly that he wanted nothing for himself; Mr Lloyd George, unaccustomed to such language, asked what he would like.

'I would like you to do something for my people.' Mr Lloyd George, unlike Pharaoh, agreed. From the acetone, maize and conkers of 1915 came the Balfour Declaration of 1917.

In order to break through German positions, built at leisure deep in the chalk, something more than crude iron and TNT were needed. Infantry must never again be asked to walk into the storm of steel with no more protection than dust-coloured suits of Dewsbury shoddy. Sir Henry Rawlinson tried the first ever night attack; it was a successful ploy, but would not stand repetition.

There remained one last hope of effecting something dramatic before winter closed in. Men with immense personal knowledge and first-class brains have differed utterly over whether Sir Douglas in putting in his tanks was using a legitimate device to procure his breakthrough or criminally throwing away the secret of a weapon that might have won the war almost on its own. Baker-Carr asserts that he, Elles and Fuller 'were definitely convinced that the benefits derived from the lessons learnt in battle more than compensated for the obvious disadvantage of "premature disclosure".' Winston Churchill, Swinton and others took a diametrically opposite view. 'To achieve this miniature success, and to carry the education of the professional mind one stage further forward, a secret of war which well-used would have procured a world-shaking victory in 1917 had been recklessly revealed to the enemy.' Mr Lloyd George put it even more vituperatively. The last word must go to one of those directly affected. Charles Carrington, commanding his company of 5th Royal Warwicks, had been in the thick of things since the beginning. He, of all those who have left their views in writing, probably speaks best for the infantryman:

'The lesson to be learned from the battle of 15 September was that the Mark I tank had almost no value except for the lift given to our morale and the shock to the German morale by the rumours about our secret weapon. Haig had to use the material that was ready; to suggest that he should have closed down his operations and given the enemy a free hand for nine or twelve months while the inventors cured the teething troubles of their new baby is to talk neither politics nor strategy. He believed, and for what it is worth I and my friends believed, that there was still a chance of fighting the decisive battle before the autumn and for such a prize everything must be staked.'

When men such as these conflict in their opinions it is barely on the south side of impudence for this generation to express one. What happened was this. At the second demonstration by Mother on 2 February, 1916, there had been senior Staff Officers from GHQ charged with assessing whether this was something worth while or just another piece of crankiness by civilians. Amongst them was Major-General Richard Butler, a member of Haig's 'G'

Staff who had somehow incurred the displeasure of Mr Lloyd George. Presumably Butler reported favourably of what he had seen, for letters began to arrive at Swinton's office asking when some tanks were to be expected in France. On 26 April Swinton replied. He refers to having met Sir Douglas on 14 April and to having told him not to expect anything for the month of June. By July, 'Some practically finished machines will have been delivered at home which will be in a fit state to move and so to instruct men to drive, but owing to their design they will not be fit to take the field, even if they are manned by machine-guns (sic) and armed with MG supplied in France.' By August 'some will already have been shipped to France — strikes and acts of God excepted.' He adds that the training area at Thetford was not ready; he hoped that by the end of June some partially completed tanks would have been 'rushed there as soon as they are capable of movement, to train men to drive'. Plainly Butler had been pressing for quick results. The letter ends with 'I am afraid this letter does not contain what you would have liked to hear, but it is the cold truth and shows the real situation.' Stern's committee can not be accused of complacency. In addition to Mother and her progeny they were at work on two machines of potentially great importance; though called tanks for want of a better name, they were the artillery of the future. Two models of gun-carrier, one for a little obsolete 5-inch howitzer and the other for a 60-pdr medium gun, were ready. The gun-carriers were potentially quite as important as the fighting tanks. Fifty of them were built, by Kitsons of Leeds, and in appearance they were far more modern than Mother. The track frames were much lower and the forward part consisted of an open well; in it was a sliding cradle for carrying the gun and winches running off the engine for loading it. The machines were rigorously tested and no fault was found in them that could not easily be rectified. There was plenty of room for carrying ammunition, the smaller gun could be fired from the carrier and far less men and effort were needed to bring the larger one into action than with horsed equipment. The Royal Artillery refused to have anything to do with it and there was nothing more to be said. Twenty-five years later, under names like Priest, Sexton and Bishop, something very similar was sought after by every gunner officer. The gun-carriers were not completely wasted; without guns they made splendid supply carriers, for their capacity was far more than any ordinary tank. Three were handed over to the Royal Engineers to be fitted with cranes for use in salvage. Certainly the gun-carriers, one of which could do the work of a hundred fatigue parties, did something towards reducing the drudgery of it all, but at the price of losing a considerable asset to the army's weaponry.

At the end of July a message arrived saying that the War Office had decided to send 'a few' tanks to France at once. Stern protested that the only tanks the Heavy Section possessed were in perpetual use by men under training and out of repair. A couple of months would be needed to make them battleworthy but he would try his best to oblige. This did not alter his view of the matter and he told Mr Lloyd George bluntly that to send the tanks out as they were would be 'courting disaster'. Nonetheless, Bertie Stern and his co-adjutors produced what the Army seemed to need. Nobody could remain obdurate when it was urged that 'The heavy casualties in the Somme offensive of 1 July, the want of success against the German lines since then, and the approach of winter without any appreciable advance having been made, all tended to lower the morale of the troops, and it might therefore be necessary to use these new weapons in order to raise it again. Our reasons for desiring to wait until the spring were understood, but we must be prepared to throw everything we had into the scale. The slightest holding back of any of our resources might, at the critical moment, make the difference between defeat and victory. Such were the arguments used.' The French were very cross, complaining that the premature disclosure would deny Nivelle the opportunity of surprise. Knowing what one knows of French ideas on security, the charge cannot be taken too seriously.

Stern allowed himself to be persuaded. The first party from the Heavy Branch left Thetford for Le Havre by way of Avonmouth on 13 August. The tanks followed. Moving them was a hard business. Each sponson weighed 35 cwt, including its gun; between leaving Thetford station and arriving at Yvrench, near Abbeville, every one had to be unbolted, lifted off, lifted on and re-bolted five times. 'C' Company, 25 tanks and 280 tankmen, was the first to arrive. There was enough to be done in the way of putting some very imperfect machines into working order, checking the presence or otherwise of a multitude of stores and pondering exactly how the tanks were going to make themselves useful when they were sent into battle. They were not helped by GHQ. Swinton complained later, when told about it, that his crews had been treated with amused tolerance or contemptuous scepticism, as cyclists might have been at one of the more expensive Meets. The tanks were made to perform evolutions for the amusement of visiting grandees after the fashion of performing animals. There was a circus atmosphere about the whole thing, with one commander writing bitterly that it reminded him of Hampstead Heath. In intervals of enforced, and resented, clowning with antics like knocking down trees and scaling walls, the crews had somehow to carry out their essential maintenance, do a little training and, if they could, snatch some sleep. Swinton meditated on what would have happened to the RFC if its first half-hundred aircraft had been treated like this before going into action. It seemed impossible to explain that 'the New Arm was a mass of complicated, and in some ways delicate, machinery in an embryonic shape and not the foolproof product of long trial and experience'.

In a vast headquarters such as GHQ had become there were, inevitably, among the good officers many others determined that their ranks and reputations would be assured without venturing into front-line trenches, save occasionally as very temporary guests. The friends of the horse still insisted, or affected to insist, that its place in the Order of Battle remained as important as ever. If intercourse of any kind with oil-stained men in canvas suits was necessary it had to be on a *de-haut-en-bas* footing. Swinton was warned that Brough was unpopular at Montreuil because he was 'difficult', a synonym for saying that Brough had firmly deprecated the use in battle of a couple of companies of tanks with untrained crews. One senior Staff officer — Swinton does not name him — begged that the operation be called off. 'I endeavoured to do so; but those in control were in no mood to pay attention to me, or, indeed, to anyone from home.'

The second Company, 'D', disembarked in France two days before the attack. The long train arrived at The Loop — a siding near Corbie — and each tank crawled off the truck under its own power, had its sponsons brought up from another train, and went once more through the routine of bolting each one on. That done, it got out of the way whilst the second tank scrambled over the empty truck and down its ramp to the ground where the same thing happened. The last one had to crawl over a great many empty flat cars before it reached terra firma. The crews were dog-tired, dirty and unshaven; they would readily have agreed that their performance lacked the panache of a Royal Tournament turn. All the same they had performed quite a feat, certainly one never before seen in France. GHQ showed its appreciation. 'Not quick enough' was all that its representative had to bark out. Such behaviour by an ignoramus was furiously resented and the Heavy Section, reasonably, took this to be a sample of the type of officer who would be the arbiter of its destinies. Time was to show that they were not far wrong. There was no such thing as a chain of command. Sections of tanks were, in effect, hired out to formations as agricultural contractors hire out their machinery to farmers. So long as they were engaged on the agreed job, the owner had no further control over them.

Perhaps at this point of the war it could not have been otherwise. Baker-Carr, as senior Machine Gun Corps officer on the spot, took a considerable interest in the debut of its Heavy Section. 'The first thing that struck me was the appalling lack of knowledge concerning battle-conditions. Few, if any, of the officers had had experience in France and that probably was completely out of date. Most of the officers and crews had been suddenly pitch-forked from the calm, almost academic, atmosphere of a training camp in England into the ear-splitting, nerve-racking tornado of the front line. Operation orders by divisions and brigades, simple and easy of comprehension by the initiated, were unintelligible to the newcomer from

England. Even the spoken jargon of war required explanation and amplification, to the detriment of the young Tank commander, already overawed at finding himself in conversation with a major-general. It is amusing to think how, a year or 18 months later, this same young officer was to lay down the law to division and brigade commanders, but, before this came about, much blood was to be soaked into the ground. It must be remembered too that a Tank, once it has joined battle, is completely cut off from the world and must rely entirely on itself to find its way.' As Baker-Carr went on to explain, the setting up of a Reconnaissance Department after this battle was a matter of life and death. It was not only its absence that made the Somme battle memorable for the tank commanders. 'Harassed almost beyond endurance by their domestic troubles of packing equipment, ammunition, food, water, blankets and a hundred other items into a space already overcrowded with machinery and human beings, [they] were called upon to answer at a moments notice a hundred conundrums which were suddenly hurled at them. Not only were they given orders which they did not fully comprehend but these orders were constantly being modified or even completely changed. Maps, which had been carefully studied, had to be discarded at the last moment and an entirely new set was issued in their place. Up till midnight on 14 September, the eve of the battle, several tank commanders were not quite clear in their minds as to what they were to do or even at what hour they were to start.' There were other unforeseen difficulties. Captain (later Lieut.-General Sir) Philip Neame, VC, was not captivated by his first experience of armoured fighting vehicles. 'Out of six tanks allotted to us [56th Division] only one crossed our own front line, and that stuck in the first German trench. The tracks of most of these were worn out in practice and training. One of the tanks was not bullet-proof; it came crawling past our HQ with a very frightened officer inside whose first sight of fighting this had been. The steel walls were riddled with bullet-holes. I imagine that by mistake inferior boiler-plate instead of armour plate must have been fitted.' The future commander of the Desert Army added that 'The 30 or 40 tanks used on the whole made such a poor impression on the Germans that they did not worry or attempt to copy them.' Here and there the Heavy Section had done more than earn its rations, but, taken in the round, it had been a disappointment. 'Every new invention has to meet the criticism of sceptics and the mere force of inertia so powerfully operated by second-rate men who don't like change. The strongest opposition to the tanks was, as might have been expected, in Whitehall', remarked Charles Carrington, adding that 'Nevertheless, four days later Haig asked the War Office for a thousand tanks of better design.' The Commander-in-Chief saw further than most of his advisers and subordinates. One other passage in Carrington's account demands space: 'In France many of Haig's best commanders, who had seen the poor performance of the early tanks, disliked them. Even a year later the Australians were distrustful, taking the view that they gave more trouble than they were worth, and even at Cambrai there was one commander who preferred to have no tanks with his infantry.' Pray remember this, especially the possessive pronoun. The commander is not hard to identify. Since September, 1915, a translated 'Uncle' Harper had been commanding the 51st (Highland) Division, TF, regarded by itself and some others as the pick of the bunch. By this stage of the war several Engineer officers had been given high commands. There were no eyebrows raised. Both Marshals Joffre and Kitchener had been Sappers. The flash of HD in a circle was universally taken as standing for 'Harper's Duds'. Division and commander were well pleased with each other.

It has to be admitted that the score card for 15 September was unimpressive. Employed, 49: reached starting point 32: 'pushed ahead of infantry and caused considerable loss to the enemy, 9: did not catch up with the infantry but did good work in "clearing up", 9: became ditched, 5: broke down from mechanical trouble, 9.' The purple prose of the newspapers was hardly justified. Nevertheless it had been quite a feat for an utterly untrained force using very imperfect machines running on infamously low-grade fuel.

It was not good enough to save Swinton. For the moment everything seemed *couleur de rose*, but it did not last. Stern came to join him in France. The lanky Swinton and the rather tubby Stern made a pleasing contrast; Swinton referred to them as Mutt and Jeff. Together they went off to compare notes with Colonel Estienne, who had been working on his *chars d'assaut* for much the same time; each side had been happily unaware of what the other was doing until quite recently. On their return Swinton was summoned to wait upon the CIGS. All that Wully had to say was, 'Ugh! You look as if you'd been up all night'. 'I replied that I had. "Ugh!" repeated the CIGS as he retired to his own room.' More productive conferences followed and Stern was given an order for 1,000 tanks. A few days later, on Wully's insistence, it was cancelled. Stern, in a great rage, went straight to Mr Lloyd George and the order was reinstated. Swinton was to have no part in it. The rumour came first to him from Maurice Hankey over the telephone. Swinton, being a very senior man, went straight to the CIGS who told him the worst. 'France wanted a big expansion of the Heavy Section and I was not considered the man to carry it out.' Swinton was bitterly hurt, even when Wully tried elephantinely to heal the pain with fair words. The tank operations were transferred from Elveden to Bovington Camp in Dorset, where they took root. Command there went to Brigadier-General F. Gore Anley, late the Essex Regiment and aged 54. Anley had seen much fighting from the days of the Khalifa until the Somme. His brief was more or less that of Barrington-Kennett, first adjutant of the RFC: to combine in his new command the professional excellence of the Royal Engineers with the smartness of the Brigade of Guards. The perceived scruffiness of tank crews must go; they would have to look more like proper soldiers from now on. Feeble excuses, like tank business being a little different from horse business, would not be listened to. No doubt General Anley did his good and conscientious best; very possibly he was not happy at the task. He was soon given another infantry brigade, this time in Palestine.*

The changes in France, on what was called the Fighting Side, were more permanent. Ernest Swinton had been the son of a parson. Hugh Jameson Elles came of a family as military as could be wished. His father was a General with much Indian frontier experience and his mother's father had commanded a Sikh regiment in the Mutiny. After Clifton, Haig's old school, Elles had been through The Shop and commissioned into the Royal Engineers in time to see some service against the Boers. Soon after that his experience widened. From the Staff College in 1913 (where Harper had been an Instructor) he went to France as DAQMG to the 4th Division in time for Le Cateau, became Brigade Major to 10th Brigade and was wounded on 25 April, 1915, when his Brigade made its great counter-attack at the time of the first German gas-cloud.

At the age of 35 he was a GSO 2 at Montreuil and was selected, more or less at random, to go and watch Mother's first performance. His credentials were the right ones for command of a new arm: an engineer, though not a mechanical engineer, militarily educated, with recent battle experience but not an excessive innovator. Being in truth only a camouflaged sapper Major he would not be likely to throw his weight about at GHQ. Oddly enough it is Elles' sister who is probably the best remembered of his family. Under the name Patricia Wentworth she wrote great numbers of excellent detective novels, mostly still in print.

Wearing the badges of rank of temporary Colonel, Elles assumed command of the Heavy Section on 29 September. His orders were clear enough: 'The Headquarters in France is to command the Heavy Section MGC in the field, to be responsible for the advanced training and for the tactical employment of the Corps under the command of the C-in-C.' At home Stern's people (he and Wilson were no longer sailors but Majors, MGC) under the name of the Mechanical Warfare Supply Department, were charged with purveying more and better tanks. The Mk IV (Mks II and III had been only experiments) was coming along quite well. It had improved tracks, an exhaust as effective as could be expected, better armour, external petrol tanks using the auto-vac instead of gravity, and the guns had been

---

* Captain Wilson says that the 2 i/c. No 26 Coy, was Major C. R. Attlee. His CO, Major Poe, thought him an ass; he did not go to France with the rest.

shortened in order to keep their muzzles out of the mud; the sponsons had been so redesigned that they could be swung inboard rather than bodily removed for train travel. With their very short ranges of activity, tanks would have to do most of their journeying in this fashion. The gears and the engine remained unaltered, though Major Wilson was hard at work on improvements that would appear before very long. The means of communication were of the rudest: flag, lamp and pigeon only. Wireless had been tried but Swinton recorded that it was taken out for fear of interference with others. It was the misfortune of the Heavy Section to be a poor relation. Had the Wright brothers failed in their aeronautical activities the tank would have had the highest of priorities for steel, skilled engineers, petrol and much else. As matters stood it had to put up with whatever the Flying Corps could spare. Estimates for production were fifty Mk IVs in each of the first two months of 1917, rising to 120 in March and April; by July that should be doubled and September ought to produce 280. By the time of the Arras battle it was only possible to field about sixty, all old models and mostly repaired Somme veterans. Both numbers and quality might have been better but for a competitor even more formidable than the RFC. The Royal Navy now demanded every square inch of armour plating and every ton of steel whether it needed it or not. Practically the whole amount produced came from Spanish iron ore and the Allies owed its existence almost entirely to one man. King Alfonso XIII was candid about it when he spoke to Mr Churchill. The aristocracy was pro-German, the middle-classes hated the French; only he and the mob favoured the allies. But for this staunch monarch the arsenals of both Britain and France would have been bare. America no longer had any steel to spare. When the United States came into the war the greatest immediate benefit to the British Army was the infusion of some 1500 doctors; very welcome they were.

The administrative and command structure of what would soon be the Tank Corps were as grotesque as could be imagined. Elles, having been given the near-derelict château of Bermicourt, near Hesdin, collected himself a Staff. Being a Sapper, he naturally picked another for his chief of operations. Giffard le Quesne Martel was another of those engineers who had turned his hand to non-Sapper things; he had been Brigade Major of one of the brigades of the 25th Division on the Somme but had seen nothing of the tank share in the battle. Since he was only 26, higher authority laid it down that he was not sufficiently mature for an appointment of the kind Elles wished and he was placed under Colonel J.F.C. Fuller, infantryman and all-purpose sage. Captain Uzielli, of the King's Regiment, was brought in to run the administrative side, Searle to be chief mechanical engineer and Captain Hotblack of the Intelligence Corps was to organize the highly important work of a reconnaissance section. Baker-Carr, whose task as pioneer machine-gunner was done, became a tankman with command first of a battalion and later of a brigade. With such an array of talent there could have been fairly quick and spectacular results. There were not. Elles explained the reasons in his Memorandum of 31 December, 1916. 'In France, the fighting organization is under a junior officer who, *faute de mieux*, has become responsible for initiating all important questions of policy, design organization and personnel through GHQ, France, and thence through five different branches of the War Office. In England administrative and training organizations are under a senior officer, located 130 miles from the War Office, with a junior officer (Staff Captain) in London to deal with the five branches above mentioned.' He went on with a phrase that has become famous (and whose style and phraseology suggest that Clough Williams-Ellis had a hand in it) about 'the tail in France trying to wag a very distant and headless dog in England.' It was still sadly true that nobody who mattered, save only an overworked Commander-in-Chief, had the least interest in or time for the tanks. Elles sensibly suggested that it would be better for the new arm to have its own directorate at the War Office as the Flying Corps already had, with a Director empowered to give orders to the Ministry of Munitions for whatever the Corps needed. He did not get his way. In May, 1917, after the Arras battle was over, a Tank Committee was formed at the War Office. It was chaired by another sapper officer, Major-General J.E. Capper. He was a considerable authority on balloons.

Arras was an improvement on the Somme but not all that of a success. As before, the tanks were left to fight a small private war with no plans depending upon whether they won or lost. At different places they did both. One of them is worth mentioning because of what followed. 'Uncle' Harper's 'little fellers' — he never spoke of his Highlanders otherwise — had much to do with the battle for what became known as the Chemical Works at Roeux. It was heavily fortified and changed hands several times. One of Baker-Carr's battalions was hotly engaged. The citation for Sergeant Noel's DCM speaks for itself: 'During the battle of Arras on April 23 this NCO took command of his Tank after his officer had been wounded. He fought his Tank with the greatest gallantry and skill, putting out of action many machine-guns and killing numbers of the enemy, besides taking 50 prisoners. His action enabled the infantry to gain possession of the Chemical Works.' Harper would not have it. Baker-Carr, who knew his old enemy's measure by now, was highly entertained: 'It was a hard-fought little battle and the infantry commanders were unable to speak too highly of the valuable assistance they received from the tanks. These reports were so eulogistic that I was much amused when the Divisional Commander in his report gave the entire credit of the successful action to the infantry and barely mentioned the fact that a tank had even been present.' Harper always ran true to form.

He did not like tanks and had the honesty not to pretend otherwise. There still remained others like-minded. In Baker-Carr's words, 'Tanks were still regarded as a "stunt" rather than as an established and permanent auxiliary arm.'

CHAPTER FIVE

WITHOUT END, REPRIEVE, OR REST

Rudyard Kipling

IT IS TIME TO RETURN to the Western Front in the weeks following Messines and to look at the plight of the various belligerents. None hoped any more for outright victory. All accepted that a peace of mutual exhaustion was the most likely terminus and that the only winner would be the United States. In accordance with tradition, information about the enemy comes first.

The German Army of 1917 was no longer that of 1914, for the men who fought on the Somme had taken the shine off it. Even the most patriotic of commentators accepted that, with the best and bravest struck off strength, no army could ever touch the heights again during its generation. Nevertheless it remained an excellent land force; its air arm, after being shaken up by General Hoeppner, was equipped with new aircraft much on a par with those of the RFC designed by T.O.M. Sopwith. Bombing, both by day and night, was becoming almost scientific and the war area was no longer limited to such parts of France as could be reached by artillery. Gas apart, the German command did not greatly interest itself in the new weapons; improvements in the existing ones along with such addition as the *flammenwerfer* and the stick grenade were sufficient. The men of the Heavy Section sacrificed at Bullecourt had served their country better than they could have known; even a calculated deception plan would not have done better. When the captured tanks were trooped through Berlin real soldiers found them objects of merriment.

The idea of a landing from the sea behind the German line had been played with long before Jellicoe had dropped his bomb on the Cabinet. Admiral Fisher had started it. When Mr Asquith convened his assembly of notables on the outbreak of war and every odd plan was canvassed the old seaman had one only. For a long time he had been boring people with his apophthegm about the British army being a projectile to be fired by the Royal Navy; his proposal to land it in Schleswig-Holstein and march it to

Berlin was hardly to be taken seriously; nor, probably, had Fisher expected it to be.

As time went by and stalemate set in the cause altered. Curiously enough it was the French, with no record of combined operations behind them, who started it all. On 10 December, 1916, Sir Douglas Haig wrote a letter to Sir Launcelot Kiggell, his Chief of General Staff, then on leave in London: 'My dear Kigge,' it began, and went on to explain how a plan had been put before him by General des Vallières, the senior officer with the French Mission to GHQ. Sir Douglas liked des Vallières and warmed to his ideas. 'I may say at once that I agree generally with the plan.... It is satisfactory that my patient talks with Joffre have at last borne fruit and he is entirely in agreement as to the desirability of carrying out the operation.' It was all a little vague. Sir Douglas spoke of using the 5th and 20th Divisions, though the word tank appeared nowhere. Kiggell was to 'speak (very secretly) to the Head of the Admiralty War Staff, the CIGS and Bacon.... The operation will take place'. He was to find a practical (this word heavily underscored) officer to take charge of it all. The freezing winter then closed in.

The French plan envisaged nothing more nor less than the capture of Ostend, followed by such a bombardment of Zeebrugge as would render the U-boat harbour untenable. The Royal Navy was, apparently, prepared to turn the heavy guns of the Grand Fleet on to the ports. This was not to be thought of. German battle-cruisers had bombarded Hartlepool and Lowestoft purely out of spite. Ostend and Zeebrugge still held their usual civilian populations, swollen with numbers of refugees. It would have been out of the question to a service brought up on the 'You will always be fools: we shall never be gentlemen' tradition to turn its guns on the brave Belgians. Des Vallières' plan, if carried out, would cost only English lives.

Admiral Bacon thought on a bigger scale. Not for him would there be a repetition of such ancient sea-landings as Saint Cast, Eupatoria or even Gallipoli. This time the business would be properly thought out. Advice, generally in favour of having a try, came from Generals Sir Henry Rawlinson and Jan Smuts. The practical officer selected to do the liaising was Captain Frederick Hotblack, of the Intelligence Corps. This was just as well. Hotblack, a civilian in 1914, was a founder member of the Tank Corps, had an encyclopaedic knowledge of the Belgian coast and of the German order of battle there, along with a strong ability to perceive the obvious. For reasons demanding only a moment's thought his friends knew him by the nickname 'Boot'.

Admiral Bacon, you will surely remember, had produced the huge tractors whose engines were now powering the machines used by Elles and his men. After they had dragged his howitzers to the Dunkirk Circus the Admiral had returned to his natural element and was guarding the Dover Straits against

U-boats. He was an energetic man and one blessed with an ingenious mind, even though some of his anti-submarine devices were found to be far less efficacious than he believed. The tools at his hand were monitors — shallow-draft warships designed for South American rivers but carrying two big guns apiece — pontoons 600 feet long by 30 wide, which the Navy would make, and a sufficiency of the best tanks. The Corps now owned two Brigades, each of three battalions with seventy-two machines. Baker-Carr commanded the First Brigade and the others (a third brigade was forming) were under the men with names to become equally famous. Colonel Anthony Courage, a Hussar, led the 2nd and John Hardress Lloyd, another cavalryman, the 3rd. Both were over 40 and had seen much fighting before tanks were so much as a dream. Battalions were designated by letters; numbering came later. Both of the two brigades in existence had two battalions in France with the third still training at Bovington. Baker-Carr's brigade had seen action at Arras and still had its original Mk I tanks, much patched and mended by now. Courage's Second Brigade, survivors of Messines, were more fortunate, being equipped entirely with Mk IVs. The principal difference to the crews lay in the fact that the Mk IV would usually keep out the new German armour-piercing bullet, whereas the Mk I would not. Until its own new models arrived, the First Brigade could not operate at much more than 50% efficiency. The workshops which had been set up behind Bermicourt had attained a high degree of competence, better, perhaps, than anything in a later war until the Royal Electrical & Mechanical Engineers joined the Army List. There was no lack of work for them.

Bacon's plan deserved to come off if only as a reward for high thinking. The landing of the 1st Division, spearheaded by nine tanks, was to take place somewhere between Ostend, where the U-boats were believed to be harbouring, and the end of the allied line at Nieuport. However sleepy the area might be in ordinary times, the German army and marines had batteries in permanent readiness capable of bringing down a storm of steel quite as thick as anywhere on the main front. They also had a considerable Intelligence advantage; the coast was riddled with disaffected or venal Belgians who could be counted on to report the smallest troop movement as soon as it took place. In the air a rough equality existed; certainly neither side could be considered master, though it was always possible for a strictly temporary superiority to be obtained over a limited area by using everything.

Bacon had his six pontoons built and a special detachment of tanks was put to studying how a Mk IV could climb up a sea wall with a curly brim and drive down on the other side. By a rare stroke of luck the Belgian architect who had designed the wall was on hand, complete with his drawings. Practical tests were carried out in the Thames estuary, with the pontoons lashed between a couple of monitors and run ashore. It strains credulity to think that all this could have gone unseen by ill-wishers, but Bacon was a Navy man; he knew of the mortal danger the country was facing and was prepared to take the risk of a bloody repulse. Williams-Ellis, who would certainly have known all about it, tells of how it was long and elaborately rehearsed: 'Officers of the Tank Corps would suddenly disappear on unknown missions, to reappear as suddenly with no memory as to where they had been or what they had seen in the interval.' Drills for leaving lighters and see-sawing over the seawall were carefully worked out. The Germans, thoroughly informed about what was afoot, decided not to wait. The trench systems scratched out by the French along the holiday beaches were feeble. It would have been possible to take them at any time; this one seemed as good as another, the relief of the French by the British having been completed only by infantry. The French heavy batteries had gone, the British not yet arrived. General Strickland's 1st Division lay nearest to the sea with a front of some 1400 yards to Lombardzyde. When the tremendous cannonade began on the night 9/10 July there were two unsupported battalions on the wrong side of the Yser. Every shell threw its geyser of sand into the air; there was no cover. When the attack came in at 7.15 both battalions died hard and its impetus was lost. For a couple of days there was some savage fighting before the offensive finally faded away. The 1st Division continued to train for a landing, wired in at a camp in the dunes at Le Clipon; the monitors practised and so did the tanks. The plan was not given up until November when the Division was sent instead to be racked to pieces capturing a few shell holes at Passchendaele.

For reasons that call for no explanation the plan could never have succeeded. Hotblack and Fuller were both dead against it. Colonel Oldfield, Harper's CRA, wrote of 'that Belgian coast thing for which somebody ought to be hanged'.

More interesting is the attitude of Sir Douglas. His reputation is not that of an Athenian, spending his time in nothing but telling and hearing some new thing, and yet he took this proposal seriously. The fact that massed German guns could effortlessly pulverize the expedition did not need to be pointed out to him. One may, perhaps, draw a conclusion that the Commander-in-Chief was not as wedded to the old ways as some would have us believe. Or, possibly, he did not wish to disoblige the French now that Nivelle had gone.

Instead of a few tanks being thrown to the guns on a sunny sea shore, the bulk of the Corps was sent to wallow in Flanders mud. Baker-Carr, regular army to the backbone but harshly critical of the Military Mind (his capitals) put it succinctly: 'If a careful search had been made from the English Channel to Switzerland, no more unsuitable spot could have been discovered.' Whether the gambit of pushing masses and masses of infantry across the swamps created by masses and masses of guns can be matter for congratulation continues to be worried out by experts then unborn. One who took a very considerable part as an infantry company commander (and won his MC there) was firm about it. Of the battle of 4 October, usually called Broodseinde, he wrote: 'What surprises me is that the historians have elevated it into a tactical masterpiece like Messines. It was just all-in wrestling in the mud.' Charles Carrington, soldier and don, wrote of what he knew.

It is tolerably sure that nobody will defend the manner in which the Tank Corps was used. It was treated with as much consideration as a mobile bath unit and given tasks so unbelievable that one is tempted to question the sanity of those giving the orders. This is not as hyperbolical as it may sound; at a crisis in the March retreat of 1918 one divisional general who had held a command at Cambrai went raving mad and had to be taken quietly away. There still stands — or stood only a few years ago — the remains of a stout pillbox named The Cockcroft where one of the few successful actions happened. The tank involved inevitably became bogged; fortunately it did so in a position where one of its 6-pdrs was pointing at the back door. A few rounds were enough to send the garrison flying. Several others were treated in the same way. These little attacks on pillboxes were of far greater importance than might have seemed likely. The spectacle of tanks abandoned, knocked about and wallowing helplessly in mud did little enough to win new admirers. A few small actions, like the Cockcroft, initiated by Baker-Carr wherever a fairly hard piece of road could be found, were observed by the Commander of the XVIIIth Corps. General Sir Ivor Maxse was a Guardsman, with a fighting record going back to Sudan days. In the present war he had hardly missed a battle; a dozen mentions in despatches spoke to this. He was a little older than Haig, well connected — his wife was a Wyndham of Petworth — and he had the C-in-C's ear. It was Maxse's good opinion of the tanks after the little battles around St Julien that probably saved the Corps from disbandment by those of lesser faith. By the end of Third Ypres, however, its existence was precarious. One other senior officer also interested himself, though to a lesser degree. 'General Harper was much in evidence at the Corps Conferences and, although he was inclined to belittle the value of the tanks, he did not fail to put in a claim for a far greater number of machines than that to which he was justly entitled.'

CHAPTER SIX

HE SAITH AMONG THE TRUMPETS, HA, HA.

Job xxxix, 25

TAKING ONE CONSIDERATION WITH ANOTHER, October, 1917, was not a happy month for anybody in the allied camp. The burden upon Sir Douglas Haig would have broken the back or at least the spirit of a less resolute man. Every disagreeable thing seemed to happen at once. First over the precipice was Italy. For a long time past General Cadorna had been kept from sleep by the fear of German troops coming to the aid of Austria. Months ago he had made a compact with General Nivelle that, should the worst happen, the railways would be ready to carry substantial British and French reinforcements to sustain him. Throughout the summer the Italians had not done at all badly, though at a stiff price in their own casualties. It did not last. In September there arrived in aid of Austria seven German divisions along with heavy guns and a strong air force all under General von Below, the victor of Riga. On 25 October they opened up with heavy mortars around the town called Karfreit by the Austrians and Caporetto by the Italians. The Italian Second Army panicked and ran. Nivelle's plan was put into operation; by 10 November six French and five British divisions were on their way. Thus, for no purpose connected with his own command, Sir Douglas lost five of his best divisions − the regulars of the 5th and 7th, the highly experienced South Midlands Territorials of the 48th and two good New Army formations, the 23rd and 41st. It was a moment when he would not willingly have parted with a corporal's guard.

Further away to the East worse things were happening. The Italian situation was rectifiable; indeed the Italians to a great extent rectified it themselves. The Russian was not. Although the October Revolution did not take place, by our reckoning, until early November it was getting into its stride by the time of Caporetto. With Lenin and Trotsky, as the true believers now called themselves, running wild after their emergence from the cellars, it was all up with a brave but over-tried army. For all practical purposes there was no more Eastern front for the Kaiser. A few divisions would have to be left to keep order but the mass of the German army could entrain westwards as soon as was practically possible. The participation of the United States in the war on land was still of less significance than that of China, an ally since August; the Chinese Labour Corps of nearly 100,000 men, most of them originally signed on by British missionaries as civilian workers, was already in France and proving of high value.

The British army in France and Flanders, including in that expression the formations from Canada, Australia, New Zealand and South Africa, along with what remained of the Indian cavalry and the young men of Rhodesia, was exhausted. Inevitably it had been the best soldiers who had 'gone west' in every battle and it was now beginning to show. Practically every divisional general, brigadier and infantry CO knew, even if he would not admit it, that the pressed men and returned wounded – some of them returning for the second or third time – were not of the value of their predecessors. It was among the junior commanders that the decline was most felt. The majority of the new officers turned out by Cadet Battalions were of good quality but there remained too many who were not yet fit for the ranks they held. Given time they would probably grow into the habits of leadership but it would not serve to throw them in at the deep end on first arrival. Too often this could not be avoided. The French seemed to be recovering a little; under Pétain they had fought a couple of middle-sized battles at Verdun and on the Chemin des Dames with fair success. They were nonetheless still suspect and could be trusted only to defend their own positions – if that.

There is an ancient military aphorism that to do nothing is to do something positively wrong. No very deep thought is needed to produce a situation making nonsense of this but it is one of the Army's Articles of Faith. Keeping his head while all about him were losing theirs and blaming it on him, the Commander-in-Chief cast about for that something. When a plan came up through the usual channels for an unusual operation starring the Tank he did not turn it down flat. This is how it all came about.

Ever since the Tank Corps, the new name of the Heavy Section since July, had been in residence at Bermicourt there had been much striking of sparks off each other by some excellent minds. At the top of the table sat Hugh Elles, the youngest of the senior tank officers at 37 save only for Martel. Fuller, already known as Boney, and Baker-Carr were a couple of years older, Courage and Hardress Lloyd a year or so senior to all of them. They were, unlike the usual entrepreneurs of novelty, mature men with a lot of soldiering behind them. Fuller, by all accounts, had the mercurial mind, Baker-Carr an admirable sardonicism and disrespect for grandees until they had earned it, coupled with a fascination for machinery unusual in his military generation. Hotblack – the name is an old Norfolk one – was in charge of all to do with Intelligence and Reconnaissance, the only one of the party other that Martel with a distinguished military career awaiting him once this war was over; finally, there was the chronicler and keeper of the archives, Clough Williams-Ellis whose war services were to be overshadowed by later fame as the architect of Porthmeirion. Elles was a strange man, a Sapper who might have been dreamt up by that other Sapper who invented Bulldog Drummond. It is not possible so long after the event to set down who took what part in the long colloquies; Fuller was always sure of himself; Elles, if one may judge from his actions between the wars, was less so and never wholly captivated by the armoured idea no matter what he might say in public. He should not be judged too harshly for his failure during the early Hitler years to throw his weight behind the rearming of the British army with proper weapons. Nevertheless he must bear some of the responsibility. When told to design a tank himself and lacking the help of Fuller he came up with the A 11, probably the most useless armoured fighting vehicle of the late 1930s. But the Elles of 1917 looked the part of the swashbuckling, rather untidy fighting man that Hugh Drummond (was it coincidence that they shared a forename?) was to make famous. Not, perhaps, an intellectual giant but a good man with whom to go tiger-shooting. Fuller, untested as a fighting commander throughout his service, provided the equipment for thinking. Helping him was Captain Martel — 'Q' to his friends — who had written down his ideas for the shape of the future warfare nearly a year before in a long paper he had entitled *The Tank Army*, much of which might have been contributed (possibly was, indirectly) by Mr H.G. Wells. Martel had been a disciple of Swinton and held his unceremonious removal to have a been a great loss to the Corps.

There was consensus of opinion about many things. Arras had taught, if it had needed teaching, that tanks demanded to be used concentrated and in mass formation. Not only must there be signal and supply tanks for their specialized purposes, but a reserve of fighting tanks, immediately on hand, was essential. The reason was tolerably obvious. Once the first flight had crashed its way through the enemy position the job was not even half done. Only more machines could complete it, for this was the moment for fast exploitation. More of the 4 mph Mk IVs would serve if nothing better was to be had; ideally, fast, light tanks with a greater range of action than anything yet invented. The supply tanks must all contain 'fills', specific quantities of petrol, oil, water and ammunition. Signals posed a great difficulty; wireless sets had been tried in Swinton's time but he had been ordered to jettison them. They could, in any event, only work at all after putting up a tall mast when the tank was stationary and vulnerable. Then there was the most serious, still not quite settled, problem of them all — Command. A tank battalion, having fought its way through the enemy wire, crossed his trenches and in the green fields beyond had to wait for the infantry to come up and for some brigadier, not half as familiar with what was happening, to give further orders. Surely it would make far better sense for the tank commander to give orders to the infantry. It was unthinkable in 1917, as much as it was in 1940. The tank was the servant of the foot; should the occasion arise it would be the servant of the horse also. This was not likely to happen. As Baker-Carr put it, 'When acting as a body of mounted troops they merely blocked the roads, badly needed for other arms during an offensive, and wasted precious tonnage of ships in order to feed thousands upon thousands of horses that were absolutely valueless in battle.'

Battle drills and planning for operations were left to Fuller. The greater part of his time was taken up in fighting GHQ and the War Office. He held his appointment for less than a year and a half of the war but friends reckoned it to have aged him by a decade.

Williams-Ellis, who had some hand in it, tells of how the idea of the first great armoured battle took shape at Bermicourt château: 'All through the later part of the Ypres struggle the Tank Corps had turned their eyes towards certain other parts of the line with a longing as for the Delectable Mountains. They imagined places in dry rolling chalk country where a Tank could travel on the surface of the ground. They dreamed of battles in which the artillery had neither given the enemy weeks of warning nor helped him to reduce the ground to a swamp or the likeness of an ash heap .... General Elles and his Staff had several places in mind in which such a battle might be fought. Perhaps they dwelt most affectionately on the thoughts of some sector of the Hindenburg Line, some high, rolling chalk plateau anywhere south of Arras. Several such delightful spots lay in the domain of General Sir Julian Byng's Third Army .... In September General Elles hopefully paid him a visit as he lay at Albert. They conferred.' General Byng had already had a plan submitted to him by Fuller on 4 August which he liked. GHQ, which presumably meant Sir Launcelot Kiggell, had said that the Ypres business must first be finished; try again in early November. Williams-Ellis avers that Byng and Elles continued working away at the plans until the green light was given on 20 October. Even then only four members of the Tank Corps staff knew anything about it.

When sanction for the attack came through it was to a Third Army whose effectiveness was no longer that of the April days. In the first place Byng was told that he must manage without the Canadians. This fine Corps deserved a rest after its part in the last battles for Passchendaele Ridge but that was not the reason. An election was coming up in Canada where the main question was to be whether or not conscription should be introduced. Many good judges believed that without it the Corps would wither away. It must not be locked in battle when the polling stations opened. Then five of Byng's divisions which had been enjoying what passed for rest were taken away and replaced by an equivalent number all of which had just returned from the meat-grinder of the October battles.

The most illustrious of these was the 29th; in spite of the high number it had begun life as a mainly regular formation, made up from battalions gathered in from India, Burma, China and even Mauritius. The Division had gained its first fighting experience at Gallipoli and had been present at almost every major battle in France since its return from there. The usual accidents of war had enriched it with two fine battalions unknown to the 1914 Army List. The Royal Newfoundland Regiment and the Royal Guernsey Light Infantry, both of them veterans now, were as good as anything in the Army and better than most. The GOC, Beauvoir de L'Isle, was regarded as one of the most competent of his rank and was given a step soon after the Cambrai battle. This was the kind of formation to be employed in the event of Third Army finding need for a spear-point. However weary it might be, the 29th Division was never known to fail.

It was the presence of the 29th Division in Byng's army that had set the tank business in motion. The reason was, of all things, polo. Back in those golden Indian years before the war Lieutenant-Colonel Beauvoir de L'Isle had commanded the Durham Light Infantry, the only foot regiment ever to win the Championship Cup. On the insistence of Lord Roberts, de L'Isle had transferred to the cavalry and became commanding officer of the Royals. The 4th Dragoon Guards also had a famous team, including one of the Army's star players, John Hardress Lloyd. Naturally enough both men were well known to Julian Byng of the Xth Hussars. All of them had served together in the Dardanelles, de L'Isle in his present appointment, Hardress Lloyd as his ADC and Byng as Corps Commander. When the Division moved to France Hardress Lloyd was given an infantry battalion; after a few months, in January, 1917, he saw the light and transferred to the tanks. Though the younger man by a dozen years, he was on terms of friendship with Sir Julian; Elles was a Sapper, Fuller and Baker-Carr both infantrymen. Only horseman can speak freely to horeseman. John Hardress Lloyd, now commander Third Tank Brigade, did. Sir Julian Byng listened — and believed.

Once the introduction had been effected he seems to have taken not only to Elles but to his acolytes Fuller and Martel. From the beginning, however, the parties were not what lawyers call *ad idem*. Fuller's plan, put forward by Elles, was of a gigantic mechanized trench raid on that part of the Hindenburg Line directly ahead of them. Its purpose would be that of other raids but magnified; smash, grab, kill as many Germans as possible, give the remainder what was called vertical wind-up and then come home. The total time needed would be eight hours; just the daylight length of a November day. Sir Julian, who did not then seek the opinions of his Corps

Commanders, reckoned this not nearly enough. He did, however, think about it very seriously. Unfortunately the higher up the Staff ladder the idea went the greater became the differences. The Tank Corps' idea of a quick in-and-out offended every instinct. Battles were not fought like that. All the same, something on those lines could and ought to be done. Whatever shape it would take, the tightest security was demanded. The Tank Corps had suffered too much already from secrets betrayed. And there was something else. The Hindenburg Lines were wide and deep. No tank yet built could cross them without some outside help. This had been the staple conversation at Bermicourt and they had an answer.

The United States had come into the war in April; China had followed in August. Ever since May large numbers of Chinese labourers, mostly officered by English missionaries, had been in the theatre. They served not as enlisted soldiers but as independent civilian contractors, each man exchanging work for wages. Part of the bargain was that they should not be taken into areas where they might come under fire, but this was not always scrupulously observed. By the autumn their strength was only a little short of 100,000 and they earned every penny of their pay. Most of the work consisted of keeping worn-out roads and railways more or less fit for use, but, being intelligent men, quite a number were promoted to vehicle maintenance. One advantage, of course, was that their language was incomprehensible other than to themselves and they could not betray anything even had they wished to. Fuller and Elles had devised a scheme for them to have an important share in making the raid a possibility.

Tanks could only move long distances by rail; were they to be massed for an attack in Third Army country something would have to be done about the lines and rolling stock. Here America came in. General Pershing (who happened to have a young ADC named George Patton) agreed to make some of his engineers available. It can only have been a pleasant change for Sir Douglas and his Staff to be dealing with a General who neither wanted something nor could be suspected of babbling secrets. That took care of one essential.

Then came the matter of Intelligence, most particularly that relating to the German army. Brigadier-General John Charteris has had much ink used about him. The one certain thing is that he meant well. With rabbit-punches like Caporetto, the Russian Revolution (the extent of which nobody knew), the attitude of Greece, U-boats and Gothas, and other minor matters, Sir Douglas might be heading for a nervous collapse. Charteris, like a good nanny, determined to keep his spirits up with soothing stories about the utter exhaustion of Germany. When the Cambrai operation was first mooted Charteris carried self-deception too far. The need, of course, was to know how many divisions the Germans could bring back from Russia in time to join the battle and what sort of shape they would be in. Also it was highly desirable to know what the German plan was vis-à-vis Italy and what was heading in that direction. Would the Cambrai offensive divert them to somewhere else?

No man now living can say what was in Charteris' mind when a week or so before battle began he informed his Chief that the enemy had no reserves opposite Byng's army. This was not what his subordinates had told him. The late General Sir James Marshall-Cornwall, then a 30-year-old Major with an MC won at Mons, had been more involved than any other officer in 'I' Branch with examining German prisoners. Marshall-Cornwall was a remarkable linguist as well as being an experienced fighting soldier. Charteris, widely known amongst the cognoscenti as 'The Principal Boy', was neither. When the younger man formed up with hard, documented evidence that the Germans had just reinforced the Cambrai front with three fresh divisions from Russia the Chief of Intelligence came near to calling him a liar. "You are mistaken," he said to me. "This is just a bluff put up by the Germans to deceive us. I am sure that the units you mention are still on the Russian front; they are not to be shown on our Intelligence map. If the C-in-C were to think that the Germans had reinforced this sector, it might shake his confidence in our success." I was so horrified that I went straight to Major-General 'Tavish' Davidson, Haig's Director of Military Operations, and gave him the facts, telling him that I could no longer go on serving under Charteris, who was suppressing vital information to suit his own ideas. Davidson told me to stay where I was, but to give him the true picture privately.' What Davidson thought privately is not known. He should have been on enquiry, for Baker-Carr had warned him at the time of Third Ypres about the failure of 'I' Branch. There had been a celebrated interview at which Davidson, after admitting that neither he nor any of his staff had been there, had plainly been convinced by the absurdly inflated figures of German losses purveyed by Charteris. Years later he expressed his view that the Cambrai battle so late in the year was too risky. 'Haig, however, pursued the course he had chosen.' The idea of a headstrong Field-Marshal pursuing his new-fangled course amidst the shaking heads of his chiefs of both Intelligence and Operations sounds unconvincing. It did not appear in that light to Charles Carrington: 'A highly speculative gamble which I find inexplicable, so out-of-character is it with the rest of Haig's career, not because it was inventive but because it was haphazard, not thought through.'

The cerebrants at Tank Corps HQ in the pleasant though bitterly cold château of Bermicourt would have regarded this as neither kind nor fair. Much thought was going on; not all of it along the same lines. Most pensive, for his mind was concentrated on one thing, was Colonel Fuller. This strange little man had been saddled with the Napoleonic nickname of 'Boney' during his days at the Staff College. The various photographs of Fuller in 1917, especially the rather famous one in the group at Bermicourt, proclaim him not to have been as other men were. Alongside the burly figure of Elles he looks dwarfish; his light infantry double-belted Sam Browne and his lion-tamer's boots set him apart from the others in conventional service dress. His wedge-shaped cat's face is not that of the common run of regular infantry officers but there is a sharpness about it that the others lacked. Fuller had come to mechanized warfare rather late in life, being nearer to 40 than 30 when he saw his first tank. Being, like Swinton, a parson's son, his conversion when it came was absolute. Far other was 'Q', the future General Martel. With a father who had been Chief Superintendent of the Ordnance Factories, Professor of Artillery and Principal Experimental Officer, Martel had grown up to the sound of military machinery. It was natural that he should grasp more quickly and strongly than other men how the time had arrived for these machines to succeed men as arbiters of battles. At Bermicourt he had represented Fisher's *totus porcus* school. His *Tank Army* paper, written at the end of the Somme battles 'to clear my mind' was a startlingly accurate vision of things to come. The text began, uncompromisingly, with the assertion that 'No present day army could fight against an army consisting of say 2,000 tanks, and it therefore follows that all the large Continental armies will have to make use of Tank armies in the future.' He treats of mines and wire, of signal, supply and destroyer, battle and torpedo tanks. Though he does not use the word, it is plainly the rocket that Martel had in mind for its main weapon. Such a one did come into existence during the last days of Hitler. There was not time enough for it to demonstrate what it could do. Tactics, organization, training, maintenance and all other essentials are covered. Though Martel came to modify his views in later years, experience proving that some of the older arms might still have places in his Order of Battle, he was a generation ahead of most during the time of the Bermicourt colloquies. Whilst not so occupied he kept up with his boxing prowess. 'Slosher' Martel, as the younger men called him, was famous in the amateur ring.

One thing, inexplicably, did not figure on the Bermicourt agenda. Fuller, when writing his book after the war, had the honesty to admit that he could have kicked himself for missing it. All training and all tactics were directed to two ends only, the killing of machine guns and the crossing of trenches. Some of the hardest infantry fighting had been and would continue to be in those small woods with which this part of France abounds. No doctrine could be evolved for tanks compelled to work in these; commanders and drivers must do the best they could by the light of nature. That was understandable. The other omission was not. Street fighting was something that had not previously come the way of British armies to any great extent. A glance at the map, if nothing more, would have shown that, sooner or later, having performed the task of trench-crossing, the tanks must inevitably find themselves in village streets flanked by high, solid buildings. The infantry had come a long way in working out drills for dealing with such a situation. Even the good brains at the head of tank business never gave it a thought. This, before very long, was going to cost both the Corps and the army dearly. It is hard to understand how anything so obvious could be overlooked, but it was. Yet Fuller's first plan of all, dated 3 August, had said that 'In order to restore British prestige and strike a theatrical blow against Germany before the winter, it is suggested that preparations be at once set on foot to take St Quentin'. There is no point in labouring this. Not even the Bermicourt brain-barn, as it was called, can think of everything. The St Quentin plan lasted only 24 hours.

This, then, was the dramatis personae for a new kind of battle. Of all the Army commanders Sir Julian Byng, the only cavalryman among them apart from Hubert Gough, was the most likely to listen to them. Although old army in its purest form, he had spent a part of his military life in more animating surroundings. During the Boer War he had commanded that highly irregular but none the less useful regiment, the South African Light Horse, with young Winston Churchill for galloper. The style of the SALH had not been that of Netheravon or Weedon (where Byng had been Commandant) but they became a unit of high value. It was experience useful to a British commander of a Canadian Corps. Unlike many Generals, Sir Julian needed no persuading that soldierly qualities existed outside the Regular army.

Up to the very last moment uncertainty persisted about what shape the battle was going to take. From Fuller's point of view the proper strategy would be a raid, something after the style of an Arab razzia, followed by more raids until the moment came for the last mighty push against a bewildered enemy. Whether raid or battle, however, there was one necessary task, the crossing of trenches 18 feet wide and proportionately deep. Fuller and his cronies had worked this one out. A couple of miles from Bermicourt stood the Central Workshops at Teneur and the tank training area of Erin — not, oddly enough, a jargon name but a real French village. The two organizations owned the services of a company of the Chinese Labour Corps. Its people could very well be put to the work of a medieval kind, the original elementary form of moat-crossing. Every military engineer knew all about fascines and gabions though hardly anybody would have happened upon either after leaving The Shop. Antiquity does not always mean uselessness. What the fascines had done once they could do again, though not exactly in the way that Roman lictors had known. Colonel Searle and his helpers at Erin designed the new model. To make even the experimental one called for

12. Mk IV Tanks at Rollencourt Tankodrome, June 1917. Rollencourt was a training area between Bermicourt and Hesdin. (*Tank Museum*)

13. Sledges—one of the aids to victory. (*Tank Museum*)

14. MkIV Male Tank leading others onto flat cars at Plateau railhead. Note sponsons swung inboard and fascines loaded (p.83). (*Tank Museum*)

15. Tanks with fascines entrained at Plateau. (*Tank Museum*)

16. "The 6th Division had the distinction of being led into battle by the Commander of the Tank Corps" (p.114). General Elles' flagship *Hilda*.

17. "There came a sound of rending metal as tank and bridge gently declined into the canal" (p.114). Lt. Edmundson's *Flying Fox* in the canal at Masnières.

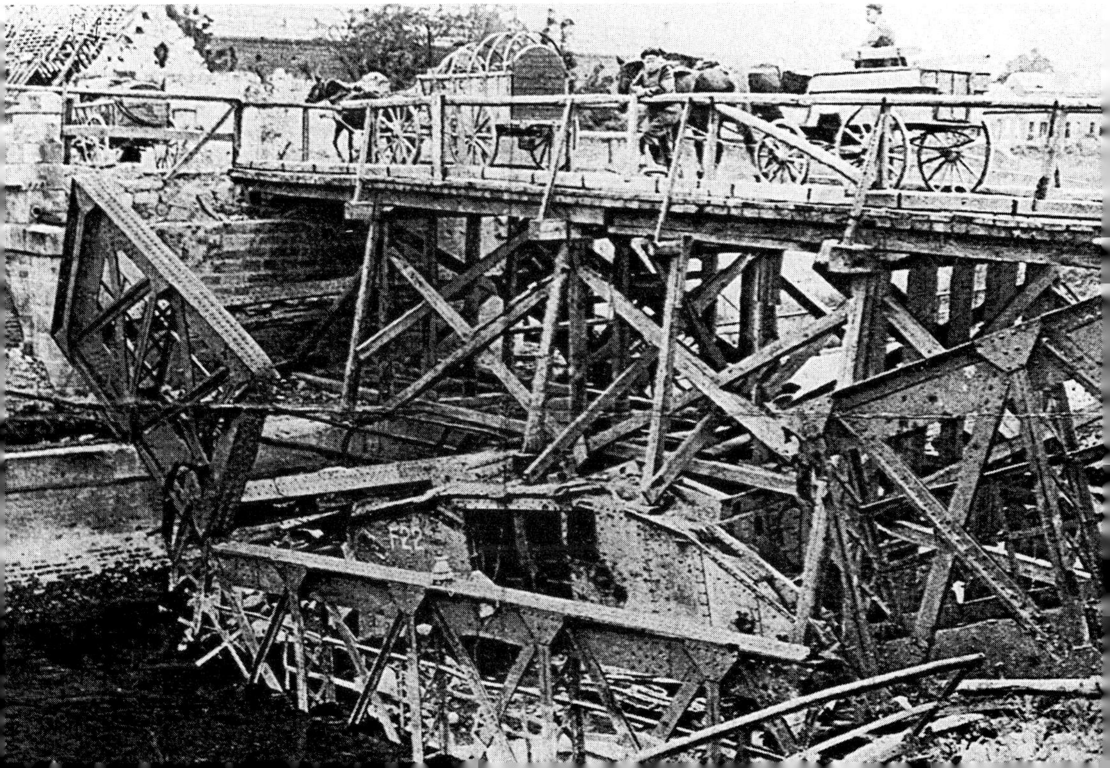

18. Female Mk IV Tank D4 towing in captured German 5.9 gun at Ribécourt. (*Tank Museum*)

19. 'G' Battalion Tanks *Grasshopper* and *Gurkha* destroyed in Bourlon Wood. (*Tank Museum*)

seventy-five or so bundles of brushwood of the kind used for road repairs. Since 350 of the fascines would be needed were the plan to be put into operation something like 21,000 bundles had to be collected up, delivered to Central Workshops and assembled. The last operation required chains and an SOS was dispatched to England praying that everything suitable be sent without asking questions. The Navy grudgingly allowed some of its precious stores to be borrowed, farms and factories were laid under contribution and even parks were persuaded to disgorge whatever they could. Once they had arrived the patient Chinese, probably wondering what imbecility their employers were meditating this time, bundled them together. The complete, still uncompressed, fascine weighed about a ton and a half. Since hand-tightness was plainly nowhere near enough, eighteen tanks were put to use, acting in pairs and pulling tight the chains from opposite directions. Twenty Chinamen (use of the demeaning word coolie was strictly forbidden) were assembled to roll each completed article through the mud. Their part in the play was indispensable; no Labour Corps, no fascines. No fascines, no tank battle.

The plan called for much more than fascines. The Daimler engines of the tanks were always thirsty; apart from ordinary lubricating oil the tracks and rollers demanded grease in great quantity; the guns and machine guns required regular nourishment and everybody, like the engine, wanted water. The Mk IV had one advantage over its predecessor; in front of the commander where once had been the petrol tank now stood a cupboard, convenient for such a viaticum as chocolate and whisky. That was the only gesture towards gracious living permitted to the eight men sardined inside. Luxuries apart, the tank lived on 'fills'; a 'fill' consisted of 60 gallons of petrol, 10 of oil, 20 of water, 10 lbs of grease, 10,000 rounds of .303 for the females or 200 6-pounder shells plus 6,000 small arms rounds for the male. Neither tank could travel very far or do anything very useful without them. 'Fills' were about the only things that infantrymen could not carry; the Workshops, as always, came up with an answer. Before the wheel was invented man had, presumably, transported his goods by sledge. On 24 October, the day the Italians were being put to the rightabout at Caporetto, the indent was submitted for 110 large ones, fit to be dragged by Mk I tanks over grassy downs. This was in addition to the 350 fascines and the same number of Erin-designed catches enabling them to be neatly dropped over a tank's bows. There was no sawn wood for the sledges. Every one had to be made out of logs, by hand. This was all to be done alongside the existing, and more important, work of patching-up and re-issuing for service 127 tanks that had been much battered already. For three solid weeks the workshops rested not by day or night. Without the Chinese workmen, many of them now skilled mechanics, the business could not have been done. As it was the nine battalions of the Tank Corps became, on the eve of the great test, a force dependent upon nobody but itself for all that would be needed in the course of a short battle. Experiment showed that a tank could pull three sledges carrying a total weight of 14 tons made up of POL – petrol, oil and lubricants – and ammunition. The few available gun-carriers, having no part written for them, were similarly employed. Each Division was allotted one. A special section of 'E' battalion was entrusted with the business of completely removing wire in order to clear a way for the cavalry. An effective drill, using a clearing anchor released by a belaying-pin, was worked out. A pair of tanks thus equipped could gather up the most comprehensive of barbed wire entanglements and deal with them as a combine harvester deals with cornstalks.

Back at home, Stern, Tritton and the rest were now able to keep up a steady supply of Mk IVs, whilst also busy making the first of a new and much better Mk V. The Landship tradition clung on; the Royal Navy, represented by 20 Squadron RNAS, collecting each tank from the factory, tested it and saw to all the entraining and detraining by way of the secret (as it was optimistically called) port of Richborough on the Sandwich River. Against the heavy and not always justifiable competition from the Navy and the RFC, Stern's and Tritton's people were working wonders. One thing, however, they could not do. The Vickers machine gun is a complicated affair and not designed for mass production. It was also in great demand and the Tank Corps had to take its place in the queue. As this was a lowly one, and the BSA Company had its production lines of Lewis guns running satisfactorily, the Corps was told that, for the time being at least, the Lewis was all that it was going to get. This was serious. The Vickers, with its armoured jacket, could take any amount of punishment and still remain a powerful man-killing weapon. The Lewis, excellent for its proper purpose, could not. One description can serve for all: 'The front gun was bent and battered in its port, looking rather like a splayed out, rusty cigarette and stuck on the ball mounting.' Tanks armed only with the Lewis could speedily be made useless, but there was no help for it. The Machine Gun Corps and the RFC had needs equally urgent — and there were not nearly enough Vickers guns.

In this fashion was the war matériel assembled for whatever kind of tank battle might be in the offing. Most of the crews were inexperienced in combat; the artillery and infantry working with them would be for the most part old soldiers, tired out already and quite unused to co-operating with these machines.

Byng had first approached Haig in August, only to be told firmly by Kiggell that however good his idea might be it would have to wait until the battles in the Salient were over. Nothing of first importance happened until, on 13 October, Sir Douglas gave his qualified approval to some sort of armoured attack. This, remember, was a month before Marshall-Cornwall's discovery of the arrival of fresh German divisions in the line. For Fuller and his people it was the training time and every day was something to be valued.

As armies settle down to their particular kinds of war they usually develop drills to deal with such new things as may appear. 'Boney', a voracious student of past campaigns, had drawn on one of the most distant in the memory of man for the method he reckoned best for the conditions of November, 1917. He had made a start in his *Training Note No. 16*, issued in February; there he laid it down that the tank was 'a mobile fortress intended to escort infantry in the attack, pre-eminently an offensive weapon, to be used in mass and in circumstances of surprise and therefore to be preceded by an artillery bombardment not exceeding 48 hours in length'. Some months later, after Messines, he expanded on this in *Projected Bases for the Tactical Employment of Tanks in 1918*. In this he posited two things, the first of them tolerably obvious. Shallow linear fronts could be defeated by an infantry advance of a few thousand yards; deep trenches had made artillery support for such movements almost useless; only the tank could cross and take the trenches. Enemy reserves, fresh and numerous, could not be taken on by foot soldiers exhausted by their first battles; a sensible enemy would, when attack was expected, pull back his guns in order to preserve them from counter-battery fire and to have them ready to deal with attackers who might have penetrated the first lines. His machine guns would remain. Thus, Fuller argued, the business of tanks would be to take over the functions of artillery once the attack had passed beyond gun range and to dispose of the machine guns along with such artillery pieces as might still be there. If all went well the last task would be to beat up rear areas, disrupt communications and prepare the ground to let the cavalry through. Cavalry was anachronistic in such a battle but there was no other arm − not counting the few armoured cars available − that could move farther and faster than a plodding infantryman. Fuller became metaphoric: 'The tank must no longer be looked upon as the spare wheel to the car, in order to meet unforeseen puncture in our operations, but as the motive force of the car itself, the infantry being no more than its armed occupants, without which the car is valueless.'

The drills he worked out to achieve this result came, so Fuller claimed, from one described by Xenophon in the *Cyropaedia* and attributed by him to Cyrus, King of Persia, in about 500 BC. It was designed to work thus. A company of tanks was made up of four sections, each of three machines. Each section would move with a single tank as its point; 100 yards behind, the remaining two would follow, another 100 yards apart. Yet a further 100 yards behind each of these an infantry platoon would come in artillery formation − extended file or single file. The point tank would move up to the edge of the first trench, flattening the wire as it went, but would not cross. Instead of that, it would turn left and enfilade the trench with its machine guns. While it was so occupied the other two tanks would be making for a pre-selected (by Hotblack or one of his officers) point in the line. The one on the left, timed to arrive first, would drop its fascine in the trench, cross over on it and also make a left turn, firing all the time. The right-hand tank would cross, using the fascine of its leader, make for the second trench, drop the fascine in it, cross, and set about the second trench in the same way as its sister had set about the first. The point tank, once all this had been done, would rejoin the fray, crossing over both trenches with its own fascine still in place and would head for the third line. While the new arm was thus engaged the oldest of them all had work to do. The first of the infantry were for all practical purposes part of the armoured force. Their job, as 'trench-clearers', was to follow closely behind, probably in single file, sort out the trenches and dugouts and put up red flags to show them as finished and the paths through the wire as clear; the second parties, 'trench stops', were the nets to the tanks' ferrets. The function of the last, the 'trench garrisons', explains itself.

It was carefully worked out and sounded splendid. Captious men, remembering Bullecourt, might have said that all should work out very nicely so long as the Germans co-operated. Hotblack himself, in an interview many years later with somebody from the BBC, made a sound point. The Mk IV tank was a frightener rather than a fighter. It worked well so long as the Germans carried out their role to be frightened. Since German soldiers seldom fled without cause there was a part in the scheme for other than tank crews. Even when their engines were purring happily and grip on the ground was firm, tanks were more vulnerable than they appeared. The German 'K' bullet would not usually penetrate the hull of a Mk IV save in its hinder parts but fire even from conventional small arms was dangerous and disagreeable. 'Splash', the tiny metal fragments broken off inside when bullet hit armour, lit the darkened interiors like sparks from a smith's anvil and were damaging enough to compel the wearing of chain-mail masks of Homeric aspect. As the Boer marksmen had cut down the gunners at Colenso so could resolute German snipers make life difficult for tank crews. The engineering that had gone into the hulls and sponsons was not refined; gaps had a way of opening up, particularly between hull and sponson. 'We had filled this up with felt packing some days back, but the packing had been shot away and bullets through this gap came right through the tank,' says one sufferer. Then there were the grenades. A single 'potato masher' made little impression but when some genius decided to bundle them up in threes and fours they became a menace, quite capable of blowing a track off its rollers. Once that had been done the only course left for the crew was to abandon ship and take their Lewis guns off to the nearest shell-hole from which they could make themselves useful. Machine-gun fire from the air was a nuisance; bombing would have been more serious but the science of tank-busting was still in its infancy. Most dangerous of all by far was the field gun, firing at short range over open sights. It did not greatly matter, from the gunner's point of view, what sort of projectile was used; high explosive, shrapnel, mustard gas or even smoke, any one of them would kill a Mk IV stone dead. This is where the infantry should come in. Stout-hearted men with short Lee Enfield, Lewis light automatics (often slung over the shoulder and fired from the hip) and Mills grenades ought to be able to take care of any artilleryman bold enough to face up to the oncoming armour. If each was to help the other effectively, some sort of rudimentary system of signals was needed. Several were tried, without much success. There was no way in which infantry could speak to tank save by walking alongside and banging on the door. The messages a tank could give were reduced to two. A red and yellow flag waved through the roof was to signify 'All clear. Come on'. The other, a shovel waved in the same fashion, meant 'I have broken down. Don't wait for me'. In theory an infantry call for help — steel helmet on rifle held above the head — existed but was quickly abandoned. No tank commander could be expected to notice it amongst his other concerns.

To be effective the infantry must keep up with the armour. The worst possible failure would be to leave the tanks unattended, lurching blindly forward into whatever might be prepared for them. Ideally, of course, this should be airman's work but the Tank Corps and the RFC still lived in different worlds. Even had they been carefully practised, as the German tanks and dive-bombers were in 1940, it needed only fog or rain — not uncommon in late November — to bring it to nothing. There was no safe place for a moving tank. Open country probably contained hidden artillery in addition to the inevitable machine guns. The fight at Monchy-le-Preux in April had shown how perilous village streets could be with resolute men on roofs sniping through interstices and dropping bundles of grenades under tracks. And in the woods with which this part of France abounds they were in permanent danger of 'bellying', as well as being as blind as Samson. Thus it was that Fuller, during the training days, taught and lectured and hammered away at the one rule which permitted no exceptions. The infantry must no more abandon the tanks than the tanks would abandon them. The tank brigade commanders, Baker-Carr, Courage and Hardress-Lloyd, preached the same sermon. Some, possibly several, of the divisional Generals, took it in. For the most part they were men tried in this war who had endured much promotion in a short time as the army mushroomed in size. Between Byng and them, however, stood the Corps Commanders.

Corps — originally called Army Corps but soon truncated for brevity — were not homogeneous affairs like divisions. They could vary in size from time to time according to the number of divisions allotted to them and only maintained permanently their HQs and such specialist affairs as heavy artillery. Their commanders were very senior men, not always ideal choices for modern battle. The two Corps in the front line of the Third Army upon whom the first demands would be made were the IVth to the north-west and the IIIrd to the south-east. Their commanders were, respectively, Lieutenant-General Sir Charles Woollcombe and Lieutenant-General Sir William Pulteney. General Woollcombe, born in the year of the Indian Mutiny, and General Pulteney, four years his junior, had one attribute which they shared with both Swinton and Fuller. All of them were the sons of parsons. How far this explains the thoughts and actions of any is hard to say; apart from memories of Victorian vicarage days they had little enough in common. Woollcombe had had immense Indian experience but had seen nothing of the then war in France until 1916 when he had commanded the 11th Division in the last Somme battles. He had the reputation of being a strict disciplinarian but he was in no case to put his opinion against that of more experienced though junior Generals. Pulteney had been in France from the beginning, arriving in command of the 6th Division in September, 1914, in time for the Battle of the Aisne and having had some hand in most of the following battles. 'Putty', who at the age of 56 had just taken himself a wife, was an easy-going man. After the war Charles Carrington asked his Divisional Commander, General Fanshawe, which was the best Corps Commander he had served under. 'Oh, Putty', he said. 'Putty let me do exactly as I liked.' When he was the guest of the famous Baronne de la Grange at La Motte au Bois his hostess had him weighed up. 'He is what we call a *bon vivant*, with a lively and twinkling eye. His Staff is a very cheerful one, and I see extremely frivolous Parisian papers lying on the tables mixed up with ordnance maps and plans of attack.' Unfortunately neither of these admirable senior officers knew the first thing about tanks. The two Generals could not be other than part-time players. The one man who possessed the vision, mental agility and technical knowledge necessary to make the plan succeed, the Australian General Monash, still awaited the opportunity to make a great name for himself.

On 20 October a draft scheme for the operation called GY was submitted by Third Army to GHQ. Sir Julian and Sir Douglas discussed it, the latter emphasizing that even were he to authorize the attack it could only be an affair limited both in size and duration. Fighting at Passchendaele was still going on, there was no knowing what further demands might come from Italy, and Russia was as much a puzzle as ever. Sir Julian, to his great credit, expounded the virtues of an armoured battle that would be quite different from its predecessors. Sir Douglas allowed himself to be reluctantly persuaded. On 10 November he gave a general approval, confirmed in writing on the morrow. This stressed the necessity for speed and surprise, the importance of securing the Bourlon heights on the first day of 'action against enemy formation and unit headquarters'. The formal Order was issued on 13 November. It was certainly clear enough: 'The object of the operation is to break the enemy's defensive system with tanks, and to pass the Cavalry though to seize Cambrai, Bourlon Wood and the passages over the Sensée River, thus cutting off the retreat of all the hostile forces holding the line north-west and west between that river and Havrincourt.' The troops available were six infantry divisions, comprising III and IV Corps, the entire Cavalry Corps of five divisions, nine squadrons of the RFC, the Tank Corps and the usual supporting cast. There would, in point of fact, be a possible second battle. The first would continue for exactly 48 hours. At the end of that time further orders would be sent. Should things have gone sufficiently well then the cavalry would be loosed, to slash and prod their way round Cambrai towards Valenciennes, outflanking the German Second Army and harrying its back area. Should the results be disappointing then Sir Douglas would call the whole thing off and everybody would dig himself in wherever he found himself. The decision would have to be made at GHQ and it would be futile to ask beforehand what it was likely to be.

Though it all sounded dreadfully amateurish, one can see how Sir Douglas's mind was working. Neither he nor anybody else could have any idea whether the tank attack would be a brilliant success, leaving the Hindenburg Line penetrated in a hundred places, a dismal failure with every machine either knocked out or broken down, or something in the middle. Plans involving the lives of tens of thousands of men can not be based upon such imponderables. At this long remove of time one may sympathize with the Commander-in-Chief. The people most concerned in 1917 did nothing of the kind.

Baker-Carr, who knew everybody, learned of it early. GHQ, he said, had no confidence whatever in the proposed plan and 'Byng had received a grudging assent, coupled with a warning that he must accept full responsibility in the event of failure'. Fuller, though he had probably not expected anything better, was horrified. This scheme bore no resemblance to the one he had put forward. Every tank the Corps possessed was to go into battle on the first day. However that day might go, the next one could only be a scrambling affair with whatever machines might have survived cobbled into some sort of ad hoc units. A battle of six divisions plus all the cavalry sounded disagreeably like a replay of every failed offensive from Loos onwards. The only hope was for the bugle to sound 'No Parade' at the 49th hour. His was not to reason why.

However infirm of purpose Sir Douglas might have seemed and however worried was Colonel Fuller, the young men of the Tank Corps were jubilant. At last all those lessons and lectures on gears, clutches, auto-vacs and the rest, all those practice assaults on mock-ups of the Hindenburg Line and all the good, Swinton-inspired training they had had at Wool were going to prove that they had not been time wasted. The fighting tanks were waiting to go, the sledge-pullers and wire-extractors were expectant. Still unsettled, however, was the question of where the commanders should place themselves in battle. Each tank had its subaltern; Captains commanded sections of three, Majors companies of twelve. One of the section commanders wrote of it for Colonel Hobart: 'Before the battle Battalion, Company and Section Commanders were fully employed in organizing, training, liaison, reconnaissance of the part to be attacked and the approaches to it, the collecting of information from all sources, and the study of air photos and trench maps and the dissemination of this information to all concerned. . . . For the most part Section Commanders followed their Tanks on foot, with the leading infantry going forward to their machines and giving them targets or re-directing them as occasion offered. They were often instrumental in getting the infantry to seize some fleeting opportunity created by the Tanks . . . or personally leading one or more machines over awkward obstacles. On other occasions they would ride in a tank but unless there had been a casualty this meant either more crowding of an already full vehicle or displacing some member of the crew. Some Section Commanders always kept one Tank with them or behind them, out of the immediate fight, with which they could influence the local situation as opportunity offered, and this was usually the most effective. After reaching and subduing an objective it was the job of the Section Commander to collect and rally his command, ready to repel a counter-attack or proceed to a further objective.' After describing the tremendous importance of Section Commanders being the proper kind of officer, he adds that all of them 'from the 3rd Battle of Ypres to the end of the war were the finest type of men, and the Corps owes them more than is realized by most. The respect in which the majority of these officers were held by their crews and the power and influence they wielded amongst the officers and men of their command was a dumb but eloquent testimony to their worth.' The Company Commander's place was, by Corps order, with the HQ of the infantry battalion he was supporting; the main task of the CO was 'preventing the misuse of his Companies by infantry commanders'.

By no means all of the Tank Corps' business was transacted from within its iron walls. Communication between insiders and outsiders was not easy. Highest 1917 technology amounted to a crowbar or shovel hung outside a sponson door with which any runner might bang for attention. For more distant communications each machine carried a couple of pigeons; when released they had a long flight, back to Divisional HQ. The 6-pdr gunners and the Lewis gunners were, in the nature of things, left to do as they thought best. No fire control was possible and, in any case, 'a crew was a team, each man knew his individual job and did it, and if one made a mistake the machine stopped until it was rectified'. All that said, the fact remained that numbers of tanks could not answer to their commanders' orders as could numbers of ships. 'Once inside the tank and the door closed one was in another world. Nothing could be seen outside, nothing could be heard, while inside one half-shaded festoon lamp gave an eerie murky glimmer in the stygian gloom. The walls represented the limits of one's world and the crew of eight its population; one was completely isolated, existence depending on the driving skill of the driver and the wits of the officer. Tanks on the left and right might be seen but they existed merely as other worlds, there were no tactics, no co-operation, and of course no external command.' So runs one anonymous entry in Hobart's chronicle. Hobart himself set out the fact of the matter: 'As the Tanks could not manoeuvre to take advantage of the situations as they arose, each machine had to be given a definite and limited objective and a definite job to carry out. To make sure that no ground which held a MG was left uncovered, the whole front to be attacked had to be covered by the Tanks. Each Tank fought an individual and isolated combat without much hope of assistance from its brothers except by chance, and numbers had to make up for the lack of control and the power of manoeuvre.' Because there were no reserves for him to direct General Elles was a free agent. Viewed from this distance of time, his entry into battle in the manner of Sir John Chandos and bearing the mud, blood and green fields flag made for Fuller in a Cassel shop seems a piece of flamboyance not to be admired. That was not how the Tank Corps saw it. Lieutenant Mitchell's remark that 'the brave flapping of that lonely flag was, that day, easily worth another hundred tanks to the enheartened Tank Corps' pitches it rather high; but it was the kind of gesture, like Nelson going into battle starred and gartered, that is not felt unseemly when the bullets are flying and victory far from certain. However it may look now, Elles and Fuller were probably better judges of such things than their successors can ever be. Their young men certainly approved. And so did the war correspondents. The day, 20 November, 1917, was one to be marked at Bovington with a white stone. The future of war had arrived and with it *dies irae* for the Kaiser and all his legions.

'If the Boche doesn't tumble to it before the show it's an absolute gift,' wrote a subaltern of A Battalion. It was not necessary to cerebrate about the second phase. Once the Hindenburg Line had been breached in hundreds of places the tanks, or their survivors, would, obedient to orders, return to their designated rallying points with their battle over and done with.

Even though the confidence of the Tank officers was not shared by everybody, it was still necessary to plan for a success. General Woollcombe convened a conference of his senior commanders. His Corps consisted for the purposes before him of the 1st Cavalry Division of General Mullens (behind his back always known as 'Gobby Chops'), Baker-Carr's Brigade of Tanks and two Territorial divisions. Of necessity every part of all of them would have to be employed throughout, for there were no reserves. There was a contrast in the reputations of the divisions. The 62nd, men of the West Riding of Yorkshire, had no particular standing within the Army. It was a formation made up almost entirely of men who had for one reason or another not volunteered for overseas service in August, 1914. Though the 62nd had existed as a formed body since the early days of the war it had arrived in France only at the beginning of 1917 and had received a rough baptism at Bullecourt. It was a battle that brought no opportunity of distinction anywhere. The great county of Yorkshire, however, has always produced soldiers of quality, even though they may not proclaim the fact as stridently as some others do. The West Riding men this time had the advantage of being commanded by a General Officer of outstanding professional ability and personal qualities. Walter Pipon Braithwaite (yet another parson's son) came from the Somerset Light Infantry, was 52 years old and a practised hand in battle. His war had begun at Gallipoli where he had been Chief of Staff to Sir Ian Hamilton. Sir Ian was a man slow to anger. One may judge the depth of his feelings from a diary entry he made on 4 October, 1915, when matters there were at their worst: 'K must have a splendid sacrifice but by the Lord they shan't have the man who stood by me like a rock during those first ghastly ten days.' The man was Walter Braithwaite, guilty by association for the Dardanelles failure and working his way back on probation. Nobody expected much of his Yorkshiremen, for second-line Territorials ranked very low in the batting order. It soon became plain that, under Braithwaite, the 62nd Division was one of the best fighting formations in Haig's army.

Major-General Harper's credentials have already been mentioned. He had been a good 'Q' Staff officer and had learnt the elements of infantry business as commander of 17th Brigade during some minor actions early in 1915. His two Somme battles as commander of the 51st had been of the hardest. High Wood, on 20 July, had failed, but on 13 November the taking of Beaumont-Hamel proclaimed that much had been learned during the months between. Unfortunately tanks had formed no part of his further education. That there might be changes at hand in the way battles would be fought in future was something about which he appeared serenely unconscious. Knowing what all men now know of the manner in which he employed his Division on Flesquières Ridge, it is hard to do justice to his memory without violence to the truth. The natural inclination is to write harshly of him as what the French used to call '*un bon Général d'Afrique*', the only one in step and wrongly convinced that he alone understood the new way of making war. Before doing so, however, it is necessary to consider the case put by his advocate. The CRA of the 51st Division, Colonel Oldfield — eventually Lieutenant-General Sir Louis — was an officer of the highest quality, experienced and level-headed. On 27 November, 1917 — mark well that date — he wrote to his friend Miss Whitaker that 'My General is really wonderful. He thinks years ahead of others. I think he finds me a very useful counsellor because I am not afraid of him and give him lines of thought. But it is wicked waste not to promote him to high command. Unluckily he simply cannot work with some fellows and has to fix his own environment.' Perhaps it was common memories of The Shop; perhaps the natural clannishness of technical officers in the face of the simpler orders had something to do with it. Such admiration from such a man is far more than mere courtesy. 'Uncle' Harper was a more intricate character than might be thought.

Kilts and bagpipes are irresistible to journalists. Putting aside all the nonsense, however, there is no denying that the 'little fellers' thoroughly deserved their reputation as good men in a rough house. The 62nd Division was made by Walter Braithwaite; 'Uncle' Harper was made by the 51st. During Woollcombe's Corps Conference he sat mumchance while the operation was being discussed. As soon as it was over he grabbed Baker-Carr by the arm and 'blackguarded the whole conception as a fantastic and most unmilitary scheme'. Though he could well have said as much to Woollcombe, and to Sir Launcelot Kiggell who was also there, Harper preferred to say nothing but quietly to sabotage the whole attack. 'Up to the very last moment he was completely lukewarm and, as I learned years later, had not hesitated to communicate his apprehensions to his brigade commanders.' Harper appears to have seen the Highland Division as an ally rather than a subordinate. What other commanders might do was up to them. His infantry would cross No-Man's-Land as tradition expected of them — in waves, led by their pipers. His only contribution to the Corps conference was recorded by his Divisional Machine-gun Officer, the young Douglas Wimberley. Secrecy, however necessary, had made the job of 'Q' side — supply and transport — almost impossible. 'Uncle' had something to say about it. After tactfully reminding Woollcombe that IVth Corps had seen little fighting recently, whereas the 51st had experienced hardly anything else, he went on. He had always seen to it that his Highlanders were well fed, even to having fresh meat every day. The Corps Commander assured him of his intention to do the same. In fact, for the duration of the battle, Harper's men lived almost entirely on biscuit plus what they were able to liberate from the enemy. Only troops not engaged enjoyed the fleshpots. Much rancour followed.

Braithwaite, on the other hand, was at pains to find out what tanks could and could not do. The Tank Corps at Wailly, unused to appreciation, did everything they could to enlighten him. Barbed-wire obstacles, built by the infantry themselves, and trenches of unprecedented depth and width were constructed. The best weapons were demonstrated, the 6-pdr gunners showing how they could either blast a machine-gun position to pieces with HE or, by firing case-shot, turn the guns into gigantic buckshot 12 bores. Then the tanks trod the wire contemptuously underfoot and fascined their way over the trenches. Although it would not be like that on the day, General Braithwaite was convinced. His personality was felt amongst men of the West Riding quite as keenly as that of Harper amongst the Jocks. 'His faith was reflected throughout the Division and the Tanks units co-operating were loud in their praise of the whole-hearted support given' was how Williams-Ellis summed it up.

Far other was the state of affairs in the 51st. Its commander set himself to devising battle drills of his own, drills which had nothing to do with the unmilitary idea of tanks and infantry working as one. Harper knew better, nor did he find himself under the necessity of sharing his own superior plan for the coming fray. Everybody knew that tanks drew fire; the 'little fellers' would be much safer if they kept a long way behind. As for the tanks, they could go hang. Tanks were none of his business. Let them go on ahead and keep out of his way; much the same orders as had once been given to machine-gun sections. If other divisional generals felt obliged to follow orders that again was no concern of his. Nobody but 'Uncle' should be allowed to order the 51st about. The last Division, in IV Corps area but not a part of it, avoided such problems. Oliver Nugent's 36th (Ulster) Division, away on the left of the line, would have no tanks at all to bother it.

At the right-hand end of a two-corps front stood Pulteney's IIIrd, descendants of the heroic remnant Baker-Carr had seen in 1914. Three years of war had brought their changes. Instead of the pick of the army, Capper's 7th Division and Hubert Gough's 3rd Cavalry Brigade, it now consisted of formations of different quality. Only two of the four divisions that made it up were regulars, even by courtesy — the 6th and 29th which constituted the left fist. On the right were two good and experienced Kitchener divisions — 12th (Eastern) on the extreme right where the line joined with VIIth Corps, the 20th (Light) alongside it.

There remained the matter of artillery. Although the cutting of wire was this time to be entrusted to tanks, it remained unthinkable that infantry should go over the top without a barrage to lean on. The man responsible for the slightly off-key voice of the guns, son of the sub-Dean of Exeter Cathedral, was CRA to a division with no part in the battle. Brigadier (later Major-General) H.H. Tudor was as well-tutored a Gunner as ever left Larkhill. It was from barrages put up in his 9th (Scottish) Division — and doubtless in many others also — that came the famous 'Ye could have lighted your pipe at it'. Tudor, of all men, was the proponent of the idea of using the guns unregistered and uncalibrated; the argument being that it were better to put up with a few casualties from a ragged barrage creeping ahead than to lose surprise. If the usual routine of bringing up great numbers of huge guns over inadequate roads and laying down equally huge dumps of ammunition for them were followed it would only remain to buy space in the Berlin newspapers and advertise the forthcoming offensive. Nobody but a gunner would have dared make the suggestion. So excellent was the technical competence of the Royal Regiment that Tudor's novelty was accepted without dissent.*

This, then, was the plan as it came out of Third Army HQ. On the right, in Pulteney's Corps area, the 12th and 20th Divisions and on the left in Woollcombe's 6th, 51st and 62nd would all move forward, each on a two-brigade front. These brigades would advance as far as the Brown Line, the second objective beyond the Hindenburg Support Trench; that done, the reserve brigades would pass through 'to carry out their special tasks'. Defensive flanks would be formed by the 12th on the right and the 6th and 20th to the left and through this wide gap would come the 29th on a three brigade front. De L'Isle's objective would be the vital bridges of Marcoing and Masnières to begin with; those taken, he was to cross and break the last German line on the other side of the canal. The 'special tasks' for the reserve brigades of the 51st and 62nd were to take the villages of Cantaing and Fontaine with Yorkshire on the flank storming Bourlon Village and occupying the Wood. The 36th had its subsidiary operation around Moeuvres while the flanking formations would keep the enemy in his trenches by ingenious forms of diversion. Given what the tanks and artillery could do, it was a very good plan. There were adventurous roles for the cavalry, including the surrounding of Cambrai and the cutting of all the railway lines leading into the city. This part read less convincingly. The warnings were hardly needed: 'The town should be damaged as little as possible. The enemy may attempt to set it on fire and you should prevent this as far as possible.' After commanding that the five railway lines should

---

* Cyril Falls, Captain of Foot and Professor of History, was there with the 36th Division. He has always maintained that Tudor deserves as much credit as Elles for the entire conception of an armoured attack.

be 'broken as effectively as possible', General Vaughan, Byng's MGGS, added a thoughtful caveat: 'The CAMBRAI-DOUAI railway may be required by us at a later stage, but as it is liable to be used by the enemy for withdrawal or reinforcement, it should be cut temporarily in as many places as possible.' One has to suppose that he meant this to be taken seriously. Optimism is not something to be cried down.

CHAPTER SEVEN

'WAS EVER A BATTLE LIKE THIS IN THE WORLD BEFORE?'

The Revenge

Alfred, Lord Tennyson

The parcel of France selected for the new battle was not new to the British Army. In the years after Waterloo both Cambrai and Valenciennes had been garrison towns, the former housing the Grenadier Guards under Colonel the Hon William Stewart and the latter Colonel Woodford's battalion of the Coldstream. Harry Smith, Rifleman and husband to the famous Juana, was Town Major of Cambrai, whilst Charlie Beckford held the equivalent position at Valenciennes. In Bourlon Château lived the Duke himself, his hounds sharing Bourlon Wood with those of the Smiths. When Colonel Hobart came to see it for the first time in 1935 he remarked that it reminded him of Salisbury Plain: 'As a rough comparison the battle could have been fought in an area bounded by Upavon-Amesbury-Shrewton-Urchfont Clump.'

The names of Caudry, Inchy, Cambrai and Le Cateau had appeared in the newspapers of 1914 when Sir Horace Smith-Dorrien had fought von Kluck to a standstill and saved the BEF from annihilation. The six miles of chalk down running south-east from the Bourlon heights had seen some fighting earlier in 1917, especially round the heavily-fortified La Vacquerie, though not on the Flanders scale. For the Tank Corps they were the nearest thing possible to nursery slopes. As soon as the participants came under starter's orders a mighty secrecy afflicted everybody. Surprise was the word of power. Those officers whose business it was to go forward and inspect the ground over which they were to operate denied their identities with false badges and plain burberries: 'One well-known Staff Officer even went to the length of wearing blue glasses; in fact in the matter of disguise the line was only drawn at ginger whiskers.... Staff and Reconnaissance officers slunk about, above all avoiding Headquarters and those other social centres which etiquette enjoins must first be called upon by all who visit other people's trenches.... At the First Brigade Headquarters in Arras there was a locked room with

"No Admittance" written large upon the door. Here were ostentatiously hung spoof maps of other topical districts and a profusion of plans lay spread about.' The Tank Corps was in merry pin, seeing at last the opportunity of doing what it had been intended for. Highlanders about the place were made to wear trousers. The part of the artillery, in order not to excite alarm in the Hindenburg Line, was to keep up exactly the daily amount of shell fire and of the same kind as had become customary. It was of the highest importance that the men of General von der Marwitz, commanding the Kaiser's Second Army, should be persuaded that their adversaries harboured no evil intentions towards them.

The two divisions in the line, 20th and 36th, were kept busy. For the moment the most important man in each of them was the CRE and his Pioneer battalion. Havrincourt Wood, about four square miles in area before the Germans felled much of it for trench revetments, was crammed with little wooden hutments. In them lived the men whose task it was to metal the roads and, as in such places as Trescault, to fill in with tons of chalk the craters blown during the enemy withdrawal. For once the weather could not have suited the British army better. 'It was fine, but morning after morning dawned with a thick ground mist which hung about all day. Foden lorries carrying stone and light steam rollers to lay it were enabled, beneath this shelter, to work at a proximity to the Germans that had otherwise been out of the question. Night after night the tanks, upon which all hinged, moved up into Havrincourt Wood. Here again the mist was a godsend, for the track of a tank across country is plain enough on an aeroplane photograph and not hard to distinguish with a glass. Contrary to the general belief of those who have not heard them on the move, the tank is not very noisy. It was the artillery tractors, dragging up the big howitzers which frightened everyone by their clatter.'

The Germans declined to take the season of mists and mellow fruitfulness as a rest period. They felt no apprehension, nor needed they to. Deep, concreted trenches with deeper, comfortable dug-outs, the whole fronted and sometimes flanked by wire should have made for some degree of insouciance. The wire alone, acre upon acre of it, the autumn sunshine giving back fitful gleams of blueness, was no ordinary farmer's stuff. Cores as thick as a man's thumb, with barbs to match, should have allowed any man to sleep with his boots unlaced. German infantry, it hardly needs to be said, were masters of their trade and that trade included an insatiable curiosity. It was highly necessary to know what the English were up to. Patrols went out with the irregularity that patrols should, avid for prisoners. On the night of 17/18 November, at the village of Trescault, one of them picked up a sergeant and five men of the 1st Royal Irish Fusiliers, a 36th Division unit. At this distance of time it is impossible to say whether they, or at any rate two of them, were loud-mouthed select bar boasters or Irishmen prepared to betray comrades to death for their own reasons. Easter week, 1916, was not all that long ago. They talked, volubly. An attack was indeed being prepared. They had seen the tanks in Havrincourt Wood. It would all begin on 20 November. Fortunately the German Intelligence also had memories, of the Casement fiasco amongst other things. It would need more than the babbling of traitors — just possibly honest men planted for the purpose of deceiving them — to give them seriously to believe that any attack could go in before a fortnight or so of bombardment. There were, however, some shreds of confirmation, largely signs of extra traffic in the rear reported by the air; von der Marwitz saw it as only sensible to thicken up his line in the most vulnerable place. He ordered an increase in the reserves around Havrincourt.

By this time Sir Douglas's plan, if it may be attributed to him, was complete and on its way to being carried out. The actual battleground was to be the stretch of grassland six miles deep by seven miles wide and bounded on either side by a canal. To the West it was simply a great dry ditch, for the Canal du Nord had only just been dug out when the war began; on the other side the Canal de L'Escaut was very much an operational affair, about 70 feet wide and deep enough to float the big self-propelled barges to which the French are addicted. Though farmland, it was a fairly well populated locality; the villages, Ribécourt, Marcoing, Masnières, Flesquières, Graincourt, Cantaing, Fontaine-Notre-Dame and Bourlon were, or had been before the Germans painstakingly wrecked them, substantial settlements with large, solid houses and an occasional château. The grain of the country is made up of undulations without any particular theme, as if the surface of a moderate sea had become frozen, calcified and sown with grass. By late November, of course, the uncut hay had degenerated into a sad-looking mass of vegetation, valueless to the farmer but just right for the furtherance of the Bullock Creeping Grip. In this great tilt-yard there were four features of utmost importance to the attackers. All were as obvious to the Germans as to General Byng. The two bridges over the Escaut Canal, (also called Canal du St Quentin), at Marcoing and Masnières, were quite essential to the passage of cavalry in large numbers. Lacking them one might as well let the horsemen stay at home. Both were certain to have been prepared for demolition and, in the event of the line being breached, it would become a race to see who could get there first. The most valuable prize would be Bourlon Wood, from which any temporary owner might do as the Duke had often done and survey the country over to Cambrai and beyond. Before any attacker could even think of taking Bourlon he must first become master of the ridge of Flesquières where the village with its château sat impregnably just behind the Hindenburg Support Line. If the tanks were to perform as they had promised, seizure of the ridge ought to be carried out almost at a run. That accomplished, the taking of Bourlon by much the same method should be within the bounds of the possible. And with the British Army firmly ensconced there, probably almost embarrassed by a great haul of prisoners and guns, it would be hard for the German Army to continue to hold the strong Drocourt-Quéant Line. The stakes were higher than they had been for a long time. Sir Douglas, though disappointed that the Canadians would not be there to be rushed through the gap in motor-buses and lorries, had no intention of letting it go outside the family. Pétain had to be told, and, for whatever reasons, he wanted to take a seat at the table. On 4 November he offered to put a Corps plus a Cavalry Corps, the whole under General Degoutte at Péronne, into the system. Sir Douglas, possibly wishing instead for the army of ghosts who had died in Flanders to keep France in the war, declined with thanks. For this he has been criticized of recent years. To an armchair savant it probably looks odd that, at a time when the lacking element was reinforcement, a commander should turn down such a gift. To scour archives for the reason would be futile. Sir Douglas knew what he knew of the state of the French army even then. He could take no risk of using any tool that might turn in his hand. And there was more to it than distrust. Just for the once Sir Douglas was going to be master in his own house. This battle was going to be fought only by the British, and as far as was humanly possible, by the home-grown British at that. Were it to end, as it might, in fiasco nobody should be able to say that his mad freak had left many empty chairs in Toronto or Melbourne. When it came to exploitation then General Kavanagh with his cavalry divisions must do the business or it would have to be left unfinished. The weather, a powerful factor in all the planning, would then take it out of anybody's hands and close the war down until next spring. Thus the preparations were made. In all the animation that was caused to some by the introduction of a new arm it must not be forgotten that Cambrai was still mainly an affair of guns and foot. Havrincourt Wood was filled along its rides with artillery pieces of all kinds standing wheel to wheel. In all 1,003 guns stood ready to open the ball — a small force compared to some other battles but still as many as at El Alamein. Nor was it only conventional artillery that took its share. In some places, in particular on the front of the Ulstermen, other new aids to the attack chimed in. The 6″ Newton mortar and the 4″ Stokes had been designed for the purpose of cutting wire. Their great bombs, packed with thermit, exploded in showers of white phosphorus and melted to nothing such metal objects as stood in the way. Only uncommonly brave men would stay in a trench when the thermit bombs began to drop. They had a tremendous moral effect.

Nevertheless it was the tank that stole the show, as it deserved. The combined efforts of the Fighting Side in France with Swinton and Stern at home had brought the sum total available to a figure little short of 500. They varied from the newest, barely run-in, machine from the Metropolitan Carriage & Wagon Works to the most patched-up and bullet-scarred veteran laboriously dredged from the Ypres mud, but they all worked and their attendants did not spare themselves to be ready. If it was the Chinese whose fascines made the battle a possibility then something of the same must be said about the Americans. With Russia and Rumania gone, Italy probably going, Greece likely to change sides at any minute and both France and Britain running out of men, the sound of Mr Cohan's deathless 'Over There' was the music of the spheres. Colonel Hoffman's 11th Engineers (Railway) probably never went back to a ticker-tape welcome but they could do things beyond the powers of any other troops available. Miles and miles of Decauville light railway came into existence through the efforts of these skilful and amiable men. It was never intended that they should be the vanguard when olive-drab first squared up to field-grey but thus it happened. It was, after all, becoming an engineer's war.

For the moment it was largely a railwayman's war. Only railways could ship the vast quantities of everything needed for a battle and the capacity of the existing lines was hopelessly inadequate. The Railways Operating Division, the child of very Temporary Major-General, about to become Temporary Vice-Admiral, Eric Geddes, with American help, brought into existence new great railheads, one called Plateau just by Albert and the others at Ytres, Bertincourt and Royalcourt in the rear of the Cambrai battlefield. In order to keep them going Geddes requisitioned a number of Great Western Railway locomotives; every one was essential, for the tanks alone needed thirty-six trains, each one loaded with a dozen machines, often on rather shaky French rolling stock. Loading and unloading them was not amusing. The only way to carry out the latter operation, usually in the dark, was to uncouple the engine and move it back to the rear of the line of flat-cars in order to give the tanks an uninterrupted passage along the length of the train to a ramp at the end. Timing was wonderfully precise, only once interrupted when an ASC driver was foolishly allowed to cross the metals in front of an approaching train. Driver and lorry were squashed flat, several trucks derailed and the permanent way ripped up. The Battle of Cambrai would probably have ended there but for the arrival of Baker-Carr. Like Hotblack, he always seemed to materialize from nowhere when most needed. With the help of Captain Hulsant of the US Engineers he sorted the matter out with remarkable speed. There was no noticeable delay.

The great muster of the tanks, the first glimpse of what war of the future would be, was nearly complete. There were 378 fighting machines, fifty-four supply tanks with sledges, thirty-two fitted with grapnels for dragging wire out of the way of the horses, two more carrying bridging material also for use of the cavalry, nine fitted with wireless and the last carrying telephone cable for Third Army. In addition to tanks and guns the divisions were arriving. 6th, 12th, 29th, and 51st all reached Péronne by train between 15 and 17 November, encumbered to some extent by General Degoutte's unwanted XXIst Corps which detrained almost simultaneously and marched into their Corps area during the following nights. The West Riding men of the 62nd moved in silently during the night of 13/14th and took up their positions to the West of Havrincourt Wood. Sir Douglas himself passed the same three days watching infantry and tanks trying to get to know each other's ways. 'I had occasion to point out that the two arms must be of mutual assistance and that the covering fire of Lewis guns and rifles must be used at all stages of the advance.' He does not say in terms whether he pointed this out to General Harper.

The line-up of the formations of the British Third Army on 20 November, 1917, was this. From left to right, the Ulstermen of 36th Division to the East of the Canal du Nord with Moeuvres as its objective; next to them, the 62nd, making across the Hindenburg Line for Havrincourt, Graincourt and Anneux. Then came Harper's 51st, heading for Flesquières Ridge and whatever lay beyond. The 6th, still recognizable as a Regular division, would make for Ribécourt with, on their right hand, the 29th whose veteran troops had the supremely important task of seizing the canal bridges at Marcoing and Masnières. The last pair, 20th and 12th, completed the tally with Welsh Ridge and Lateau Wood as their targets. Each of these last two divisions was allotted a company of 24 tanks. The 'F' battalion machines with 12th Division were to make straight for Masnières. Intelligence reports asserted that they would find there 'a wooden bridge to the sugar factory taking infantry in file, a lattice iron girder bridge, 26'4", including footways and footbridge alongside'. On the western side was another wooden bridge capable of taking infantry and cavalry. The other bridge, at Marcoing, was the responsibility of the 'B' battalion tanks with the 6th Division, whilst those from 'A' battalion with the 20th Division would range the couple of miles or so in between, shooting up every enemy thing they could see. To complete the tale of arrangements for crossing the canal and setting the cavalry to work a couple of Field Companies RE, the 497th (Kent) and 455th (West Riding), were 'made responsible for the preservation and restoration of all river and canal crossings from Masnières to Marcoing inclusive'. What was expected of them in places certain to be swept by machine-gun fire at all times is hardly clear. A pontoon section was kept in reserve on the Fins-Gouzeaucourt road, warned that its services were not likely to be needed until the following day. There it remained, unused and unuseable.

So much for the assault of the Canal bridges. Away to the left the 51st had the lion's share of the tanks, seventy in all, and Braithwaite's 62nd were allotted fifty-six. The IIIrd Corps formations, unlike the other, had set aside a number of machines to be used as reserves should be, but it made no difference. Every tank in the Army was put to work at once. On the extreme left the 36th Division had to manage without any at all, simply because there were not enough to go round; its objectives were reckoned to be less formidable than the others, though General Nugent would hardly have agreed with this. Further north, beyond the Third Army area, General Haldane's VIth Corps would lend a hand by keeping such German troops as might be on their front pinned to their trenches. An attack — a genuine one — would be mounted around the old battlefield of Bullecourt whilst the 56th Division in between them would enjoy itself with what was called a Chinese attack — much noise but little else — upon that part of the Hindenburg Line that lay opposite. In order to make this more effective 600 of Captain Livens' gas projectors were added to the usual arsenal.

The cavalry remained a respectful distance in rear, around Fins, the Divisions including a Canadian Brigade and two from the Indian Army, the Ambala and the Lucknow. They were spared one worry usual in cavalry circles. This was Artois, home of the Artesian well. Hundreds of them, brim full, were to be found everywhere. At least the horses would not go thirsty.

Inveigling some hundreds of noisy and conspicuous tanks into safe harbours from which they could emerge in time to reach their forming-up places on the dot was not an easy task. Havrincourt Wood, sanctuary to Baker-Carr's 1st Brigade, was not too difficult, even though the Germans held the eastern side of it. Courage's 2nd was reasonably fortunate in being given quarters in Dessart Wood, a couple of miles south of Havrincourt village, but Hardress-Lloyd's people were less so. 3rd Brigade had to hide its tanks as best it could under camouflage nettings around Gouzeaucourt and Villers Guislain. Some artistic work had gone into this; netting and canvas painted to look like brick and tile was rather effective. Track discipline was rigidly enforced, tank crews being furnished with bass brooms and enjoined to sweep away any marks that might suggest to a German airman that the new arm was lying before the Hindenburg Line, crouched to spring. Though fewer in numbers than their British opposite numbers, the German air service, operating mostly from Awoingt, just to the south-east of Cambrai, was very much a force to be reckoned with.

The Royal Flying Corps, excellent in many ways, was not of very much value to the troops on the ground. In part this was due to the vile weather of the first couple of days; in other part to its commander. Brigadier-General Higgins was known to his friends as 'Josh'; to the others, the majority, he was 'Bum and Eyeglass'. Further comment would be superfluous. Although technically still a part of the army, the Royal Flying Corps had for a long time been living a life of its own. Its interests focused for the most part upon the rival airmen of the German service and interest in the ants toiling below was not greater than was needed. Artillery spotting and aerial photography were, of course, of first importance and by now highly efficient. Attacking ground targets was unpopular, not greatly studied and rarely effective. It would be quite unfair to blame the brave young pilots and observers, most of them with very short flying histories behind them. To watch the progress of a tank or an infantry company and to set about the guns and machine guns that held them up was beyond the ability of most of them, even in sunny weather. Clouds and mist, the conditions prevailing for most of the time, rendered their part in the ground battle of little value. That is hardly remarkable. Pilots of the reconnaissance aircraft were obliged to climb to 5,000 feet, something that took about 45 minutes, in order to get a grandstand view. By the time the climb was finished they were frozen almost to death and still, often enough, could see nothing but swathes of dirty cotton-wool. Communication with the ground, theoretically by wireless, was usually a dialogue of deaf mutes. Only the reliable pigeon remained.

Criticism long after the event by those whose information has to be less then complete risks doing injustices, but it must be made. The Battle of Cambrai failed in its purpose because the German army was able to switch powerful forces into the line without much interference. Their own History states that 'In the period 20-29 November, 13 Infantry Divisions and over 600 smaller units and formations were brought to the battlefront. 730 trains in 9 days'. This was carried out without any hindrance worthy of note; nor does it include the very considerable arrivals by road. The Air Instructions issued by Third Army set out as bombing targets firstly enemy aerodromes, second Headquarters at Caudry and Escadoeuvres and only at the last 'Rly. junctions in order of importance'. Five are named, Douai, Denain, Busigny, Le Cateau and Valenciennes. Cambrai is not mentioned. Why the arriving troop trains were not hammered by every gun and bomb that could be turned on them is inexplicable. Had Hankey's 'Grasshoppers' been taken seriously they might have come in useful as extras to the tank but the serious work of the Flying Corps was to interdict the coming of more and more troops and this was demonstrably unsuccessful.

There was no thought of failure among those who were wide awake to see the dawn of 20 November, the most important day in any year for the Tank Corps and its children. Its temporary headquarters were in Albert, occupying at *numéro huit* in the aptly named *Rue Carnot* what appeared to have been a rather depressing night club. The usual aspect of the little town suggests that no night club there could expect a bright future but it may have seemed livelier in 1917. From there Elles, Fuller and the others had made their arrangements. The light railways had moved up for them 165,000 gallons of petrol, half a million rounds of 6-pdr ammunition and five million of .303.

It ought to be enough for a short battle. In its unheroic surroundings Fuller and Elles put the finishing touches to the famous Special Order No 6* and the equally famous mud-blood-and-green-fields flag was made ready. When Elles announced his intention of leading the advance in the style of Drake or Farragut there were furious protests from his Brigadiers. Baker-Carr alone preserved the record: 'I, personally, also felt slightly resentful as I had, on more than one occasion, suggested to him that I might go into battle in a tank and was promptly threatened with every sort of pain and penalty if I did so. Elles was wise enough not to disclose his plan till it was too late for his superiors to object.'

Zero hour was 6 am. The sun would, according to the almanac, rise at 7.30 and set at 4.03. All hands settled down in the hope, usually misplaced, of something like a night's sleep. Bitter cold was not the only obstacle. Fear, not for oneself but of letting the side down, had as much to do with it.

The approach march of the tanks was carried out in the utter darkness of a night with no moon. Keeping direction, even when it meant no more than following the tape, was hard enough; where the tape had been ripped up it became near to the impossible. In some places, certainly in the area of the 12th Division, there was an order, as blood-curdling as it was silly, that any man lighting a cigarette should be instantly shot by the nearest officer. The Tank Corps officers alone were privileged; a quick tobacco-reddening draw more often than not gave light enough to pick out the tape-ends, as well as affording one man a little comfort. 'H' battalion, the one chosen to furnish Elles with his flagship and, more importantly, to clear the path of the 6th Division, took seven hours, beginning at the one when people at home were sitting down to tea, in covering the four miles between Dessart Wood and the start line. Before the crews could think of rolling themselves up in blankets, tarpaulins and whatever came to hand for a few hours sleep there was the messy business of greasing rollers to be carried out. One may imagine that the rum ration did not come amiss. Cold makes tiredness even more tiring; it was greatcoat weather but greatcoats have no place in fighting order. There were several hours to go before the engines needed to be swung into life and warmed up. There was no wind, the clouds hung low and heavy. By western front standards, it was a quiet night.

* Set out in Appendix I

CHAPTER EIGHT

'BESIDE HIM STALKS TO BATTLE THE HUGE EARTH-SHAKING BEAST'

The Prophecy of Capys
Thomas Babington Macaulay

MR CHURCHILL, FOR THAT HE WAS at the time of writing, says somewhere that an attack may fairly be compared to the dashing of a bucketful of water across a floor. It begins with a great whoosh, is followed by a steady stream and then gradually peters out; all that with no action save the thrower's own. The truth of this pleasing simile can never have been demonstrated more clearly than in the series of operations called for brevity the Battle of Cambrai.

Half an hour before the freezing dawn broke, as in the half-hour before every other one through the war, thousands of infantrymen stood to in their trenches, blowing on fingernails in order to get a grip on a bayoneted rifle. Everybody knew that something out of the common was about to happen but exact knowledge was denied them. As bloodshot eyes stared into the mist, the balloon, as men used to say, went up. This time there was no 'Stand Down'. On the front of General De L'Isle's 29th Division the Point of War was proclaimed in proper fashion. For want of a herald to carry defiance to the German, the General's personal bugler sounded three 'G's. The rest of the line was alerted by a single gun, its message as clear as any crashed out on Armistice Day. Before it had died down the world erupted in noise, reboant and earth-shaking. The RE Survey Companies, working alongside the Royal Artillery, had scientifically laid each gun by instrument; bombardment by 1003 pieces was almost the last thing the German troops of General von der Marwitz were expecting. It ought not to have been possible; the usages of war, if not the laws, had long laid down that a fortnight of this sort of thing should elapse before the first foot soldiers moved out over the bags. Battery after German battery was overwhelmed, mostly without their being able to fire a shot in return. This was the first great surprise of Cambrai. If the tank had never been invented the unregistered barrage was a feat of novel military technology well worthy of recognition.

The sudden tempest of steel and explosive was not, of course, the only surprise that Sir Julian Byng had for the King's enemies on that morning. As the smoke barrage thickened around the Hindenburg Line the tanks rumbled forward. Every one had had its course charted as far as possible; Hotblack and his reconnaissance sections, men wearing special jackets with red and green lights on the back, had paid out several miles of black and white tape in order to give each machine its own axis of advance. For the most part the tank commanders walked in front, an unenviable place between tank and wire. It would be time enough for them to embark when the bullets started to fly.

The left, or northern, end of the battle was largely Irish business. Far away to the north-west the 16th (Southern Irish) Division of Sir Aylmer Haldane's VIth Corps set about that part of the Hindenburg Line around Bullecourt, with the regular 3rd Division on their right. Tunnel Trench and the large pill-boxes called Mars and Jove fell to them, all without the benefit of a single tank. The 56th, London Territorials with much sterner work just ahead of them, provided their firework display. Then, on the left of the area marked out for the big operation, Ulster took over. The part allotted to the 36th Division was different from all the others. Its first task was to seize those German trenches west of the Canal du Nord and south of the Bapaume-Cambrai road from the Spoil Heap to Moeuvres. That accomplished, a bridge across the dry gulch would have to be built by the divisional sappers on the Demicourt-Flesquières road substantial enough to carry field-guns and wagons. A second, smaller, one was to be put across some 1500 yards to the south. The German defences consisted of two main lines with a frontage of about 1500 yards and a depth of 300. The dominating point was a 60-foot-high spoil heap, made by the canal diggers, where the line west of the Canal really began. This had to be taken before anything else. It was well wired in, the Division had no tanks, and it must make the best of the 6″ Newton mortar for wire cutting. As it was plainly wise to have the defenders looking anxiously over their shoulders before the infantry were to go in, a careful timetable was prepared. Zero hour for everybody else would be 6.20. For the 36th Division it would be 8.35. The intervening hours could be usefully employed by the guns and mortars, working on the wire with thermit and other things.

The right of the line was taken by Major-General Scott's 12th Division, one of the oldest of the Kitchener formations and having the rare distinction of a General killed in action.* It held for a further record. By the end of October it had been for an unbroken 18 weeks holding the line on an active battlefront. The heavy Arras casualties had been replaced, but the new

* Major-General F.D.V. Wing, at Loos in 1915.

arrivals, most importantly the new junior officers, were for the most part green. The Division had counted itself fortunate to be sent off for a rest, even in the cold and rain around Hesdin. Rest is, of course, a term of art. In this instance some part of it was taken up by training with the tanks nearby but it did not amount to much. Nobody expected it to be put to the test in a fortnight's time. It was. Within that short period every unit was marched to the station at Doullens or Frevent and detrained at Péronne. A couple of days' foot-slogging took them to Fins, Sorel-le-Grand and Heudecourt where they took over trenches from the 20th Division. Scott's task was to penetrate the Hindenburg defences by two bounds each of about 2,000 yards, forming a defensive flank to the south-east and taking firm hold of Lateau Wood, about a mile and a half due south of Masnières. Douglas Smith's 20th Division would move in step on Scott's left with Marden's 6th keeping level. The general direction was north-east, across the Hindenburg and Hindenburg Support Lines; 20th Division was given the front from La Vacquerie to Welsh Ridge, whilst the 6th would make for Ribécourt, the spur to its south-east and then on for a further mile to Premy Chapel ridge and Nine Wood. Defensive flanks were to be established by the 6th towards Flesquières on its left for the benefit of Harper's Highlanders and another on the right in order to make a safe passage for the 29th whose business it was to seize the bridge at Masnières and the heights south of Rumilly. On the extreme right and intended only to create a diversion there stood the 55th Division of Sir Thomas D'Oyly Snow's VIIth Corps.

The tanks, seventy-two fighting machines to each division (wireless tanks were allotted to some infantry brigades) would open the ball on both Corps fronts. The IVth Corps divisions, 62nd on the left, 51st on the right, would move behind them through Havrincourt, Graincourt and Flesquières on to the richest prize of all, the Bourlon heights. The 1st Cavalry Division of General Mullens was first to take Bourlon Wood and village; that done, it was supposed – expected seems hardly the word – to advance north-west and cut off the German troops that would be trapped in the salient. It was given no task beyond that.

All began famously, as the bucket of water was thrown across the floor. The roar of the guns took on a certain rhythm, the air quivered with the passage of great shells, bursting encouragingly on the German positions. The tanks waddled forward out of the wood, their companies in line ahead until they reached a given point about 1,000 yards from their first objective. There they deployed into line abreast. Such a sight had never been seen before; probably only a very few of those witnessing it would have taken in the fact that they were looking on the face of future wars.

The whole tank force, almost every driver, gunner and commander in France, moved forward in a long line, the point tanks 150 yards ahead of the rest. For a while there was an air of finality about the business. The tank crews were quite unworried by the belts of wire or any other obstacles. Had they not practised all the drills of Elles and Fuller ad nauseam? The sound of scraping against the side was nothing new, nor did the trenches worry them. The belts of wire were usually about 50 yards deep, not in straight lines but angled thoughtfully so as to shepherd advancing infantry on to the waiting machine guns. 'It neither stopped the tank nor broke up and wound round and round the tracks as we at first feared, but squashed flat and remained flat, leaving a broad carpet of wire as wide as the tank over which the following infantry were able to pick their way without great difficulty,' remarked one of Hobart's contributors. The fascine, of course, was not designed as a bridge. Once dropped, however, it served well enough. The tank would go down in what Bovington called the swallow dive, begin to nose up on the other side and push its back paws on to the bundle; this would give just enough purchase to see it over the top. The next wave turned along in front of the trench and the defenders' heads were best kept down by enfilade fire from front and rear, while the bayonetmen and bombers behind poured through the beaten lanes and attacked them hand to hand. No effective resistance was possible and no help came from their own guns in the rear. In this fashion, 'Within 2½ hours of zero hour the whole of the Hindenburg Line outpost zone and front system was in our hands; masses of prisoners were streaming back to our cages, and leap-frogging battalions and tanks were passing forward for the attack on the enemy second line.' Thus wrote Colonel Hobart. And the crossing destroyed for ever one of the dreaded gifts of this war. Even after all these years its most haunting song is the one that ends with 'If you want the old battalion, I know where it is: 'anging on the old barbed wire'. Armies had not quite finished with this horror, but, after Cambrai, it could never be the same obstacle to an attacker.

Behind the line of German forward defences there rose a pall of black smoke contributed by Byng's gunners. Into this great numbers of panicked German infantry were heading in search of sanctuary. 350 pathways had been made through the entanglements in which they had trusted and, in most places, the British infantry was moving through them. Braithwaite's Yorkshiremen took Havrincourt; another of his brigades, leap-frogging through, carried the fortress village of Graincourt and moved on to the outskirts of Anneux. By dark, teatime in England, they had covered 4½ miles and bagged thirty-seven guns along with some 2,000 prisoners.

On the right flank, Scott's 12th Division, following its tanks at a steady 50 yards a minute, captured Bonavis, Pam Pam Farm and, most importantly, Lateau Wood. Had that strongly held position remained in enemy hands it would have been able to enfilade the 29th Division as it advanced on

Masnières. The co-operation between guns, tanks and infantry worked admirably in spite of the small opportunities of practising it.

Forty-two tanks of 'C' Battalion went on ahead of 12th Division. By great good fortune the account of the doings of some of them remains. Second-Lieutenant W.P. Whyte's report is still in the file where it has been since the day of battle: 'Tank 2882 being hopelessly ditched I at once took over Tank 2877 with the crew of C34 as 2/Lt Rew had just been wounded. Went to the right of Bleak House into the hollow SW of Pam Pam Farm. Silenced 2 machine-guns then turned north to Pam Pam Farm. Just as we swung North 2 vision plates got blown in with MG fire and 2 of the crew badly wounded also 2 guns knocked out leaving us with only 1 gun. As no infantry could be seen I returned and got in touch with them.... I dumped the wounded and again proceeded to the right of Pam Pam Farm where MG were holding up the infantry. I cleared that lot out and got on to the Brown line (the second objective) by 11 a.m. Here our last gun got over-heated and seized thus leaving us helpless.... An enemy battery got on to us and blew in the door and a hole in the tracks and bullets came in where the vision plates should have been and punctured the return water pipes. This we patched and as all our guns were useless I thought it best to rally. This we did and on our way back pulled out 2 Lieut. Morris's tank which had got badly ditched. We got to R 17 Central about 2 p.m. The ground was excellent and also trenches.'

Mr Whyte, having casually reported how his tank picked up fifty prisoners and turned them over to the infantry went on 'draw special attention to the excellent driving and calmness although hit with splinters of Gnr. Street and L/Cpl Paterson who, equally knocked about, had calmly mended the return water pipe'. The taking of Lateau Wood produced one of the more enduring tank stories. As one of them clanked into the undergrowth the crew of a German 5.9 howitzer contrived to depress the muzzle quickly enough to get one round fired point-blank at the intruder. It blew off most of the starboard sponson but left the vitals undamaged. Before the gunners could re-load the tank was on top of them and their gun crushed to scrap iron. One account says, unkindly, that the crew had left the tank which did the work under its own power. It hardly matters now. The infantry of Kent, Buffs and Queen's Own, took the bayonet to the German garrison and Lateau Wood passed into English hands.

With all that accomplished the day's work on the right flank was over, save for the necessary consolidation of captured ground. Of the seventy-six tanks that had started at zero fifty-five were still fit for another round. Only a dozen were battle casualties. The remainder were ditched in a sunken road. By skilful co-operation between old and new the Division had, in a little over three hours, captured more than three miles of line. The work of consolidation was enlivened by the sudden irruption of a large party of French civilians, released from Masnières after three years of captivity and forced labour. As they marched down the Cambrai road bawling out the *Marseillaise* the unappreciative English huddled round fires in the trenches smoking German cigars and speculating about the Cup Final. The Division had lost about 1300 men, 144 of them killed. This was considered a very moderate bill for the temporary ownership of a piece of land some 2,000 yards wide by 5,500 deep. And so it was, by the terrible arithmetic to which our grandparents had become accustomed.

Next in line on the left came Douglas Smith's 20th (Light) Division, the 'Light' being a word of no meaning save an historical one. For a start the share of the business given to them went like good machinery. The tanks hove into sight through the murk at 6.10, the barrage opened up along the entire front at 6.20 and the steel helmets and bayonets followed at their proper 100-yard distance behind. By 7.30 the men of Somerset had taken the strongly fortified position of La Vacquerie and by 9.25 the first objective, a track from Banteux to Ribécourt, had been reached and taken. The second, and final, one comprised the whole of the feature called Welsh Ridge, from a point in the sunken road nearly 3,000 yards north-east of La Vacquerie to the railway, 1200 yards south-west of Marcoing. This had been taken by about 11 o'clock after some of the fiercest fighting yet seen. Though the training at Wailly in working together had been short it proved just sufficient. Infantry sections, now often close alongside, used their very mobile Lewis guns to see off artillery pieces that could kill tanks with ease. Two VCs were earned during these hours, Rifleman Shepherd of the 60th and, posthumously, Captain R.W.L. Wain of the Tank Corps. At that point Smith sent in his reserve brigade; it had left the old front line at 9.10 following behind the assaulting battalions and now advanced to its main task of the day, the seizing of Marcoing bridge. By this time, a little after midday, the tanks had long ceased to be in orderly lines and were operating with individual virtuosity. The whole assaulting force, from section to division, had swiftly changed into a body with hands and feet but no nervous system. Communications had almost completely broken down. The standard form of message sending, the DIII field telephone, demanded mile upon mile of wire to be trailed behind it. The 20th Division alone paid out 137 miles of armoured cable. It was not, however, proof against being churned up by tank tracks and the like and only in those few places where it had been possible to raise the wire on poles did it survive. The wireless tanks, in which nobody reposed great confidence, started off well enough to suggest that they might have a future but for the moment they were almost useless. Captain E.F. Churchill, commanding 1st Tank Brigade Signal Company RE, wrote a report on it all later. Two forward stations and a directing station were set up, one of them in the so-called Grand Ravin (it was no more than a ditch) behind Ribécourt, the other in the Hindenburg Support Line. The bulky apparatus was carried up by the fighting tanks, two being needed for each. This, of course, made them practically useless for their proper duties but it could not be helped. A 30-foot mast was needed; it had to be carried outside the tank and if it did not fall off it was quickly destroyed by machine-gun fire. The two stations ran for a time, starting at 1.30 pm, but, although 'Several messages containing valuable information were obtained by these means', the accumulators soon expired. It was all, as Churchill said, 'most unsatisfactory'. The sets were 'only makeshift and exceedingly clumsy'. On occasions as soon as men emerged to erect the mast machine-gun fire came down on them and it was necessary for the tank to drive the gunners away before the signal work could begin. For the first couple of days only the pigeons worked, in spite of the weather. It was a pigeon, fluttering in to Brigade HQ, that brought the news of Lateau Wood being taken. After its arrival in the loft RE telephonists passed the news backwards over such lines as were still working.

The important village of Marcoing along with its bridge were taken by the Tank Corps practically unaided. One of its officers, Lieutenant T.A. Crouch, wrote of it to his mother on the back of a German operation order: 'Yes, I went over in a tank on the 20th and had no end of fun and I also met with a certain measure of success. No doubt you have read about the 12 tanks which attacked and held Marcoing. Well, I was in one of these and the whole thing was the most extraordinary operation I have ever seen or heard of. The Bosche simply ran for his life.' No soldier is on oath when writing to his mother. The citation for Tom Crouch's DSO — a great rarity for a subaltern and generally reckoned a near-miss for the VC — expands a little: 'On arrival of the tanks in Marcoing without infantry support this officer's conduct was most gallant. He moved across the open space on foot, all alone under heavy machine-gun fire and succeeded in getting his tanks through the village.' For a full hour the tanks had the place to themselves until the advance guard of the infantry arrived. Most accounts of the action tell dramatically of how an officer emerged from one of the first tanks and snatched a fizzing fuse from the German engineer about to blow the bridge, having pistolled any number of them in the process. The Report on Action of No. 1 Coy., A Battalion, does not quite measure up to this: '2/Lt. J.M. Bayley (No. 2 Coy) examined the railway bridge over the canal at Marcoing soon after 11 o'clock and, finding it was mined, cut the leads of the fuse and brought them away.'

There were compensations. Bayley's Company Commander, Major Justice Tilly, arrived at the same moment mounted on a mule, accompanied by two orderlies, his Reconnaissance Officer and two German prisoners with a pot of stew slung from a pole. Tilly wrote of it that 'when I saw Bayley he was crossing the bridge with a French woman hanging round his neck. He had one arm round her which held his revolver and in the other he was waving the leads; they were both laughing and shouting'. As well they might be. Just over the ridge, about half a mile away, Captain R.W.L. Wain was engaged in a desperate battle at the building called Good Old Man Farm; it ended with his death, charging alone with rifle and bayonet, and a posthumous VC.

Major Lakin, commanding another company in 'A' Battalion, soon arrived on an unaccountably acquired horse. Then came a third company commander and finally the CO. Lakin and Tilly set off complete with horse and mule to see what lay ahead, reaching the outskirts of Cambrai practically unmolested. As nothing was to be gained by going on they turned about and were back in Marcoing at about 2 pm. By then the village was full of troops from the 29th Division. One section from Lakin's Company drove forward to Rumilly without infantry support and came to grief there. The Cavalry Brigade that had off-saddled to the south of Marcoing made 'no attempt to go forward then or later, although invited to do so in no uncertain terms by Lakin, himself an ex-Cavalryman'.

At Masnières matters went equally well to begin with. This was the parish of 'F' Battalion whose commander, Major Philip Hammond, has left one of the fullest accounts of the battle. He tells of his protests at being compelled to halt once the Hindenburg Line was crossed and how his urgent request to take three tanks as fast as they could go and seize the all-important bridge was refused, 'because the King of the local gunners did not like me'. The picking up of useful things was no substitute; not even 'a whole dump of Boche hot ration containers... like huge thermos flasks meant to carry on a man's back and held a full dixie of tea or stew so hot that after 24 hours you could hardly sip it. They were wonderful things'. The poverty-stricken British Army did what it could with home-made hay boxes. On the way to Masnières, on foot with a party of runners, he observed that a great deal of fire was coming from La Vacquerie and 'I knew that someone was held up and that the Boche had got his belly up to the bar and was firing as hard as he could'. Though La Vacquerie was not in his parish, Hammond 'ran across to my four left tanks, turned them left and we came in by the back door.... When we got to the concrete line the electric light was still on and it was plain the Boche had just jumped out of bed and run in his socks holding his pants up.' Hammond, determined to get to Masnières bridge without further waste of time, handed over the Company to his second-in-command ('Say I was believed to be dead or missing') and set off alone with 'a man called Roberts, a ship's fireman from Musselburgh... a stout-hearted bloke'. The self-constituted vanguard of the British Army set off, armed with a revolver (Hammond) and somebody else's water-bottle of whisky (Roberts), 'across country as hard as we could run'. Roberts picked up the rifle of a dead German and eventually they reached the outskirts of the village. 'Everyone was on the run, and we ran too.... There was a bit of a curve hiding the bridge and as I was on the right side of the pavement and Roberts on the left I could see down the street before he did. I had just time to see a Bosche standing waving his arms in the street and turning the crowd of running Huns down a side lane (which I afterwards found went over by a footbridge by the lock). Then there was a heavy thump, a cloud of dirty white dust and the bridge had gone. So I was beaten by only a few minutes and a few yards.' Then came more troops, a section of three tanks, Major Martel and 'a great deal of clattering, galloping and shouting and a lot of our medieval horse soldiers came charging down the street'. After a while they trotted off. 'I asked for some men to go over the bridge with me but I could get no help from them.' They looked at two other bridges passable for cavalry but complained 'that they couldn't get over because there were machine guns there'. Hammond sent for a tank which demolished the house where the guns were. 'Still these people wouldn't do anything. They had no sense of proportion, of what was too dangerous and what wasn't, in fact they had been living for years in back areas and had no experience of real war.' 150 feet above flew Captain Donald Marendaz of the RFC in his little AW scout plane, charged with spotting for the cavalry. Looking down on the bridge, the absolute essential to any cavalry sweep, he observed it to be bending beneath the weight of a single tank. He wound down his signal wire, tapped out his message in Morse telling his horsemen to go back, when a salvo of shells from some 12″ guns nearly dropped him into the canal. Whether his message ever arrived is something that will never now be known. The tank had made the trial on direct orders from Martel, who had probably expected something of this kind to happen, and it completed the work of turning bend into break. The bridge was about 70 feet long and, even in its partially demolished state, several feet above the water. Lieutenant Edmundson drove slowly down the bank with all his doors open. There came a sound of rending metal as tank and bridge gently declined into the canal accompanied by great hissings and clouds of steam as cold water and red-hot exhaust pipe met. The bridge was effectively closed to cavalry and would remain so for a long time to come.

The 6th Division of Major-General T.O. Marden had the distinction of being led into battle by the commander of the Tank Corps mounted upon a tank named *Hilda*.* He can hardly have been other than a nuisance to the crew and sensibly parted company with it after a few furlongs. Then he walked back home, testily refusing many German offers of surrender. The

---

* *Hilda* became ditched shortly afterwards and had to be extracted by Harvester.

20. MkIV Tank FI demonstrates wire-cutting at Wailly, 21 October, 1917. (*IWM*)

21. The real wire to be crushed. A segment of the Hindenburg Line. (*IWM*)

22. Abandoned Tank used as gunner OP. The initials proclaim it to have been one of the Wire Clearers. (*Tank Museum*)

23. 'H' Battalion Tank *Hyena* knocked out near Bourlon Wood, 21 November, 1917. (*Tank Museum*)

24. Lancers cluttering up the road at Trescault. (*IWM*)

25. Traffic near Ribécourt, 22 November, 1917. (*IWM*)

26. 'G' Battalion Tank passing knocked-out German battery on the Graincourt side of Flesquières Ridge. (*Tank Museum*)

27. Uncompleted German defences at Flesquières, 23 November. (*IWM*)

Division followed closely on its protectors, its left on the 51st and its right on the 20th. On Harper's side the Hindenburg Line lay 750 yards ahead; on the other it was no more than 250. This was only the outpost zone, hidden from sight by the reverse slope of the ridge. Half a mile further on stood the main position, two lines of deep trenches. In between were formidable belts of wire, each stretching back about 150 yards. Dotted about in the middle were carefully-sited and well-concealed machine-gun posts. Such a fortification ought to have been inexpugnable, as it would have been in any earlier attack. The two tank battalions, 'B' under Lieutenant-Colonel E.D. Bryce and 'H' under the Hon. Claud Willoughby, made all things possible. Everything went, as it usually does with the Regular Army, like clockwork. 'The Division had a most successful day, with very light casualties (about 650), capturing 28 officers and 1227 other ranks prisoners, 23 guns and between 40 and 50 machine guns and many trench-mortars.... The artillery had pushed forward to advanced positions to cover the new front. Before darkness came on the machine guns were likewise established in their new forward positions thanks to careful arrangements and the use of pack animals.... The Tanks, which had made surprise possible, were most gallantly handled and all arrangements most carefully thought out by Col. A. Courage.' There was another story to tell — the cavalry: 'At 3.15 p.m., the cavalry, which would have been of the greatest assistance in capturing the enemy guns holding up the 51st Division, reported that they could not advance owing to snipers in Ribécourt. That village had been in our possession since 10 am and the 18th Infantry Brigade had passed through it at 11.30 and were now two miles beyond it. However, the cavalry pushed through patrols before nightfall to Nine Wood.' The note of exasperation is hardly undetectable.

Though some elements of 6th Division entered Cantaing they lacked the strength to hold it and were forced to withdraw at nightfall. Nine Wood was another matter; few episodes in military history can be so well documented as its capture: 'There were large numbers of Germans strolling about in and around the edges of Nine Wood. They were taken completely by surprise and suffered heavy casualties from the long bursts of Lewis gun fire from the leading tanks!' When the tank Hiawatha and her consorts had finally cleared them all out the Section Commander, Captain Rex Davis, took the precaution of obtaining a receipt for the wood from the Guernsey Militia. A prudent man, Captain Davis.

There is a story, so well authenticated that it must almost certainly be true, of the last minute before 11 am on 11 November, 1918. A German machine-gunner sat down behind his gun, fired a complete belt into the air, got up, faced the British Army, took off his cap, bowed, turned about and walked slowly into history. He, and many thousands like him, earned their exit line. But for the mishap of Lieutenant Edmundson's tank on Masnières bridge they would have collected vastly more scalps. Fortunately for themselves, the British cavalry did nothing. Had Sir Douglas been able to hire the Mongol hordes of Genghis Khan as he was hiring Chinese labourers something might have come of it, but even that does not seem likely. 'When the time came for the cavalry to move,' Sir James Edmonds recorded, 'the cavalry commander said that the evening was too dark and made other excuses.' Voices were heard saying, 'Pity Goughy wasn't there'. If, indeed, any military advantage might have followed unleashing large numbers of animals and their riders there could have been something in this. Evidence suggests otherwise. At 3.30 pm, when the light was certainly thickening, the Canadians decided that they had had enough of hanging about. A squadron of the Fort Garry Horse crossed the canal by way of a lock used by the infantry, put itself together again on the far side and roared off towards Rumilly. They overran a German battery, lost their squadron leader and about two-thirds of their number and straggled back into Masnières next morning after turning their horses loose in order to create a diversion. It was a miniature of what would probably have happened to the Cavalry Corps. Lieutenant Harcus Strachan was awarded a VC; Seely, the Brigade Commander, survived for a little longer. Sir Douglas, General Kavanagh and his Divisional Commander, Macandrew, had all been trying to get rid of him for the past year as unfit for command. It took some more months before they were able to shuffle him off to the Ministry of Munitions.

Lieutenant-General Sir Charles Toler McMurrough Kavanagh, late Xth Hussars, is not always numbered among the Great Captains. Nevertheless, he deserves to have his name written in letters of gold for, by masterly inactivity, he saved four divisions of cavalry from massacre. There was, as the surviving operation orders show beyond doubt, another Masnières bridge almost equally serviceable for horse. It stood 1600 yards away to the south-east, hard by the farm called Mon Plaisir and was marked on the maps. Whether Major-General Greenly of the 2nd Cavalry Division (himself a Staff College instructor contemporaneously with Harper) knew this, as he ought to have done, nobody now can tell. It was nothing to him; only General Kavanagh was allowed to give the order for his Division to cross, form up into line and charge for the guns. Had General Kavanagh seen himself as Lord Cardigan reincarnated he might have sent far more than 600 into the Valley of Death. Whatever his reason, he did nothing. Thanks to this defiance of military assertion that 'to do nothing is to do something positively wrong', there was a reserve left to be employed passim when the German counter-attack came.

When news arrived that there was no longer to be what a very distinguished officer of the XIth Hussars called 'if not a gallop at least a nice hard canter to Berlin' they all went home. Which was just as well, for they would have been as useful as HMS *Victory* at Jutland. The tone would not have been raised by Hussars, Dragoons and Lancers trying to take on Richtofen's Circus. The effect of bombing and machine-gunning upon acres of terrified and uncontrollable horseflesh is not pleasant to dwell upon without even considering such refinements as phosgene and mustard gases. On this occasion at least everybody would have been better off had the cavalry remained in their stables.

That is how it appears over a long distance of time. Not everybody in 1917 took the same view. Captain (later Brigadier) A.E. Hodgkin was a sapper with an ungrateful appointment at Third Army. He wrote in his diary that 'people are daily more annoyed with our cavalry.... The Anzac School at Aveluy here have sent a message to 'G' offering to ride straight for Cambrai if only the cavalry's horses could be given to them.' The offer was quintessentially Anzac but it was just as well that they could not be taken up on it. 'Light Horse Harry' Chauvel himself could not have made much of this depressing business.

At the other end of the line the 62nd Division had done splendidly, thanks to its own soldierly qualities as well as to outside help. Havrincourt had proved a tough nut, its over-running taking a full hour. The tanks had not had an easy passage. The upward slope from Havrincourt Wood was cluttered up with fallen tree trunks left behind by the German engineers needing timber. Six tanks had been hit by shell fire and rendered *hors de combat* before Lieutenant McElroy came on the scene. His 6-pounders quickly saw off the German guns that had been firing from the reverse slope of the ridge, his Lewis guns accounted for three more and he would certainly have done even greater damage but for one of those absurd accidents of war. In the middle of Havrincourt's one street was a shell-crater, full of rain-water and uncrossable. While commander, driver and gearsmen were doing all the complicated things necessary to back a Mk IV tank a bullet hit the reserve petrol tank on the roof. Blazing petrol poured down the interior; fire extinguishers could not cope with this and the crew, having little choice, abandoned ship. From their cover in a shell-hole they watched German troops trying to swarm over and capture their tank, where the flames looked to have subsided. This was too much for McElroy. Back into the tank he went, revolver in hand, and began firing from the doorway. The Webley ·455 revolver, at close range, is a formidable weapon. McElroy shot down eight before his crew returned, followed by a party of British infantry. Something over 100 German soldiers promptly surrendered. The tanks and infantry moved on to Graincourt. By 11.30 most of the sections of Hindenburg Line under attack had been taken.

In spite of the failures, there were all the elements now of a very considerable victory. The cavalry certainly failed. One highly-regarded General Officer commanding a very good Division failed also. Harper, you will remember, had ideas of his own over how this battle should be fought. The tanks, which were under command and not merely in support — Elles had no authority over them in action — should go ahead on their own. An hour later his Jocks would follow. They would move forward in waves, as they had done on the Somme when all of them were green in judgment. The formation is simple for half-trained troops to adopt, but the Highlanders were by now far better than that. Quite apart from presenting the waiting machine-gunners with unmissable targets there was another drawback. Men spread out in this fashion and under fire were not going easily to find the clearways through the wire so painstakingly prepared for them by the Tank Corps.

The two battalions, 'D' and 'E', both began the move forward at 6.10 am. Ten minutes later the British barrage came down on the German lines. Moving in waves and meticulously carrying out the drills of King Cyrus, they crossed the Hindenburg Main Line with hardly any resistance; prisoners, low quality infantry by the look of them, gave themselves up in great numbers and were shepherded away. By a little after 7 o'clock the Hindenburg Support Line had been reached and opposition was strengthening. Up to that point the infantry had wandered along behind the tanks, smoking and with little else to occupy them. By eight all resistance seemed at an end and the Grand Ravin was reached. Then came, as instructed, a halt, while the artillery changed over from time concentrations to a creeping barrage. Halts during advances are always to be avoided unless no other course is open. This one resulted in 'serious loss in momentum of attack and much disorganisation'. Part of this was caused by the need to put out, and then bring back again, the protective machine-gun positions. Even worse was a factor that neither Third Army nor GHQ had bargained for. For many Highlanders, and quite a few others, there was an ancestral tradition that had to be honoured. 'Looting, which went on all through the battle, also slowed the infantry up seriously.... I met a sergeant of the Argyll and Sutherland Highlanders who had collected 18 watches and 24 gold rings by the time he had got as far as the Grand Ravin.' The tanks, too, indulged themselves. One commander 'walked on ahead of the Tank to have a look at the Grand Ravin, which turned out to be a harmless ditch — no obstacle at all — nor were there any defences there, except a line of dugouts. On returning to my Tank I found to my horror that its crew consisted only of the driver, Cpl Hoggard: the rest were absent. He said he had thought they were outside walking alongside the Tank (a common custom if things were quiet and the atmosphere inside became unbearable). I searched frantically right and left, and in a few minutes the crew trickled back in ones and twos, laden with the most amazing collection of loot I have ever seen, chiefly consisting of field glasses, greatcoats, pickelhauben and such likes. A particularly tough little Scotch Lance-Corporal came back with a frying pan full of sausages which he said he had got from an officer's dugout. Having collected the crew, we mounted once more; the Tank in the meantime had been going slowly on, driven by the faithful Hoggard.' This is only one of quite a number of anecdotes on the subject.

When they moved on again at about 8.50 the tanks began to encounter much more serious opposition. They were advancing into the area considered by the Germans to be the most vulnerable of all and heavily defended. Flesquières Ridge had already been reinforced by an infantry brigade and two batteries; the artillery of the 107th Division was at that moment detraining at Cambrai station and would be hurried forward. As both battalions topped the rise they came under direct fire at short range from a mass of guns. This was the moment when infantry ought to be clearing the way for the tanks with Lewis gun and bomb, as had been practised by other Divisions. 'By the time the Tanks of 'D' Battalion had reached the crest of the ridge there were very few infantry in support behind them. 'E' Battalion, attacking with two companies only, was in much the same predicament. 'There were no infantry behind the tanks by the time the Flesquières crest was reached. Efforts were being made to get hold of another regiment, the 4th Gordons, to leap-frog the 8th A & S Highlanders but by the time it had got up the disaster had occurred.'

As the tanks came slowly over the brow the German gunners got to work. There was nobody to disturb them and they could aim steadily. The battle was uneven but the tanks did not perish unresisting. By some fine driving and gearsmen's work they made a notable fight for it but there was only one possible end. 16 tanks were destroyed by direct hits, 'brewing up' their crews and smashed as tanks would not be smashed again until Mortain in 1944. One commander told Hobart long years later of the acts of gallantry performed, the getting out of dead and wounded under fire by men often wounded themselves — 'One Company I know suffered 60% casualties, 30% of whom were burnt to death if not already killed' — and of 2nd Lieut. Atkinson, who had played full back for Cambridge in 1913, going for one of the guns with a large track spanner until they got him.

There are, inevitably, conflicting accounts of what really happened on Flesquières Ridge. The most convincing, because it was written by a participant with no motive for the least deviousness, is the account given by the then Corporal W.T. Dawson of 'C' Battalion. After he and his crew had carried out their part in the 12th Division battle and were on their way back to the rallying place they stopped, quite legitimately, for a little sightseeing. 'On the right of Flesquières on top of a ridge were about a dozen or so of

'E' Battalion tanks knocked out. They extended on a line which would be about 150 yards and presented a ghastly sight, being not only knocked out but some hit by four or five shells, being completely smashed – tracks standing up in the air and burnt out.... A battery of concrete gun emplacements with accommodation for the gun crews below and built into the side of the sunken road with openings for gun muzzles, all commanding an unbroken view up the sloping ground to the top of the ridge.... All carefully camouflaged and put there in anticipation of the attack round that side of the village.' Hardly a place to be attacked by tanks on their own. The heavy machine-gun fire from Flesquières Château, surrounded by a brick wall like Hougoumont, was indeed a formidable obstacle but, had Harper obeyed orders, it might easily have been overcome as similar obstacles were. As things stood, it proved a tough nut. Several tanks, their petrol gauges reading too low for comfort, wandered up to the edge of the demesne, broke the château windows and shot up everything they could see. Though tanks could do all manner of things, they could not yet capture substantial buildings strongly held. Most of those which approached the château went home bearing the marks of it. One feat by a tank crew deserves better than oblivion. Lieutenant William Bion, in a tank ominously called *Edward II*, was attacking a machine-gun position nearby when it received a direct hit from a heavy shell. The only possible course was to leave quickly. As the door of the side away from the enemy was jammed, somebody had to jump for it in the face of the machine-gun fire. Private Richardson dived out, carrying his Lewis gun, brought it into action and kept the enemy's heads down long enough for the rest of his crew to emerge. They found shelter in a communication trench where Bion organized his garrison. Ten Gordon Highlanders, appearing from nowhere, joined them. Since the German machine gun continued to pepper them, Bion decided to see it off himself. Taking the Lewis gun with him, he scrambled back on to the roof of *Edward II*, still bearing its fascine, and from that shelter he killed the German crew. Then about a company of German infantry debouched from the village and charged. The Lewis guns stopped that, but, as the attackers went to ground, ammunition ran out. Bion, a resourceful young man, spotted an abandoned German Maxim gun with boxes of belts; for some hours he and his small party kept all assaults at bay until they were relieved by a company of Seaforths. Even then their troubles were not over. A sniper shot the Seaforth Captain through the head and Lieutenant Bion of the Tank Corps ended the day commanding a company of Highlanders. Subalterns are not often awarded DSOs. Bion was.

Though the German gunner officer praised by Sir Douglas Haig in his Despatch was fictional, the German army can claim one genuinely heroic figure from this battle: 'Major Krebs, [of the 27th Reserve Regiment] who took over the defence of the village when the Brigade commander was wounded.' The German history tells how 'during the night of 20/21st he successfully evacuated Flesquières with the remnants of several battalions and three batteries'. In addition to these the British army salvaged twenty more field guns from the village and the wood around the château.

Harper was widely reckoned a good divisional General. His soldiers liked him, his senior staff admired him. Nonetheless, one cannot avoid feeling that this war had passed him by. His clock seemed to have stopped somewhere about 1870 and in nineteenth century battles he would have done well. Here he was above what General Montgomery would have called 'his ceiling'. He had ruined a plan beyond his understanding and that not merely by a refusal to work properly with the tanks. At Flesquières the 51st had a reserve Brigade that was not in action at all on the 20th; both Braithwaite and Marden made offers of help, with or without tanks. Sir Julian Byng's BGGS, Major-General De Pree, gave it as his opinion years later that a well-organized attack of infantry and tanks working from the north-west could probably have taken Flesquières at any time. It is hard to contradict him.

Harper's faulty tactics meant that Flesquières remained in German hands until the following morning. But for the fact that the 62nd Division had cleared the left flank and the 6th the right it might have remained so for even longer. The damage was done, the timetable so painstakingly worked out wrecked. Bourlon Wood, empty though it was, would remain untaken that night. Braithwaite, his offer to help Harper by attacking Flesquières from behind having been rebuffed, was not going to advance into the blue with his right flank wide open. It would be quite unjust to criticize him but it must be matter for regret that the General decided as he did. The Ulstermen were moving up towards Moeuvres without any great trouble; one of Braithwaite's own brigades was in Anneux, and a section of three tanks, part of the Company whose help the 51st had declined, had been sent to find out what was happening in front. Their commander's report was unequivocal and, as events were to prove, correct. The Germans were in full retreat towards Cambrai. Bourlon Wood was empty and waiting to be occupied. So ended the first day. A handful of German snipers and machine-gunners, assisted by a British general officer, had held up an entire division, a tank brigade and all the cavalry.

For a long time the story was told of the brave German artillery officer at Flesquières Ridge who had personally accounted for sixteen British tanks. It was completely untrue, and one can not help suspecting that it was cooked up either by or on behalf of General Harper. It might have made his behaviour seem less culpable than it was. The yarn was taken up by Colonel Boraston, so despised by Winston Churchill, and featured in Sir Douglas's

Despatches. Even Baker-Carr and his Signals Officer, the other Churchill, believed it and wrote as if it were Gospel. So did Williams-Ellis (with the implied approval of Elles) and any number of respectable historians. It was left to Hotblack, writing in the *Royal Tank Corps Journal* for March, 1933, to puncture it. There was no Siegfried; instead several batteries of good gunners all took their share. History was to repeat itself in 1944 when much the same thing happened in Villers Bocage.

Nothing much has been said about the cavalry, for there is nothing to say. Divisional cavalry regiments, using their horses as unarmoured personnel carriers, earned their rations here and there by reinforcing hard-pressed infantry; the formed divisions, expected by some 'to be passed through to raid the enemy's communications, disorganize his system of command, damage his railways and interfere as much as possible with the arrival of his reinforcements', did none of these things. Henderson's *Stonewall Jackson* had been a set book at the Staff College for many years; everybody, including Harper, knew all about J.E.B. Stuart and his great raids during which all these things had been done. General Kavanagh was no J.E.B. Stuart. Nor were Stuart's adversaries his adversaries. Baker-Carr, up in IVth Corps area, told of what he saw: 'Surely masses of galloping squadrons had passed through the "gap" and were riding *ventre-à-terre* through village and hamlet, cutting down the fleeing enemy amid loud cheers from the down-trodden and enslaved peasantry. Not a bit of it. The cavalry, after blocking all the roads for miles, sat down behind a hill, remained there all day and then returned homewards, again blocking up the roads which were desperately needed to bring up every sort of supplies for tanks and infantry. What a chance that day was missed! Never before and never again was such an opportunity offered. On each section of the front, gaps in the wire, a quarter of a mile or more wide, had been made; the "going" was splendid, and from midday onwards, except in a few isolated spots, organized resistance had ceased to exist. Bourlon Wood, Bourlon Village and even Cambrai could have been captured. The only reason why the 62nd Division failed to capture Bourlon Village was solely due to exhaustion.'

Baker-Carr blames the failure to stir on General Kavanagh who had strictly forbidden anything to be done without his orders: 'The 1st Cavalry Division, under Major-General Mullens, was allotted to the front on which I was working and he and every officer and man of the division were eagerly looking forward to coming to grips with the enemy once more. And yet the only cavalry man whom I saw that day was the cavalry liaison officer attached to the 1st Brigade of the Tank Corps, who sent back message after message reporting the successful progress of the battle. At the end of the day he was almost in tears of disappointment and mortification. The one great chance in the War for mounted men came and went on 20 November, 1917, never to recur.'

This was the considered judgment of a highly experienced officer who was not accustomed either to concealing his opinions or fearing to make them known. Nevertheless, it can not be mere impertinence to wonder, three quarters of a century later, whether he was wholly right. The misadventures of the Fort Garry squadron showed what might be expected in General Pulteney's part of the field. IV Corps' front might have been more promising, though cavalry has never been the ideal arm for holding ground. Very possibly they could have clattered into Bourlon Wood and village along with Anneux and Fontaine-Notre-Dame. But what then? Only Braithwaite's 62nd Division, already leaning on its chin-strap, could have supported them. And the Germans, thanks to an excellent railway system, were already winning the race for getting there fustest with the mostest. Idle speculation, of course, but interesting in showing the difficulty for a commander in trying to combine troops of the 20th Century with those of prehistory. The 19th Century inventions of barbed wire and the Maxim gun would have routed them. Add the diving squadrons of Richtofen and the rest, guns blazing away into masses of screaming animals. This, at least, is not *arrière pensée*. Major Hammond wrote that 'those poor horse soldiers were a pitiful sight in a modern war. If they had known how to get down and fight it wouldn't have been so bad. If they had been the least use and understood how to act at once I could have taken them over.' It would be futile to count on the cavalry for anything: their day was done and past. The last criticism seems aimed at the Indian regiments which were not trained to dismounted action.

Brigadier-General Crozier*, commanding a Brigade in the 40th Division, returned from leave just in time to witness the events of 20 November. A couple of days later, in a deluge of rain, he fell into conversation with 'a Corps Commander through whose formation we pass'. It was probably Sir Aylmer Haldane. On being asked whether he could take Bourlon Wood Crozier replied that, 'We'll take [it] on our heads'. 'I'm glad to hear it,' answered the General, 'but I fear the cavalry have lost all their thrusters; they have gone to the tanks and the Flying Corps and the Infantry.' It was probably just as well. The outskirts of Cambrai were no place for a Rupert.

All the same, the results of the first day were impressive: three German defence systems penetrated to a depth of about 4½ miles on a wide front and more than 5,000 prisoners taken. Crozier's Corps Commander was not wrong

* Crozier, though a good soldier, was a deeply unpleasant man. After the war he gave grave offence by writing a booked entitled *The Men I Killed*, telling of how he had personally shot soldiers for what he deemed cowardice. All was not lost, however. He ended his military career as he deserved with the rank of Major-General – in the Lithuanian service.

in saying 'we have done wonderfully'. Nor did Byng stint his praise to the Tank Corps. He wrote to Elles that 'No Army has ever been so splendidly led and so fully assisted as mine was by your Corps'. Colonel Boraston, Sir Douglas Haig's despatch writer, whose work, said Mr Churchill, 'is marred by small recriminations by an air of soreness, by a series of literary sniffs and snorts', adds that 'but for the wrecking of the bridge at Masnières and the check at Flesquières, still greater results might have been obtained'. At Flesquières, very probably; the bridge may have been a carefully disguised blessing. Twenty-four hours remained at the end of which Sir Douglas Haig would have to give the last order. Do we stay where we are, or do we go on?

Those tanks still capable of movement that had not done so already made for home, their day's duty performed. Guns and infantry settled down to a bitterly cold night under a half-hearted moon. The less fortunate collected up their patrols and set quietly out into the unknown, listening for any sound that might give a clue as to what the enemy was about. Those with no specific duties tried to cat-nap for a few freezing hours. The cavalrymen fed and watered their horses in preparation for another futile day.

Third Army HQ at Albert was drinking in the most encouraging of reports. Captain (in due time Brigadier) A.E. Hodgkin, RE, condemned to what he considered unworthy tasks as Chemical Adviser, noted some down in his diary: 'Intelligence says that the enemy cannot possibly get more than one division up to Cambrai tomorrow, so there should be an excellent chance of our getting there. Rumour has it that St Quentin is being evacuated.'

Brigadier-General Charteris had, one imagines, been busy. Next day's entry reads even better! 'Today we have taken Bourlon Wood and village.... There is a possibility of the battle ending tomorrow.' The congratulations were premature. GHQ's instructions to General Byng had been clear: 'He [the C-in-C] desires to lay special emphasis on the following points:- (a) BOURLON WOOD is to be turned and its capture assured on Z day.' Third Army's own Order lays down that 'It is very important that BOURLON WOOD be captured by us on Z day.' Thanks entirely to Harper, Bourlon Wood had not been captured. Nor would it be until ten more months had passed.

The second day of the battle demonstrated how the steam had gone out of it. The great armada no longer existed. 179 tanks were *hors de combat*, though only sixty-five had fallen to the German guns. A bare forty-nine could be mustered for the second day's work. During it four German divisions, fresh and businesslike, arrived on the scene. Prince Rupprecht moved his reserves with a despatch that only Major Marshall-Cornwall had thought possible. Seven more divisions from Russia were on the move and Byng would soon be the attacked rather than the attacker.

Everything now turned on the Fontaine-Notre-Dame − Bourlon Wood end of the line. Pulteney's Corps had made itself reasonably secure; the

German light railway system, similar in gauge to the British, had been joined up near La Vacquerie by the American engineers and both guns and shells were moving freely over it to Masnières.

Woollcombe's people, however, were in less happy case. The rains had come, the tanks were few and his infantry tired. Nevertheless, it was not all bad news. The small German garrison had pulled out of Flesquières during the night and the Highlanders moved in unaided. The Division, now able to fight in its own fashion, moved forward to the next objective, the German line around Cantaing. The position had been thickened up in the dark hours, there were no tanks to crush down the wire and, so far as the rain permitted, German gunners on Bourlon Ridge could watch every move. The plan was for thirteen tanks from 'B' Battalion to lead the attack, but, having encountered every imaginable difficulty, they arrived late. There had been no possibility of the commanders making even the swiftest reconnaissance of the ground on which they were going to fight. The Highland Brigadier, impatiently refusing to wait for them, ordered the assault by his brigade to begin. The time was 10.30.

The attack on Cantaing was a classic of its kind. The guns pounded steadily away, the RFC swooped low over houses with machine guns blazing and there the 20th century ended. Battalions of the Gordons and the Argylls marched proudly forward, Colonels, Captains and Adjutants on their chargers with their men following in company columns. Out in front, where the tanks should have been, strode the pipers, the interesting noise they made rising high above all else. Here and there horsemen galloped about brandishing swords. For a while it was undiluted Edinburgh Tattoo. Bagpipes are not compatible with short rushes. The gunners of the German 52nd and 232nd Divisional Artillery, having watched fascinated, eventually decided that enough was enough and opened fire. The Highlanders, brought down to earth in every sense, dived for cover. Their attack, magnificently brave though it was, had never had the smallest chance of forcing a way through the defences and into the village. Among the defenders now was Major Krebs and the former garrison of Flesquières.

At noon the tanks arrived, cantering down from Premy Chapel Ridge, and took over the battle. In the space of a little more than one hour and after some savage fighting they had smashed their way into the village, destroyed the machine-gun posts, and taken 400 prisoners whom they turned over to the Highlanders, the Queen's Bays and a battalion of Durham Light Infantry from Marden's 6th Division.

The shifts to which Third Army was put after losing the impetus of the first day appear from the forces employed for the taking of Cantaing. In addition to the Highlanders and Captain Raikes' section of tanks there was a cavalry brigade. What it was expected to achieve is unclear. 'An officer who watched the attempts of Cavalry and Infantry to co-operate with the Tanks in the open ground south of Bourlon Wood was much impressed with the difficulties of co-ordinating cavalry and Tanks. When MG fire was met the horsemen had to go so far back to get cover that they lost touch and the Tank was left alone on the objective for a long time before the Cavalry could be communicated with and got forward again.' This should hardly have come as a surprise; there was no place for animals in such a battle. Nor was it only horses that were vulnerable. Captain Raikes' own tank, 'which had several defective armour plates' was perforated by forty-three bullets, several of which went through both sides. The casualty list, apart from 'splash', amounted to one cut finger. Having done more than enough, the tanks turned for home. Two others from the same battalion had also been busy. The infantry in front of Noyelles had been pinned down, like the rest, by the ubiquitous German machine-gunners. Learning of this, 'B' battalion took a hand. 'In half an hour,' says the record, 'they succeeded in crushing all resistance, setting fire to an ammunition dump and patrolling the village until the infantry took over. Neither Tank was in the least hurt and there were no casualties amongst the crew.'

Later in the afternoon the 'B' battalion tanks were relieved by eight from 'H' battalion, commanded by Major A.G. Pearson and with orders to push on as far as Fontaine-Notre-Dame. First they took out Cantaing Mill, a fortress whose machine guns were holding up any further advance by the 51st; then they set out along the open ridge between the two woods of Bourlon and La Folie. About 4,000 yards of bullet and shell-swept open lay between the tanks and their objective. The same two infantry battalions that had started off so bravely that morning fell in behind them. Nobody had told them that General Harper had just issued orders for them to stay where they were until General Braithwaite had taken Bourlon Wood. 120 Seaforths out of 375 reached Fontaine; the totals for the Argylls were much the same. With, quite literally, cannon to the left of them, cannon to the right of them and cannon in front of them the tanks travelled the six miles at top speed — about 4 mph. Speed is armour, as Jackie Fisher had proclaimed, but 4 mph can hardly be reckoned speed. Only by constant zig-zagging, with all that that implied in a Mk IV tank, could these sixty-four stalwarts keep their fleet from serious damage. Steady clattering of metal on the hull was hardly audible above the banging away of the tanks' own 6-pdrs as the gunners spotted through their telescopic sights something deserving of their attention. Many German machine guns were eliminated along with three field pieces, two to the south of Fontaine and another near Bourlon Wood itself. Captain Hickey, a veteran of 22 who but for the war would have been a harmless chartered accountant, led in his section. The tanks deserve to have their names perpetuated as much as other warships. *Hadrian*, *Havoc* and, rather surprisingly, *Hong Kong*, rattled into Fontaine at dusk. As usual mist was rising from the ground. Fontaine was deserted. Hickey scoured the street for half an hour, pondering that it was only a couple of miles to Cambrai and the town might have been theirs. It was a dream. Petrol and ammunition were nearly all finished, the Daimler engines were running hot for lack of oil and the crews were done up.

The German defenders, the 52nd Reserve Regiment, had fled in the direction of Cambrai, and Fontaine-Notre-Dame was, for a short time, empty. Nothing more could have been expected of Highlanders barely capable of speech and movement, but, everybody on both sides later asserted, this was the cavalry's chance. One has to be sceptical about this. To have expected them to spur away into the darkness in the textbook hope of turning retreat into rout was hardly realistic. They might have given their animals to keepers and got down to consolidating this most precious gain, but one doubts it. All they could have mustered would have been rifles and a few Hotchkiss light automatics; cavalry can not dig, nor is the turning of houses into strong points their vocation. There was a further factor. The darkness would not last for ever, the Germans would soon be back in far greater strength ('The Boche is a good hand at coming back,' Major Hammond observed in Masnières) and the topography was against them. Bourlon Wood towered over the main road from a height of some 150 feet; not a great elevation, but enough to make the owner of the ridge master of the village below. With Fontaine strongly garrisoned it might have served as a jumping-off place for more tanks to move into the Wood from the south-east, but the garrison would have had to be something more solid than dismounted cavalry. If General Woollcombe wanted Fontaine he must first have Bourlon Ridge, and that could be taken only by a regular assault using all arms. He had none − only a few exhausted and abandoned Jocks.

The tanks remained with them for as long as they could but by 5.15, in the dark, it was time for them to go. They trundled off to Cantaing, leaving Fontaine garrisoned by a few hundred men already written off by their General. Harper had no intention of using his fresher units to relieve them. He was probably right. There was no reason for him to suppose that anybody was going to relieve the 51st and he had to keep such reasonably fresh battalions as he had for the next task, whatever it might be. The tanks, of course, could go hang. They were no business of his. Until somebody else should have taken Bourlon Wood the Highland Division would stay where it was.

The Yorkshiremen of the 62nd Division made a very brave try. In a letter, Colonel Oldfield remarked that his Brigadiers in the 51st were the best in the Army. Admirable though they were, there was a Brigadier of Braithwaite's who stood head and shoulders above the rest. Boys Bradford,

25 years old, commander of an infantry brigade and holder of the Victoria Cross, was not of the common run of men. On that same afternoon, just as the battles for Cantaing and Fontaine were at their height, his brigade was ordered up from Graincourt to the assault on Bourlon; his battalions could not have been better chosen. All of them, now bearing the proud name of the Duke of Wellington's, were his much loved 33rd. Eighteen tanks from 'G' Battalion would lead them into the assault on their old Colonel's château. Some squadrons from the 1st Cavalry Brigade would also lend a hand after their own fashion.

The first fine careless rapture of 20 November seemed long ago. Units were not where they should have been, liaison officers from the Tank Corps, soaked, frozen, hungry and worn out, searched in vain for the headquarters they needed. As often as not, once they had been found, a wall of misunderstanding about what tanks could or could not do confronted them. Bradford was quite another matter. Once the shivering Tank officers had found his HQ in the catacomb under Graincourt church, operations began to take shape. First Bradford insisted that they eat, drink and thaw out a little: then they talked plans, so far as they could be made without even the pretence of reconnaissance. Under Graincourt there were no exhibitions of petulance such as they had found elsewhere, but a quiet confidence and an expressed faith in the tanks and their crews. 'Bradford was the ideal General for work of this kind. One of Hobart's 1935 party wrote that 'Bradford made a great impression on me and though I have forgotten much about Cambrai, I shall always remember him and his great powers of leadership'. On the day of the German counter-attack he was killed by a shell just outside Graincourt.

The attack, delivered by men already near the frontiers of exhaustion, made better progress than it would have been reasonable to expect. The Germans, having got their second wind, were fighting back hard. Anneux and Anneux Chapel, this last standing by the roadside, were taken but at a great price in Yorkshire blood. The guns of half a dozen tanks drove the defenders out and Bradford's men actually reached the edge of the wood. It was enough; the German trenches of the Cantaing Line which they were supposed to be taking over had been no more than spit-locked. The attack, like so many others, gradually came to a halt.

There was little encouragement elsewhere. On the left, Nugent's 36th Division had reached Moeuvres but lacked the strength to take it. A neighbouring Brigade from the 56th had been pushed in and held some of the Hindenburg Support Line. In Pulteney's bailiwick matters were even worse. Details of the toing and froing along the canal bank are less important than one single factor. The German infantryman was getting the measure of the Mk IV tank. Once the shock of the first encounter had worn off it soon became clear that tanks were more vulnerable and less horripilant than they looked. The antidote was to keep down whilst the things passed and then shoot into the hinder parts where the petrol tanks were fixed. The target was easy; all that was necessary was cool heads. The drill was soon further refined. Let the first line of infantry merely avoid contact, leaving the second to do the shooting. By these means the first line could open rapid on the British Infantry as they came unsuspectingly onwards and cut them down. Separating armour from infantry was always a sound idea. Under the spur of necessity it was revived in France during the brief campaign of 1940 when the roles were reversed.

An attack on the 2,000-yard-long sector of the Masnières-Beaurevoir Line failed utterly. After a cold winter's night without blankets a brigade of the 29th Division alongside one from the 20th was ordered to move off at noon led by sixteen tanks. The tanks arrived several hours late; it was not their fault, for the system had once more broken down and order reached them only when it was time to start. The 29th, with three battalions across the Canal by Masnières and its suburb called Les Rues Vertes in its hands, decided nonetheless that it must go in. Its own History tells what followed: 'The volume of German machine-gun fire was immense. Armour-piercing bullets riddled a number of the tanks, knocked out the crews, and indirect fire caught the troops as soon as they reached a certain height. The SWB and KOSB suffered many casualties. Next morning it was found that the SWB had hardly any officers left and Captain Ewbank from the Borders was lent from Brigade headquarters.' The tank casualties were proportionately worse. Many were holed and set on fire, two were killed by direct hits from field guns and one, which had somehow reached Rumilly, ran out of everything and was captured. Matters fared slightly better at the 20th Division end merely because the commanders of the four tanks that had arrived said firmly, and no doubt rightly, that the bridges would not take their weight. German confidence was growing by the hour and Pulteney was hard put to it to cling on to what he had won. There was no longer any question of exploiting the gains of yesterday and putting the cavalry through. The cavalry, at any rate the 18th Hussars, had left their animals behind and were fighting on foot with rifle and bayonet. Along with a battalion each of the Royal Fusiliers and the Middlesex they engaged in a ding-dong street fight among the houses of Noyelles for several hours. By sunset the Germans, 23rd Reserve Regiment of 107th Division, had had enough and left the English masters of the village. For what that was worth. They deserved their victory. The men of de L'Isle's division had had no rest for three nights before the battle, had put in three night marches, sometimes as much as 12 miles at a time, and had gone into battle, carrying 60 lbs of equipment, with a further 10 miles to go before reaching the canal. The others were in much the same case. Pause a moment, and wonder whether later generations could have done it.

For the Tank Corps as a formed body of three Brigades the Battle of Cambrai was already over. In the coming weeks small numbers would be making themselves useful but from now on they would be ancillaries. Fuller's great raid never was. Sir Douglas, left with an indefensible salient, had to decide one way or another and without any waste of time to go on, regardless of cost, and acquire more real estate of little use towards winning the war or to beat an ignominious retreat? After all the bell-ringing in England, said to have been inspired by Lord Northcliffe, this would hardly be well received. As Colonel Oldfield said in one of his letters, after unflattering remarks about allies, 'It is England v Germany now and no mistake.... Matters look very serious everywhere.' In a passage slightly surprising to read, for Oldfield was Harper's second-in-command in all but name, he added, 'The tanks did very well, far better than I thought. The cavalry a complete failure, as you will have read. The Boche fought us bravely and recovered from his surprise very quickly.' Possibly wondering whether he had not gone too far, he ended the letter with, 'The world is about to go mad on Tanks, whose possibilities are very limited in reality.'

CHAPTER NINE

'DESPITE OF ALL YOUR GENERALS
YE PREVAIL'

The Crimean Heroes

W.S. Landor

SOME TIME DURING THE NIGHT of 21/22 November Sir Douglas made up his mind. The battle would have to go on. Considerations of a political kind, mostly affecting the Italians, clearly outweighed the military. Experienced senior officers, some of them much affected by this decision, condemned it. The historian of the Guards Division did so roundly. After reciting Colonel Boraston's eulogy, he added, with much truth, 'At the end of the day's fighting, however, the situation was not particularly satisfactory, so far at any rate as the contemplated scheme of exploitation was concerned. Bourlon Wood had not been reached. A decided check had been experienced in front of Flesquières; the enemy's troops in Moeuvres and north of the area of attack showed no sign of withdrawing; and the British cavalry had failed to make use of its fleeting opportunity to push through the German lines and isolate Cambrai. But, in despite of this partial success, the British Commander-in-Chief considered that the results which had been obtained were sufficient to justify him in continuing the offensive – and this, although he had failed to gain possession of the all-important Bourlon – Fontaine-Notre-Dame ridge and could no longer count upon the advantage of surprise.'

The Official Historian asserts that Sir Douglas 'displayed no hesitation in closing down the IIIrd Corps operations on the St. Quentin Canal, for he had from the first regarded the advance eastward as primarily of value in safeguarding the flank of the northward thrust.' Presumably he had never taken too seriously the prospect of mounted torrents raging around Cambrai by way of the Marcoing and Masnières bridges. Few would censure him for that. One of that few was Marshal von Hindenburg: 'Strong bodies of cavalry assembled behind the triumphant leading infantry divisions failed, even on this occasion, to overcome the last line of resistance, weak though it was, which barred the way to the flanks and

131

rear of their opponents. The English cavalry squadrons were not able to conquer the German defence, with the help of their tanks, and proved unequal to decorating their standards with that victory for which they had striven so honourably and so often.' Fähnrich Paul von Hindenburg in 1870 had charged at the head of his company against the Chassepots at St Privat. The Generals, on both sides, still refused to believe that war was no longer the same thing as it had been when they were subalterns. Perhaps this is one of the eternal truths.

The events that followed do no credit to the Commander of IV Corps, the General Officer Commanding Third Army, or the Commander-in-Chief himself. Still less can anyone compliment their Staffs, at any rate in the highest stratum, on their professional skill. Once the first day was over and the tanks had shot their bolt all that remained was the old story. Bravery that seems superhuman to us who have led more sheltered lives compensated for muddle and something less than even ability of the middling sort on the part of those whose business it was to plan and conduct battles.

For a start, it was needful to replace the exhausted men of the 51st and 62nd by fresher ones. There were none. Almost every division in France had been hammered on the anvil for a long time. The new men, especially those in the commissioned ranks, probably had the heart of the matter in them — they would not otherwise have been there — but they still had so much to learn that some of them were almost passengers. The veterans, after months of fighting in the vilest conditions, were often more cautious than they had been. All the same, the British Army of late 1917 was the biggest and the best ever to have worn out boot leather.

The relieving soldiers would have to come from Fanshawe's Vth Corps. It comprised three divisions. Two of them were to go first and no pair of formations could have presented a greater contrast. The division of all arms had been the basis of all European military organization since Wellington's day. At the peak of his power the Duke commanded seven. The British Army of 1917 numbered ten times as many, by no means all cut to the same pattern. This was inevitable from the way that army had been raised. Cavalry apart, only a dozen or so were regulars; the Territorials contributed fourteen first-line formations with three more from the second joining later. The Kitchener divisions — properly called New Army and enlisted or commissioned as regulars for the duration — made up the rest, except for the 63rd which came from the Navy. Sir Douglas complained regularly and not without reason that he did not have an army at all, only a collection of divisions. Colonel Oldfield explained it to Miss Whitaker in a letter dated 14 November: 'The thing to be is to be in a dud Division in a good Corps. Then you don't fight and are well looked after.' Divisions came to develop personalities as distinct as those of the regiments that made them up.*

Nobody, except the most bitterly envious, would have denied that the Guards Division was the best of them all. Since its formation in 1915 it had been in most battles and had always carried itself superbly. That picked recruits should mature into the best infantry on earth was not all that surprising; slightly more so was the equally high quality of even the humblest of their divisional ancillaries. If ever there was a Guards Blanket Delousing Unit it would have been a model of what such things should be. The Guards were always expected to do well, to behave when under the stiffest fire as if marching down the Mall and, above all, to perform each smallest task as if the fate of the Empire hung on it. As an important part of Guards mystique the Household troops must always execute nearly impossible feats of arms whilst making it all look absurdly easy. In a letter to Kiggell, dated 4 January, 1918, from Eastcott, Kingston Hill, Sir Douglas wrote that, 'As you know I look on this Division as the *only* really reliable one out here.' Almost exactly the same form of words as the Duke had used from Spain nearly a century before. Each writer, if pressed, would probably have agreed that there was some small poetic licence in this. But it was near enough to the truth.

Nobody expected much of the 40th Division. It came late into existence, the last but one of the Kitchener divisions, and its method of recruitment was vastly different from that of the Household troops. By the time the 40th was raised the supply of men was running out. The minimum height for infantry recruits, 5' 2", did not demand a race of giants but even midgets were becoming hard to find in late 1915. Then some unknown genius in 'A' Branch came up with an idea. Was there not a race of men, most probably in coal-mining counties, who were short, squat, wide, thick and brawny beyond the common run? South Wales in particular had been spoken of. Lower, then, the height barrier and you would have an untapped supply of new and serviceable fighting men. Thus came the 35th Division, the Bantams. On the Staff of one of its brigades was Captain B.L. Montgomery. The idea was sound but the sums were wrong. Such men certainly existed but the mines could not yield up all their best pitmen; for every brawny Bantam who enlisted there were three or four undersized corner-boys. In the early rush of optimism, however, orders went out for the making of a second formation of Bantams; thus began the 40th Division. In order to show that the rest of the Army looked down upon it only literally, the 40th was given

* Obviously some divisions were better than others; but let it be remembered that, even when battered to the point of ceasing to exist, no Division in Haig's army, unlike some in Montgomery's, ever suffered the ignominy of being certified unfit to be sent into battle.

a Guards General, Sir Harold Ruggles-Brise, for its commander. His first task was to order a mighty weeding-out. One battalion with over 1,000 men forming up on pay parade was cut down to under 200. Battalions were amalgamated, complete new ones were drafted in from outside and in May, 1916, the 40th Division embarked for France. One brigade was almost entirely Welsh; otherwise no part of the Kingdom claimed it. The new GOC, Major-General John Ponsonby, was a Coldstreamer who had lately been in command of the 2nd Guards Brigade. At 51 he was rather old for the appointment but experience, hard and recent, made up for this. The Division were not strangers to Third Army country. On 20 April, 1917, it had found itself by Gouzeaucourt, in sight of the roofs and spires of Cambrai; looking slightly to the west men could see a ridge thick with trees. The name of Bourlon Wood meant little enough then. Between April and October there had been a good deal of shapeless fighting in what was later the right of General Pulteney's line, much of it around La Vacquerie and Gonnelieu. Not the kind of war that divisions sentenced to the Salient had endured but wearing enough. By 11 October, when taken out of the line for what was euphemistically called a rest, the 40th had been six full months in the line without relief.

The Guards had been in every Flanders battle from Pilckem to Passchendaele and were tired. Three weeks in rest billets had hardly been much in the way of recuperation; the Divisional Commander, Major-General Feilding, was not pleased to be told by V Corps Staff early in November that the rest was over and he must start marching south. That was all. The Division moved to the St Pol area, concentrating there on 12 November, still unaware of what was going on. On 11 November, at the first of several meetings, General Feilding was told. The general outline of the attack by III and IV Corps was revealed and 'it was confidently anticipated that the continuance of the advance towards the Sensée River would turn the whole of the German defensive positions to the north'. One matter was certain: 'The Third Army Commander assured the Major-General on this occasion [16 November] that the Guards Division would not be employed in the offensive unless Bourlon Wood were captured the first day of the attack [when it would be used for exploitation]. In the event of the failure of the IV Corps to capture the wood, he told the Major-General that there was no intention of continuing the operation and that the plan was to withdraw to a line through Flesquières.' The Guards, along with the 40th, would be kept in hand to move across the captured wood and 'pass through the gap in the enemy's defences and attack north in rear of the German front line', accompanied, and probably hindered, by the 1st Cavalry Division.

The events that followed demonstrated that Staff college training hardly produced perfect Staff officers and commanders. Feilding and his

Guardsmen had been mercilessly humbugged since the first orders had reached him. By late on 19 November, after two nights on the road, marching through freezing rain among the traffic blocks, they had reached their billeting area around Achiet-le-Petit and Gomiecourt, worn out and very short of sleep. Their Major-General, not entirely reassured about the intention to leave him in peace if Bourlon Wood was not instantly captured, received a succession of new and contradictory orders from IV Corps. First, on the morning of the 21st, the Division was to move to an area round Beaumetz-les-Cambrai; by afternoon it was ordered instead to concentrate at Barastre. Buses would be supplied. The First War by now was taking a shape undreamt of in 1914 but to be disagreeably familiar next time round. The traffic jam had been invented — not on the scale of Salerno, Anzio or other famous ones but solid enough to block all the highways. Training of traffic control police had hardly begun; individual drivers did the best they could. The buses, genuine solid-tyred London General Omnibus Company, painted grey and with boarded-up windows, arrived late. Once on the road they became stuck; the rain continued to fall. A brigade which had preferred to march got there first. By the early hours of 22 November the majority had arrived, even tireder, colder and wetter than at the beginning. Most of their machine guns, all the smoke shells for the artillery and much besides was stuck in traffic somewhere down the road.

As the fight for Fontaine-Notre-Dame rose to its crescendo the Guards Division tried to get a little sleep in horrible billets. At 8.30 on the following morning General Feilding asked General Woollcombe whether his Division would be required to relieve any division in the line. He was told that it was 'most unlikely'. The day was instead employed by moving his brigades from one set of villages to another. It was not restful. Beaumetz, Doignies and Lebucquière, straddling the main Bapaume-Cambrai road, had just been vacated by the 40th Division, on its way into the furnace.

At 1.30 pm (the Army did not take to the 24 hour clock for another twelvemonth) a conference took place at Beaumetz where the 40th Division still had its HQ. An outline was given of a proposed further attack on Bourlon Wood, beginning with that Division taking over from Braithwaite's 62nd. For the moment 40th Division was still part of V Corps which had nothing to do with the battle. At 4 pm, just as it was getting dark, further orders came for all three of Ponsonby's brigades to move forward at once. Almost as an afterthought the General was told that he now came under IV Corps.

The GOC 119 Brigade, Brigadier-General Crozier, had dashed on horseback for Graincourt, his appointed headquarters, with a cavalcade some sixty strong of his COs and their necessary attendants. The reconnaissance, such as it was, proved valuable. Not much of Graincourt church remained

135

above ground but underneath were the great electrically-lit and comfortably finished catacombs upon which the Germans had lavished both labour and materials*; the descendants of their peasantry worked hard for the enemy clearing space between tombs of long dead Sieurs de Havrincourt, the old Lords of the land. It became a popular place. A tank officer wrote that 'There were a round dozen of us at the conference, a muddy, rather blear-eyed party, some in tin hats and trench-coats, revolver girt — some in honorific red and gold — all with slung gas masks. General Ponsonby and his GSO1 sat on an old packing case with a map spread out before them on another, lit by the dancing flicker of two guttering candles stuck into German beer bottles. General Elles and Colonel Baker-Carr were there with a chorus of Commanding Officers, Company Commanders and Reconnaissance Officers of the 1st Tank Brigade.... One felt uneasily conscious of forming part of a Graphic picture entitled "Advanced Headquarters" or "Planning the Battle".'

During the night the 40th Division took over from the 62nd, holding a line from Anneux village, along the sunken road behind the Wood to a point in front of the Sugar Factory where the front of the 36th Division ended. On the right stood the 51st, its line making a great bulge towards Fontaine-Notre-Dame from whence it fell away sharply to the south. Just before midnight of the 22nd/23rd orders came. There was to be an attack, starting at 10.30 on the morning of the 23rd, in which the 51st, 40th and 36th Divisions would all participate. Its objectives sounded optimistic: high ground north-east of Fontaine; railway line north of Bourlon Wood and Bourlon village. Fontaine was to be attacked yet again by desperately weary Highlanders. It is hardly necessary to say that the Germans had got there first.

They were to be led by the tanks of 24 Coy, 'H' Battalion, then harboured in a sunken road just east of La Justice. The quality of Staff work at a higher level had not fallen off at all. During the night the Company was ordered to attack Bourlon Wood in the morning. Later this was cancelled and instead the attack was to be against the western side of Fontaine and the eastern edge of the Wood, by which means the 51st would storm Fontaine and the high ground in between. 'There was little opportunity to prepare for this attack and the co-operation with the infantry of 51st Division was indifferent.'

The tanks of 'H' Battalion set off at about 10.15 am, moving down the low ground about 500 yards west of the La Justice-Fontaine road. Two Sections swung right, towards the western edge of the village, whilst the remainder headed for the eastern slopes of the wood. 'The infantry followed up to

* During the final withdrawal the RE blew the whole place up.

136

within a few hundred yards of the village, but were then held up and unable to advance further owing to machine-gun fire.' The tanks cruised to and fro between village and Highlanders but could achieve nothing. Small arms fire from the Lewis guns and occasional short bursts from the commanders' Hotchkiss could do no damage to brickwork. Only the 6-pdrs could penetrate the solid walls and they, having no elevating gear, could seldom hit the upper windows where German machine guns were clustered. The only chance was to find some means of canting the entire tank on one side in order to cock the muzzles up a little. Here was work for Stern and Wilson's self-propelled guns, work that a little more thought should have expected. Instead of smashing down houses, they were degraded to the useful but unheroic duties of mechanized coolies. 'H' Battalion's crews did all that men could, but their efforts were little rewarded. One crew's story must serve for all. The tank *Horsa* (2/Lieut. A. Mustard) on 20 November had 'left starting point at 6.10 am and continued running until its return to final rallying-point Ribécourt at 4 pm, a period of 10 hours'. There had been little enough rest in between. Now, on the morning of the 23rd, *Horsa* was fighting again. 'Another interesting incident occurred on the edge of Fontaine village to 2nd. Lieutenant A. Mustard's tank who was attacking the village with No. 9 Section. On reaching the outskirts of the village, his tank experienced engine trouble and stopped. The Tank was surrounded by the enemy who bombed it and fired at point-blank range through the gun-mountings and loopholes, three of his gunners being wounded. He was called upon by the enemy to surrender, but ordering his gunners to keep up Lewis gun fire, he himself worked at the engine and after three-quarters of an hour succeeded in starting it and finally brought his Tank out of action. None of the infantry were in Fontaine during this period' — a few bald words that can do scant justice to high adventure and magnificent bravery by all hands.

Then came the second foray of the day. This time the tank part was given to 'B' Battalion, soon to be reinforced by elements of 'C', from which two companies under Captains Price and Hedderwick came to join in. Price, who rose to high rank in later years, was not convinced of the soundness of the plan. 'We had lost several Tanks on the 20th and many others were in a bad mechanical state owing to the fighting but Hedderwick managed to produce five and myself six. With my Tanks I proceeded to La Justice and reported to the Infantry Brigade Commander. The renewed attack began at 10.30 am. I sent one section into Fontaine under Captain Henderson and one under Captain Purdy in to the gap between Fontaine and Bourlon Wood to work round the back of Bourlon Wood. We had, of course, no wireless in those days and no means of communication with sections once they were launched. I waited for about two hours at La Justice and then as I had had no reports back I set out on foot towards Fontaine to try and get information. En route

I met Colonel Hotblack who was then Corps Intelligence Officer and whom like Colonel Martel one always seemed to meet roaming about the battlefield.... It appeared that my Tanks had got into Fontaine and round the east end of Bourlon Wood but that the infantry had been unable to follow them. Colonel Hotblack and I found that the infantry were mostly holding on on a line just in front of us and several Tanks of different battalions were cruising about the neighbourhood so I sent to collect them. I collected three Tanks of 'H' Battalion and one of another battalion together with a platoon of Argyle [sic] and Sutherland Highlanders of the 51st Division and made another advance on Fontaine. The Tanks again reached the village but the infantry were unable to follow owing to MG fire mainly from Fontaine Church. I then withdrew the Tanks and the attack fizzled out. Of my original six Tanks only two rallied; two received direct hits on reaching the high ground east of Bourlon Wood and two were hit in Fontaine. Six men of the crews of the Tanks hit on the Bourlon Wood side managed to get back. In Fontaine the whole of one crew were lost but the Tank which got away from the village was able to get alongside the other disabled Tank in the main street and while keeping up intensive fire on the houses to transfer the crew of the disabled Tank under cover of this fire and bring them back.' Take, if you will, a moment to consider what these few words mean. A tank, crowded enough with its crew of eight, stops dead, under fire, and crams aboard eight more. It is almost beyond imagining, but it is true. Price ends his story with 'I got back with my remaining two Tanks to billets in Ribécourt at about 8 pm after a tiring day'. Hardly an exaggeration. Price's Field Message Book survives, in the archives of the Tank Museum. It is more eloquent than anything written a decade and a half later. The book begins with 'First Message 12.50 pm'. Then 'Orders received. Capt. HEDDERWICK has taken his five tanks on left aaa Capt HENDERSON with C46, C47, C48 is going to mop up the village of FONTAINE aaa Capt. PURDY with C58, C57 and C43 is going between the village and wood to BOURLON aaa Have marked route for each Tank commander on map aaa All is going strong just crossing trench in F266 b aaa T Reginald Price, Capt., La Justice.' A later message, timed 4.15 pm, is less cheery. 'Under orders received from Captain HOTBLACK I have come forward to find any Tanks that might be coming back (of any Battalion) and send them on to the village of FONTAINE and endeavour to get the infantry to follow aaa I have collected HWB, HELEN, HELAN (sic) LADDIE, and C13 and they are all now returning to FONTAINE aaa I have collected a party of Argyll and Sutherland Highlanders and they (about 50) are advancing behind the Tanks under two subalterns aaa They have just reached edge of village (map reference given) aaa E battalion 12 in number are just crossing road about F20b38 with infantry in rear of them (152nd Brigade 5th Seaforths) aaa My own Coy C57

direct hit aaa HENDERSON 3 Tanks entered village 1 p.m. not seen since aaa
PURDY 2 Tanks crossed crest in F8D 12.30 p.m. not seen since aaa Infantry
damn windy.' Hotblack, as usual was everywhere. This was the day when
he won the Bar to his DSO. The citation observes that it was for
'Conspicuous gallantry and devotion to duty during an attack. He
reorganized infantry whose officers had become casualties, collected tanks
and succeeded in launching a fresh attack under heavy fire. He set a splendid
example of courage and initiative on this and many other occasions'. Price
himself finished the war at the age of 23 with DSO and Bar and MC.

The experience of the 'B' Battalion Section under Captain C.W.G. Grimley
were much of a piece. His zero hour was 10 am, postponed twice in order
to get some smoke shells up with which the artillery could provide some
sort of a screen. Grimley, probably aware of what had happened during the
last tank attack on Fontaine, 'asked the Infantry Brigadier if I was to pay
any attention to La Folie Wood on my right flank and was it held by the
enemy? and he said "No".' The Brigadier was wrong; La Folie Wood and,
even more importantly, La Folie Château, were bristling with German guns.
Grimley, having watched with his battalion Reconnaissance Officer, Captain
Dillon, had his suspicions that there was a battery on the road, 'plumb in
my line of attack'. He gave his tank commanders orders not to drive straight
into the village as he had been told to do but to go round the backs of some
houses along the garden walls. So long as the smoke lasted they might have
a little cover from fire also. He also laid down a fire plan. No one was to
fire anything until he had loosed off his own 6-pdr. On that signal every
Lewis gun was to spray the point where the houses finished on the road
'whether targets could be seen or not'. The ploy worked. The German history
later acknowledged that the battery on the south-east side of Fontaine was
'smothered by MG fire'. 'We were doing a good 4 m.p.h. when on nearing
the village German infantry ran out of a shallow fire trench. First a few and
then about two Companies got up and legged it for the village.... We bowled
over quite a few.' Going round by the garden walls also paid off. Of the three
field guns waiting for them there two were crushed and the third wrecked
by shell fire. 'At this moment hell was let loose as we turned into the street.
We were being fired at from the roofs, front, back and sides. A combination
of splash and armour flaking made it most difficult to see anything when
handling a gun.' Difficult or not, Grimley's tank demonstrated how a tank
should be used in street-fighting. 'In order to put sufficient elevation on the
gun, we had to get the Tank on the other side of the street. Bateman and
Chappell on the port side 6-pdr put three out of action in one house, the
shells going below the sills and taking gun and crew I should imagine most
successfully.' With every Lewis gun smashed to pieces ('with Vickers
machine guns we would have given them hell') and 6-pdr ammunition nearly

finished, with his tank on fire — three pyrene extinguishers put it out — and nearly all hands wounded in some degree, Grimley decided that the time had come to seek infantry support. He found the Gordons 400 yards short of Fontaine, held up by enfilade fire from La Folie. There was only one thing to be done: 'I went over to within range of the Wood and fired my few remaining 6-pdr rounds. I could see no target. The enemy were too well hidden.' Leading his tank back on foot, making it jink as it came under fire from a field gun, he met Major Hotblack (everybody was vague about his rank at the time). 'It seemed that no matter where one was one could always meet Hotblack.' Then the engine seized for lack of water and they found the tank to have been pierced in several places. Having somewhere found a pram into which a wounded man was bundled they all walked back to Marcoing in search of a tow. The business had occupied, Grimley reckoned, about five hours. Fontaine was still even more firmly in German hands.

Whether Harper's conscience was troubling him or whether there was some other reason why his CRA was risking himself amongst a couple of depleted infantry battalions is uncertain. Colonel Oldfield was certainly there. 'I got mixed up in the Boche counter-attack at Fontaine and got away with some difficulty getting a good thump in a most dishonourable spot from a piece of Boche shell. It was lucky I was there as I was able to get ammunition up to the hard-pressed infantry and to keep all the guns on,' he wrote on the 27th. In spite of everything Fontaine remained in German hands.

The 40th Division was slightly better off. There were thirty-four tanks mustered for its support during the taking of Bourlon Wood; tanks were not at their happiest amongst buildings, but forests ran them a close second.

In the Mk IV tank there was only a small clearance between flywheel and floor; drive over a tree stump, bend the bottom plating and you have a job for the salvage men. Bourlon Wood, so long hammered by the guns of both sides, had great numbers of stumps apt for the purpose. The only safe place for a tank was in one or other of the rides where it became a target for everything an enemy could fire or throw at it. They, naturally enough, hated the tanks as the Boers had hated the Cavalry. Once immobilized, a tank and its crew were in serious trouble. Neither side offered or expected quarter.

The 23rd of November saw hard and unrewarding fighting for both tanks and Bantams. The barrage came down at 10.30 along the southern edge of the wood where the German front-line trenches were. Every ten minutes it lifted for a couple of hundred yards. The divisional artillery had been thickened up by four medium batteries, two of 60-pdrs and the others 6″ howitzers, making a grand total of 158 guns. At 10.50 the tanks were to move forward, twelve of them on the right with Crozier's Brigade making for the wood and twenty more with Campbell's, whose objective was Bourlon village. Their task was to pass through the infantry, who would follow 100 or 200 yards behind, whilst a barrage of HE, smoke and shrapnel preceded them all. The ultimate object, as orders stood, was to seize and dig in on the railway line north of the Wood; the tanks were not to withdraw until that had been done. Bourlon Wood was pretty much typical of the hunting pleasaunces of the French nobility before the Revolution. The Historian of 40th Division and the Official Historian both put its area at 600 acres; Cyril Falls, of the neighbouring 36th, says it was half that. No two maps are identical but the Comte de Franqueville, who owned it, was not constricted for space when he and his friends pursued animals along its many tracks and rides. The trees, untended for a long time, clustered thickly together and a thriving undergrowth of hazel and aspen grabbed at ankles nearly as well as did wire. The assault on it began as it had been planned, save for the absence of smoke in the barrage. All the shells were stuck somewhere in the great traffic jam stretching back almost to St Pol. Brigadier-General Crozier packed his men off into battle (or says that he did) with winning words: 'Remember Spion Kop. If I want you to come back, come back. I decide your fate. You hold on or die.' He also pointed out that tanks were a luxury. The job had to be done with or without them. Crozier was perfectly right. The tank battle contemplated by Fuller and the others had finished by teatime on the 20th. What remained, from a tank standpoint, was a tidying-up operation.

There was little tidiness about the events of Day 4. No reconnaissance of any kind had been possible and, against all the canons of experience, thirteen tanks were tossed into the battle with no hope of any achievement. The Grand Ravin was crossed and Graincourt reached. By the time they could see their objective three had expended all their ammunition and did not go on, two had been knocked out by machine-gun fire, one had broken down and seven made their way into the Wood. Writing of it many years later, one Section Commander, Captain L.N. Johnson, remarked that 'Although we got about a mile into enemy territory our "supporting" infantry never left their trenches and we had to make our way back'. Nobody sees much of his own battle, nor can all experience be the same. Williams-Ellis, in a good position to know more, wrote of a 'brilliant attack by the 40th Division'. Even the historian of the Guards Division, seldom rushing to say kind things about 'the Feet', tells of their 'stout resistance'. There was a lot of country, swept by every sort of German shell and lashed by uncounted machine guns that the Welshmen must cross before they could take to the bayonet. Casualties were very heavy indeed, even before the main German line in the sunken road zigzagging across the wood from east to west was reached. The noise was deafening, trees falling in numbers as the shells hit them and German projectiles dropping everywhere, latrant and mugient. Above all rose the chatter of automatic fire as the Welsh Lewis gunners took on, stalked and gradually overcame the German machine guns. Once the straight east-west ride had been taken the confusion became a little less. Tanks bobbed up here and there, earning their rations every time, but, as Crozier had said, they were a luxury. This was old-fashioned bayonet work and 23 November, 1917, was Wales's day. Battalions with high numbers, like the 18th Welsh Regiment and the 19th Royal Welch Fusiliers, went for the pick of the German army like the veterans they were not. The last-named took on the Fusiliers of the Guard and drove them out. It was Robert Louis Stevenson's war in a woody place: 'A war of the march in the mirk midnight, and the shot from behind a tree'. Well-trained snipers on both sides found the wood a paradise, in the original sense of the word. Casualties, almost as much from them as from anything, were horrendous.

By midday Crozier's men had reached the northern edge of the wood, but they could get no further. In Bourlon Village, at the same time, scouts from the other brigade were seen cautiously seeking entrance from the south-east, but withdrawing under heavy fire from the machine guns. Three of the six tanks working with them had fallen to the 'K' armour-piercing bullets. Half an hour later the village was left to the Germans. By dusk, after much more infantry work as bloody as it was indecisive, the situation was the same. Part of the wood was held, though precariously; the Ulstermen on the left had been unable to make much progress. Plainly the battle had got out of hand. Thus huge mêlée bore no resemblance to the planned raid; worse, it seemed that the German strength was growing as our own diminished and there was now a serious danger that the battle was going to be lost.

There was no help from the air. During the last couple of days the weather had much improved. General Snow said so in his regular letter: 'It's much finer today and aeroplanes can see what they are doing. For the first two days of the push they could do nothing.' Unfortunately it was the German air force that benefited most. The Circus of von Richtofen, always on call as a kind of fire brigade, had been brought up to help; the air battle soon became a private one between his red-noses and the RFC. Only three days earlier Sir Thomas had written, 'I went to see Pulteney in the afternoon. He was full of how done the Boche is and I think he is right'. To Harper's Highlanders in Fontaine-Notre-Dame and the men of the 40th in Bourlon Wood it did not seem quite like that. Fresh German formations, supported by aircraft, had gone over to the attack. The few score of Seaforths still in the village, leg-weary as never before, were on their own. Like the heroes of antiquity they fought on after all hope had gone. Fontaine was given up at about 2.30 and promptly re-occupied. The German army, far from being 'done', was now cock-a-hoop. Ludendorff himself later remarked that it was the success they had had at Fontaine which decided him to stage his great counter-attack a few days later. His recovery is understandable; at nightfall on the 21st the gap there had been three miles wide.

Byng had thrust his stick into a wasps' nest and the wasps were buzzing angrily out. He had no reserves designated for hole-plugging. Only one thing remained to be done. Sir Julian, raised to the rank of full General the day before, sent for the Guards. General Feilding, having been told at 8.30 that it was most unlikely that his Division would be needed, can hardly have been surprised when, at midday, the telegram arrived from General Woollcombe. He was to be prepared to take over from the 51st Division that night. This was the kind of staff work now to be expected. Nobody knew where Harper's brigades were; Divisional HQ was supposed to be in Flesquières. In reply to Feilding's urgent demand, IVth Corps sent the necessary information. The Guards' General, lacking means to carry out a relief in the proper way, sent the commanders of his two advanced brigades to the places indicated in order to arrange matters with their opposite numbers. The locations given were, in every particular, wrong. After some hours, and more by luck than anything else, the errant brigadiers stumbled upon some of Harper's Staff officers at Flesquières. They knew nothing of any relief. Indeed, they were at that very moment making domestic arrangements for their own. Feilding's GSOI came back from Corps HQ with orders, given at 2 pm, for the relief to be carried out at once. Since he had no commanders for the formations concerned, Feilding sent them by march route to Lock No. 5 on the Canal du Nord. It seemed as good a place as another, north of the Bapaume-Cambrai road and within a furlong or so of Moeuvres. There the brigadiers found them.

The relief was carried out. Two Guards brigades marched 15 miles, most of it in the dark and over unknown country. The Highlanders were not expecting them, nor were their staff officers quite clear where their own units were. For their part, the Guards had no transport, no machine guns and precious few Lewis guns. All these were stuck somewhere between Flesquières and St Pol in the great traffic jam. The Highlanders gladly lent their own guns.

The Germans knew far too much about it all for comfort. Two non-combatant officers of the 51st, Dr Rorie and the Rev Andrew Grant, plying their respective trades on the morning of the 23rd, found the sunken road by Anneux. There the chaplain announced, contrary to the truth, that the short coats and woolly jackets of the men in front showed them to be West Yorkshires. When a German Intelligence Officer questioned them they virtuously declined to answer questions; it was hardly necessary as the information sought appeared on their uniforms and helmets. To the courteous question, 'And who is your Brigadier?' they remained equally politely silent. Their interrogator smiled and said, correctly, 'He is Pelham Burn; and he goes on leave next week.' Probably a Rhodes Scholar.

The relief was a scrambled affair but it did take place. It also produced another small shape of something to come. The road from Trescault to La Justice, crossing the entire Hindenburg system, imperatively needed to be made and kept fit for wheeled traffic. The first AVRE – a Mk IV tank commandeered by the Royal Engineers – cleared away the wire in a fashion otherwise impossible.

The 40th Division had done better than anyone dared to expect, but its bolt was shot. Crozier's Brigade on the fringes of the wood had fought like lions but there comes a limit to what even lions can endure. Though attack after attack had been beaten off, each one left the brigade that much the weaker. It could not go on. The Guards took over the right of the 40th Division as well, spreading their line very thinly indeed. A subaltern of the Coldstream, W.B. (Bill) St Leger, kept a very full diary, meticulously written up every day until he was killed in action the following April. He told of what happened here: 'Sunday 25 November. That attack this morning didn't come off, because the wretched 40th Division [the Bantams] which took Boulon [sic] Village retired out of it before even the Huns counter-attacked and also retired from part of the wood, running through our 3rd Brigade who were in support.... The Bantams appear to have retired in front of our 3rd Bn. as well, as Reggie Lloyd, Heartrending Harold and another officer got upon their parapet and tried to "shoo" them back. "We've just escaped from the Germans!" whispered one terrified Bantam into the unsympathetic ear of HH.' Against that, pray remember that the Division had lost 172 officers and more than 4,000 men in just over two days. The Guards moved the line towards the north-east corner of the wood but could do no more.

A fuller account exists of the day's work for the 2nd Scots Guards. Wilfred Ewart, the novelist who was to die so tragically from a stray Mexican bullet after surviving the war, wrote of it shortly afterwards: 'At daybreak on the 23rd we marched about eight miles that night across the Hindenburg Line (which was captured on the 20th) to some good German dugouts on the fringe of the village. In the morning we found ourselves in front of Bourlon Wood and saw the church spires of Cambrai five miles to the south-east, the Germans heavily shelling the neighbouring villages of Graincourt and Anneux, and our knocked-out tanks lying about in all directions. The wounded were pouring back. At 9 o'clock that evening the order came to move up to Bourlon Wood, which we did as a Battalion, getting shelled a bit going across the open. Bourlon Wood was a nightmare sort of place – pitch dark and no one knew its tortuous ways or quite where the Germans were. It is a big wood, divided up by rides and summer roads. After going half-way through it, very heavy rifle and machine-gun fire broke out in front on the farther edge of the wood, lights going up all round. Several men got hit and down the ride there came a surging mob of cavalrymen, infantry and engineers, absolutely out of control, shouting and yelling that the Germans had broken in and were coming through the wood. It was a fine example of New Army discipline. Our men fixed bayonets, lined the ride, expecting every moment a terrific German onslaught. Nothing happened. We then went on through the wood, which was pitch dark, nobody knowing whether the Bosches had been driven out or not, and eventually dug in. We then found some very windy Highlanders and dismounted cavalry, and we got orders to push on and drive the Bosches out at daybreak.'

The Guards, being perfectionists, are not always indulgent to lesser men. There are still limits to what they can do. Three under-strength companies cannot drive two battalions of the 3rd Prussian Guard out of a prepared position without even knowing where it is. Ewart tells of how the machine guns, at a range of about 15 yards, cut down his men in droves: 'After about 20 minutes the Germans got tired of shooting, and we decided to get away if possible one by one.... It was an experience I shall never wish to repeat, and it is no compensation for the loss of people like Menzies and Sergeants Fotheringham and Maclean to know that what they were asked to do was absolutely impossible. It is little consolation even to know that the Corps Commander has been sent home.'

Neither Byng nor Haig had anything to offer in the way of fresh troops. The untrusted French were never seriously considered. Sir Douglas's state of mind may be judged from the fact that he had to swallow his pride and ask Robertson to delay sending the 2nd and 47th Divisions to Italy. To Byng he telegraphed orders that Bourlon Ridge must be securely held and, to that end, as much of his cavalry as were needed should be unhorsed and sent to fight on foot. This was the last farewell to the mirage of less than a week ago. The 1st and 2nd Cavalry Divisions, less horses, were hurriedly encadred into cavalry battalions with numbers and became a part of IVth Corps. Ponsonby's Division bowed out. In all probability few people now even know that the British Army once had a 40th Division; fewer still could tell you why, in late November, 1917, an acorn and oak-leaves were added to its divisional sign of a bantam cock.

That part of its area not now occupied by the Guards had to be taken over by somebody. Since neither the 2nd nor the 47th Division was yet available there was only one thing for it. Cavalry can act as honorary infantry; their little guns, at a pinch, can do field artillery work. But they cannot act as ad hoc formations of all arms; what remained of the 62nd, Braithwaite's Yorkshiremen, must go back once more. And so they did.

General Feilding knew perfectly well what was in Sir Douglas Haig's mind. He wanted the crown of Bourlon Wood and he was quite prepared to use up the only division he trusted to seize and hold it. The philosophy was not new. In Spain the Duke, whose château now looked much the worse for wear, had used almost the same words but he would never have sent them into such a battle as this. The configuration of the wood, of course, made its continued possession every bit as important to the German army. And geography gave the German another advantage. Even if Bourlon Ridge, dug and wired, remained firmly in British hands it would still be overlooked from the high ground just south-east of Cambrai; not even a reinforcement of Michael and all his angels would have dislodged the German army from that.

Colonel Boraston, in his Cambrai despatch, is disingenuous. Sir Douglas, through the Colonel, avers that 'our position in the wood itself was a difficult one and much of the ground to the south of it was still exposed to the enemy's observation.' It was decided, therefore, to make one more effort on 27 November to capture Fontaine along with Bourlon village and the entire ridge.

Feilding was horrified. It was 'a dangerous and impracticable undertaking for which there could be no kind of justification'. He requested — demanded would be a better word — a conference. At it, next morning, he handed Woollcombe a written appreciation, ending with an assertion that the attack must fail. There was no arguing against the points he made. According to our own Intelligence the Germans had shifted their batteries to the north of the wood and to the high ground south and west of Cambrai. The Guards Division had six battalions that could, by a stretch of imagination, be called fresh. They were to be ordered to attack from a salient into a smaller salient and throughout every moment of the operation they would be exposed to fire, advancing across the open to capture an undemolished village which would be stoutly defended. The very least that must be done was 'to subject Fontaine-Notre-Dame to an intense bombardment by all the heavy artillery available'. Woollcombe's BGGS promised that this would be done.

Having explained how the proposal amounted to nothing more than the planned destruction of his Division, Feilding offered two alternative schemes — either a wider attack to include the high ground south-east of Cambrai and across the canal from Masnières, or call the whole thing off and dig in for the winter on and around Flesquières Ridge. The General did not need to add that only the day before one of his brigades had been saved casualties because a hailstorm had blinded the German gunners; or that the first snow of winter was just then falling. General Woollcombe, old and out of his depth, said that he could give no decision. They must all wait for Sir Julian who should be there at any moment. While they waited, Feilding spoke of the barrage plan, in case Byng were to order the attack against which he had advised. Neither Woollcombe nor his Staff then present knew anything about it. Before this had got far, General

28. "The Livens projector, which could drop on the enemy anything one liked" (p.13). Sappers setting up this much undervalued weapon. (*Royal Engineers Library*)

29. "Then, with all passion spent, a greater power took over ... deep snow and blizzard" (p.171). Wrecked tanks at Flesquières after the battle. (*IWM*)

30. German troops removing 'C' Battalion Tank at Banteux. (*IWM*)

31. Mk IV Female Tank presented to the City of Cambrai, with the tutelary deities Martin and Martine. (*Tank Museum*)

32. "The near-derelict château of Bermicourt" (p.66) had been restored to its former glory when the author took this photograph in 1991.

33. Group at Bermicourt, 1917. *From left*, Fuller, Uzielli, Elles, Atkin, Berry, Dundas and Butler. (*Tank Museum*)

34. Bourlon Wood from the air. Anneux Chapel can be seen in the left foreground. (*IWM*)

35. Bourlon Château, home of the Comte de Franqueville (p.141), after the battle.

Byng arrived, listened to Feilding and ordered the attack to proceed. Feilding hurried back to his waiting brigadiers and conferred. It was another scrambled affair. The weight of it was to be borne by the 2nd Guards Brigade, with two battalions from the 3rd.* The attack was to go in at the now customary hour of 6.20 am on the 27th. The brigadiers received their orders at about 2 pm on the 26th; COs had theirs by 4 o'clock; company commanders somewhere around midnight. Nobody had seen the ground; the battalions were already advancing through the snow to relieve the 1st Brigade in the line and had passed the last two nights in the open. Everybody was drenched to the skin before movement began. At 6.20 they moved forward, 3rd Grenadiers on the right heading for Fontaine, 1st Coldstream in the centre aiming for the south-eastern slope of the ridge with the 2nd Irish further up it and aiming to gain touch with Braithwaite's right-hand brigade. The artillery, other than heavy, did all that was expected of them. A standing barrage, thickened up by machine guns, came down upon the danger point of La Folie Wood. Four machine-gun companies were set to cover the ground by Fontaine railway station and the eastern exits to the village. It was all that could be done. The whole line moved forward, the creeping barrage going on before, though very imperfectly. That was hardly surprising. The Grenadiers and the Coldstream had identifiable objectives as they advanced astride the Bapaume-Cambrai road; the Irish were, in the words of Mr Kipling, 'given a compass bearing and despatched at dawn into a dense wood on a front of 700 yards to reach an objective 1,000 yards ahead'.

There was some tank support. Fourteen machines from 'F' battalion, a dozen of them being ready to go at 5 am, were put under Guards command. It was not a small feat to have any tank at all ready to fight a week after the great day. The historian of the Guards Division observes, doubtless accurately, that 'The tanks were late in crossing the line, but some of them caught up with the infantry during the advance.' Guards and tanks were, so far, barely acquainted. It soon became evident that, in spite of all the barrages, the guns and machine guns in La Folie Wood and château were as active as ever. As they had first scourged Captain Hickey's tanks and then those of Captain Grimley, so they now tore into the Grenadiers. By the time Fontaine had been reached the two companies on the south side of the main road had been almost wiped out. Every officer and NCO bar one had fallen by the time the vanguard reached the village. One indomitable Corporal and six Guardsmen reached Fontaine church and attached themselves to the next Company. The casualties in the others had also been heavy. The Coldstream had travelled less than a furlong when machine-gun fire burst out from both

* Among the COs there were names of power. Those of Gort (4GG), A.F.A.N. (Bulgy) Thorne (3GG) and H.R.L.G. Alexander (1IG) would all be heard again.

Bourlon Wood and a chalk-pit just outside Fontaine. One Company lost every officer except its Captain and most of its NCOs. The survivors rushed the place, captured three machine guns, put about forty men to the bayonet and accepted the surrender of some 200 others. By about 7.30 most of Fontaine belonged to the Guards; their numbers, however, were now so reduced that there were gaps between companies bigger than frontages held. Most were down to about fifty and the machine guns from north of the railway line and east of the village showed no sign of slackening.

The Grenadiers and Coldstream, what was left of them, had an uncertain hold on Fontaine; the Irish, pounded every bit as heavily, had fought their way through the wood but could then do nothing more than dig in where they found themselves. Tanks, once again, operated as individuals. A Grenadier officer, Carroll Carstairs, wrote of a meeting with this CO: 'Together we proceeded up the main street of Fontaine-Notre-Dame, down which machine-gun bullets are pouring with the volume of water from a fire-hose. We hug the houses to minimize the danger of being hit. We reach the cross-roads and I marvel that a man can get so far and remain alive. We are in the van of the battle. It seems a miracle has happened to me. Knollys greets us. His Company Commander has been wounded. He is holding his position with about forty men and one machine gun. Nos 1 and 2 Companies have disappeared into the blue. They were, as a matter of fact, wiped out. All officers (including both Company Commanders) killed, both Sergeant-Majors and all Sergeants were casualties, and two-thirds of the men. . . . I find Carrington with about thirty men, all that is left of No 4 Company. He looks exhausted. He is standing beside a German field gun. We should have put it out of commission. Our consultation is interrupted by the appearance of a tank. It stops, and out of it an officer descends. "Do you want me any more?" "No". I feel as though I were dismissing a taxi. He climbs back into the tank and down the street it waddles away.' Disjointed though it was, the tanks made a contribution to this unwinnable battle. Though the Coldstream complained that 'the 4 tanks, detailed to cooperate with them, were late in arriving and of no practical assistance,' the Grenadiers were more appreciative. When the party left astride the main road came under German counter-attack 'with the assistance of 2 tanks [they] regained lost ground [but] their casualties, due to the enemy's intense machine-gun fire, were too heavy for them to do anything more than consolidate their position'. It was the same story as elsewhere. The Victorian weapon, the Maxim gun, was still master.

There is no need to itemize the next sorry part of the story. Fontaine and Bourlon Wood, both untenable, were given up for good. The Guards had taken casualties to the tune of thirty-eight officers and 1,043 other ranks, all to no purpose. The three battalions making up 2nd Brigade mustered under

500 men. Sir Douglas no longer needed to take any decision about going on. The decision-makers were now Prince Rupprecht and General von der Marwitz. The bucket of water was about to be thrown over the floor again. By them.

CHAPTER TEN

THE FURIOUS GERMAN COMES

Thomas Babington Macaulay
The Battle of Naseby

IT IS, ONE MAY SUPPOSE, necessary for the commander of a great army not to open his mind except to a few chosen intimates. And, for the sake of his reputation in later ages, he does well not to leave more written evidence that can be helped when success does not crown his efforts. By lunchtime on 27 November it was beyond argument that the gamble was not going to succeed, that irreplaceable men lay dead in a hecatomb and that losses must be cut. If anything, the state of affairs was worse than that.

Sir Douglas and Sir Julian had no more troops. It is true that the two Italy-bound divisions were back under command but they were not to be used up as all the others had been. One of them, the 47th, was commandeered along with the 59th in order to give the Guards and the 62nd a little rest but there were no more divisions coming. The tanks, too, were finished; though they had done spectacular things, there was a strong school of thought holding that until something better than the Mk IV was to be had the tank had completed its moment of glory. The Guards, in particular, were not admirers. Colonel Headlam was of opinion that they were now too vulnerable. 'The SmK (armour-piercing ammunition) used by the Germans was very powerful. It is said to have gone through brick walls as if they were made of paper.' The Tank Corps took another view. From his seedy office in the street named for the architect of victory in an earlier conflict, Colonel Fuller wrote in his weekly Tank Notes something in the nature of a paean: 'Whatever may be the future historian's dictum as to its value, the First Battle of Cambrai must always rank as one of the most remarkable battles ever fought. On November 20, from a base of some 13,000 yards in width, a penetration of no less than 10,000 yards was effected in twelve hours (at the Third Battle of Ypres a similar penetration took three months), 8,000 prisoners and 100 guns were captured, and these prisoners alone were nearly double the casualties suffered by the 3rd and 4th Armies [sic; he probably meant Corps] during the first day of the battle. It is an interesting point to remember that in this battle the attacking infantry were assisted by 690 officers and 3,500 other ranks of the Tank Corps, a little over 4,000 men, or the strength of a strong brigade, and that these men replaced artillery for wire-cutting, and rendered unnecessary the old preliminary bombardment. More than this, by keeping close to the infantry, they effected a much higher co-operation than had ever before been attainable with artillery. When on 21 November the bells of London pealed forth in celebration of the victory of Cambrai, consciously or unconsciously to their listeners they tolled out an old tactic and rang in a new — Cambrai had become the Valmy of a new epoch in war, the epoch of the mechanical engineer.' Even so might King Porus have written after the first public appearance of his trained battle-elephants. Captivated by this and persuaded that the battle was over, Fuller gave orders for all those tanks still capable of movement to make their way back to winter quarters. Snow was coming at any minute.

Sir Douglas, if Colonel Boraston is to be believed, had by no means given up. 'As the result of five days of constant fighting,' he wrote, 'we held a strong position on the Bourlon Hill and in the wood, but had not yet succeeded in gaining all the ground required for the security of this important feature. The two following days passed comparatively quietly, while the troops engaged were relieved and steps were undertaken to prepare for a deliberate attack which might give us the tactical points we sought.'

It is only kind to consider the audience for whom this exercise in economical truth was intended. Certainly not for such as might read it three-quarters of a century later. Haig's position at home was under threat; he badly needed, if not a victory, at any rate the simulacrum of one. The British public, facing up to its fourth dreadful winter, had had enough of defeats and horridly costly near-victories. Then there were the Americans. Many men of high importance were firmly of the 'Wait for the Yanks and the Tanks' school, and it was not an ignoble one. General Pershing and his immediate subordinates, if we may judge from their post-war writings, had no great opinion of the British army. Were such opinion as they had to be shaken even more, there was no knowing what they might or might not do. The US Army was numerically strong but under-equipped and undertrained. Valiant hearts and stout boots are not enough; without a competent staff system no army can perform effectively. The Americans had virtually none, but were learning fast. They must not become disenchanted with Sir Douglas and his feats. One may deprecate Colonel Boraston's lack of candour even though he was a barrister by trade; but one would not have enjoyed his task. T.E. Lawrence somewhere quotes what he said was an ancient Arab proverb: 'A lie is excuseable in three circumstances. In war, to reconcile friends, and to a woman.' Colonel Boraston might have found another.

Both GHQ and Third Army refused to be downhearted. It was widely asserted that the German Army, however well it might have performed during the last few days, was not what it had once been. As recently as the end of the Flanders battles reports have been arriving at 'I' in Montreuil that made this to seem a certainty. Nor were they entirely nonsense. The German official account had told of how 'Divisions disappeared by dozens into the turmoil of battle, only to emerge from the witches' cauldron after a short period thinned and exhausted, often reduced to a miserable remnant.' Cheering though this was, it had nothing to do with those formations now hastening back from the East.

The entire German army was feeling angry and humiliated. Stories of 'Tommy' breakfasting off the hot meals prepared for Fritz who had taken to his heels were rife, and true. The formations now arriving from the Russian front had never endured the rough treatment handed out to those opposed by the British and they were accustomed to victory. This would be the opportunity to show the contemptible little army what it was to mix it with real soldiers.

The conference that settled the shape of the next phase was held at Le Cateau, where in 1914 Sir Horace Smith-Dorrien had prevented a retreat from becoming a rout. Now the boot was on the other foot and the wearer knew it. General von der Marwitz received at his Second Army HQ a pride of German Generals; amongst those present were Kronprinz Rupprecht, commanding the Northern Group of which his Army formed a part, and General Erich von Ludendorff himself. For some days he had been a very worried officer but by the afternoon of the 27th when the conference took place he seemed to have recovered all of the old confidence. For this there was one simple reason. The *tankschrecken* − 'tank funk' − that had come upon most men had not passed over the General's head. For a moment it had looked as if the British had come up with a weapon that could carry everything before it. Then had followed the palpable failures at Bourlon and, more particularly, at Fontaine. The vulnerability of the tank and the limits of its usefulness had shown themselves and there ought no longer to be cause for alarm. Indeed there was more cause for serious optimism. Byng's army had manoeuvred itself into a number of positions ill-adapted for defence against a vigorous and determined attack made more or less in the old style. So, at any rate, the General hoped. Neither Kaiser nor people were regarding him as *Alte Fritz* come again and, like his opposite number at Montreuil, General Ludendorff badly needed a victory.

Though tankless, the German army was by no means outdated. The air service was becoming much more than an extension of forward artillery observation and could be very serviceable as a machine-gun corps with wings. Massed air attack on infantry had never been seriously attempted but this looked like being an opportunity. In point of quality of machines there was not a lot to choose between the rival flying corps, nor, by and large, in the quality of pilots. What mattered, however, was not the overall position covering the entire battle-front but local superiority over the Cambrai area. The arrival of Baron von Richtofen and his peripatetic gladiators would probably suffice. So long as they could keep the RFC at a distance, knocking their balloons and artillery spotters out of the sky in the process, the main body of his airmen could devote themselves to ground-strafing on a scale never before attempted.

The other master-weapon was the gas. This was a form of warfare begun by Germany, taken up to some degree by Britain and then, so far as artillery went, abandoned to Germany again. Only Captain Livens and his projectors remained; they had now been improved to such an extent that they could deliver salvoes of 60-lb gas drums at the range of nearly a mile, swamping everybody who had the misfortune to stand in their way. A great number of them, filled with phosgene (mustard was not yet in the British arsenal) had been used during the Arras battles with gratifying results. His blazing oil projectiles had also proved effective on the Somme, though neglected since. At High Wood, on the front of a single battalion, they had wiped out all defenders. The Army found a use for them again here. An important consideration in planning the Cambrai battle was the prevention of German reserves being hurried in from places not immediately under attack. Hence the diversionary tasks of the 56th Division in the north. One division of Snow's VIIth Corps, the 24th, had no part in Act I. All the same, it had something useful to do. As the gloves were now off and there was no place for chivalry it 'discharged 200 blazing oil drums into Quennet Copse'. The Germans opposite the 24th Division gave no trouble.*

For one of the more interesting variants on this form of settling disputes between nations I.G. Farben owed nothing to anyone. They alone devised the oily fluid, diffused from shells, which gave no warning of its approach, apart from the smell, and produced in a few hours terrible burns, loss of sight and voice and pneumonia. Somebody gave it the homely name of mustard. There was no denying its effectiveness, for it could linger for days in heavy soil, making it dangerous to dig in it, lie on it or dump stores on it. The weapon, for one must dignify it by that name, was first used in the series of battles we call Third Ypres and acquired a valued place in the German arsenal — not quite the same as a tank, but useful, especially against troops unfamiliar with it. 'Gas discipline,' the wearing of respirators for hours at a stretch, became the mark of the good soldier.

---

* By the end of the war about 140,000 Livens projectors had been used. The Special Companies RE who operated them reckoned that vastly more should have been used. They were easy to set up and not bothersome to their own infantry.

With these accessories in hand and two more divisions on the way from Flanders, Ludendorff decided on an operation of some magnitude. The main thrust of his counter-attack, seven divisions strong, would be against Pulteney's Corps, taking him in both flank and rear. The general line would be by way of Flesquières and Havrincourt Wood to Metz, where all roads met. Three other divisions, starting from west of Bourlon Wood would move southwards, joining up with the remainder at or around Flesquières. There would be a two-day bombardment, much of it gas, and the attack would go in on 30 November.

Some years later, Brigadier-General Seely told of a post-war meeting with Crown Prince Rupprecht. '[He] told me that the only way to restore confidence in the German Army was to launch a counter-attack in the same place.... It was an entirely novel kind of attack. "You had overwhelmed us by complete surprise with your tanks. We wanted to try and do the same thing without tanks." It all depended on finding men brave enough to creep right up to and under our hastily constructed wire entanglements under cover of the mist.' There was no shortage of such. Leutnant Ernst Junger of the 73rd Hanoverian Fusilier Regiment left a full account of how it felt to attack Bourlon Wood. He, rightly, reminded his readers that infantry warfare was not mere butchery: 'Everyone knows that who has seen them, these princes of the trenches, with their hard, set faces, brave to madness, tough and agile to leap forward or back, with keen, bloodthirsty nerves, whom no dispatch ever mentions.' No army could, or would wish to, claim a monopoly of them. A few years later many could be seen cranking barrel organs on street corners hoping for a few pennies to fall into their caps.

Though every possible warning was given of the wrath to come only one man appears to have understood it. German guns were not yet capable of carrying out the surprise bombardments recently perfected in the British service. When they began to register on targets never shelled before, then something plainly was up; when no less than seven new bridges over the canal were openly made there was ground for more than suspicion. Gunner officers from their OPs could watch the activity going on behind the German lines, whilst RFC pilots were reporting great numbers of German soldiers to be coming up from the back areas in motor-buses. German aircraft in large numbers suddenly seemed to fill the sky. Major-General Vaughan, Chief of General Staff at Third Army, refused to believe that anything serious was afoot. The Germans were not nearly strong enough, as Charteris had said. They were merely, as the Chinese philosopher of old advised those in difficulties to do, putting out more flags.

The Cassandra was a prophet who had every claim to be respected. Sir Thomas D'Oyly Snow, in his 60th year and four years senior to the Army Commander, had held high commands in almost every battle since Mons.

Sadly, his days were numbered, not for age or doubtful competence but simply by reason of a leg injury that would not properly heal. Sir Thomas and his BGGS, 'Jock' Burnett-Stuart, were nearer to the anvil and could see the hammer poised. The historian of the 56th Division later wrote down what was generally believed among the cognoscenti: 'Early in the proceedings General Sir T.D'O. Snow, commanding the VIIth Corps, is reported to have placed his fingers on a map at the point of the Twenty Two Ravine (which led straight into Gonnelieu) and said, "If I were a German I should attack there". No attempt was ever made to reinforce divisions before the German counter-attack, although the Army was aware that one was threatened.'

There was more to it than that. Amongst the papers of the late Sir Basil Liddell Hart is a note of a conversation he had with Sir James Edmonds, the Official Historian, ten years after the battle. After railing at the stupidity of Generals, Burnett-Stuart had said flatly to Edmonds that 'Snow had full knowledge of German counter-attack coming, but Byng refused to credit it. Snow had asked Pulteney to concentrate his guns on the Crevecoeur hollow where the Germans were massing, but Pulteney would not.'

Edmonds did not admire the Army Commander. It would be unkind to suggest any connection between this and his having been passed over by Byng for a senior RE appointment. Whatever the reason, Sir James Edmonds is less than appreciative. Byng, he says, was known in those circles in which Edmonds moved as ' "Byng The Bungler", with every talent except military talent.' Other men saw him differently. It was on 24 November that General Snow wrote to his wife that 'I was very glad to see that they had promoted Bungo. It was very much his show'. Snow was not the only active participant to descry merit in his Army Commander. That admirable cynic Colonel Oldfield wrote another of his letters saying that 'I have been waiting for a real General to rise. I rather think it may be Byng. Everyone is so impressed with him who knows him.' The succeeding generation had no doubt about it at all. The future Major-General Sir Percy Hobart, writing in 1935 as a simple Colonel, observed that 'The courage, imagination and vision displayed by Lord Byng cannot be too strongly emphasized. To him falls the credit for a decision on which was to depend the future trend of the whole war in the west.' The Official Historian and his friends will have to be content with being a minority in their assessment of the Army Commander's qualities. It remains a pity that Sir Julian did not quite apprehend the nature and quality of the imminent German offensive; a few heavy batteries setting about the ravines might have made a considerable difference to the events that followed.

General Snow, fully conscious that authority forsakes a dying king, did what he could. Sir Douglas Haig's diary entry for 4 December, written up after the tumult and the shouting had died, tells of how he had visited VIIth

Corps HQ where he had been told of how the seven new bridges and the approaches to them had been made and how Snow had been worried enough to go personally to Villers-Guislain and order up thirteen extra Vickers guns for the place. He was not alone in his unease. General Jeudwine, who had well understood the purport of the sudden increase in German air activity, stepped across the Corps boundary to take counsel with his neighbour, General Scott of the 12th. They agreed in general terms on what needed to be done but neither had any troops to spare nor were their artillery resources likely to make much impression upon any irruption on a massive scale. Only Corps and Army commanders could order the twenty-nine siege and heavy batteries at their disposal to bring down the devastating barrages needed and they did not seem to believe anything to be in the wind. General Snow had put it very mildly in his letter to Lady Snow of 1 December: 'I had expected it [the German attack] but was in the minority.' This, though hard to understand, was demonstrably true. Only a couple of days previously the entire Third Army, along with its attached troops, seemed to be quite persuaded that the battle was over.

The Tank Corps, in particular, felt its work to be done. Elles had inspected 'a weary but satisfied body of men' at Havrincourt on the 29th and sent them on their way with appreciative words. Baker-Carr's and Hardress Lloyd's brigades had entrained at once for Wailly and winter quarters. Courage's would follow them in a few days' time. The divisions on the ground, every bit as tired, were reassembling themselves, as formations do after battle; there were fresh drafts to be absorbed, equipment of every kind to be replaced and work to be done, as a matter of routine, in making their positions as defensible as they might be. The posture of IIIrd Corps was succinctly described by General Marden: 'Comparing the position with the back of a man's left hand, the 6th Division occupied the third finger, the 29th Division the main finger, the 20th Division the index finger, the 12th Division the portion below the index finger down to the lower portion of the thumb when fully extended; the 55th Division occupied the thumb.'

The 55th, of VIIth Corps, was in no better case than the others. The West Lancashire Territorials had been racked to pieces in the Salient; during the last few days there, at the end of September, they had taken casualties amounting to 127 officers and 2,603 other ranks. Though the Division had been kept out of the mainstream battles of 20 November it had not been a mere spectator. Since no tanks could be spared it had carried out a subsidiary attack, to keep the Germans from moving more troops northwards, without them. In order to make up this deficiency the 55th, like the 24th, had been given 1300 of Captain Livens' gas cylinders along with 335 thermit bombs and 170 smoke bombs. These, lobbed into enemy trenches around Vendhuille, had been highly effective and 'absolutely silenced the enemy machine guns'. Along with these helpers there were a number of dummies, not only dummy tanks but dummy men; they proved equally serviceable. All the same, the operation had cost General Jeudwine the better part of an infantry brigade; when it was over his Division, what remained of it, held, or attempted to hold, a front of 13,000 yards. For artillery it possessed just two batteries, one of them borrowed from another division. Of necessity it did not occupy anything in the nature of a regular trench line — a series of unconnected platoon posts with a little depth here and there. This was the sort of defence that faced the storm troops of von der Marwitz in the area running south from the Banteux Ravine.

Of the neighbouring formations Scott's 12th (Eastern) Division had been almost continually in action since it was blooded at Loos. After the first phase of the Cambrai battle 'the infantry battalions were very short of men, reinforcements not having reached them'. Cyril Falls, never a man extravagant with praise, calls it 'By no means one of the most spectacular of the British divisions but always of sound quality'. At the end of November, 1917, it was not at concert pitch. General Scott himself told of the nakedness of his land: 'Some 700 reinforcements, who had not joined their battalions, were organized as a provisional battalion under Major W.R. Johnson, 9th Essex, and sent forward to support the Queen's.... The Northumberland Hussars were sent to Vaucellette Farm to keep touch with the 55th Division on the right and the 3rd Corps Cyclist Battalion to Revlon Farm to reinforce that part of the line ... an officer of a trench-mortar battery, a subaltern Royal Artillery and Lieutenant White, Brigade Intelligence Officer, joined the party and about 100 men of various units, with rifles, were formed into four platoons.'

When a line of sorts was established, from Vaucellette Farm, along Revelon Ridge and then due north to Gouzeaucourt, it was manned by 'Northumberland Hussars, 12th Division Details, Cyclists, Army Troops RE, details of the 20th Division, Band of the Royal Dragoons and Monmouthshire Pioneers'.

The plight of the 20th Division was, perhaps, the least enviable of all. It occupied a position on the left of the 12th, which still held Lateau Wood, along the top of the spur and then north to the canal. Like the others, it was barely defensible against any serious attack. The line formed a deep salient, overlooked by high ground in enemy hands almost throughout its length. The canal bridges were all comfortably inside the German lines; on the south-east face of the salient the steep convex slope of the ridge left an area of dead ground along the bottom. So effectively was this hidden from view that even the outposts could see nothing of either the valley or the village called Les Rues des Vignes. An advance of a mere couple of furlongs to Lateau Wood would enable the German infantry to look straight into the

English gun-line. A successful attack on Bonavis Ridge would cut off the entire salient, encircling the infantry and leaving the batteries, such as they were, outflanked.

Though Generals Scott and Jeudwine, both of them Gunners, had been sufficiently persuaded of their danger to coordinate their fire plans as far as they could, General Smith seems to have been more optimistic. So much so that when the blow fell many battalions in his 20th Division — their average strength about 300 — lacked their Commanding Officers. They had been 'sent back for a rest, as it was considered a good opportunity for their seconds-in-command to get some useful experience'. This they were not to be denied.

The artillery, on the other hand, was not over-extended. The divisional artilleries — the little 18-pdrs and a 4.5 howitzers — played up manfully but the medium guns of Pulteney's Corps, the 60-pdrs and the 6″ howitzers, remained silent. Even more to the point, the mighty 12″ howitzers around Metz, under Third Army alone, were unemployed throughout the day. These were the guns that, with their 750-lb shells, could have created havoc amongst the Germans massing in the Ravines, but they fired not a round. GHQ — to be more accurate, Brigadier-General Charteris — had announced *ex cathedra* that the German Army had been knocked about so severely in Flanders that it could not possibly manage to try and take revenge for its recent humiliation. The heavy artillery, therefore, would not be called upon. Fortunately for the British Army and its allies this was the last chance given to the Director of Intelligence to demonstrate how wrong he could be about almost everything that mattered.

It is no disparagement of the skill and determination with which the German Army attacked to remark that it had advantages. Though it possessed neither tanks nor, yet, the ability to lay down a barrage without registration it had concentrated on other matters. Local air superiority was probably the most important; Major Sholto Douglas, commanding 84 Squadron from Izel-les-Hameau, ten miles south-west of Vimy Ridge, found the air battle unsatisfactory: 'Such was the state of the weather that all our work was done at an exceptionally low altitude — anything from 300 to 2000 feet and never higher than that — and the arduous apprenticeship that my Squadron had served in the Salient bore its first fruits. We shot down five or six of the enemy without loss to ourselves.' That was as far as it went. 'November weather gave little opportunity to put into practice the formation flying techniques that we had been practising.' All the help the RFC could give was by sorties of one or two machines without distinguishable objects. As every litigant soon persuades himself of the superiority of his opponent's counsel over his own, so does the infantryman from his coign of disadvantage firmly believe the enemy air to be having the best of it. Richtofen's Circus and the rest of the black crosses seemed to be everywhere, their wheels practically brushing men's helmets. And air was not everything. The gas shells, available in unlimited quantities, were admirably suited to disorganize the best dug-in defenders; against men with little or no cover they were devastating. It mattered little that artillery techniques were not yet all that good; there had been plenty of time for registering. The infantry, as always, carried the heavy end; *Gott* certainly seemed to have been *Mit Uns* by providing the ravines, the interstices between the fingers. It was hardly possible to cover all of them by observation; quite impossible to cover them by fire. As General Snow had pointed out, this was the place for a German counter-attack, and so it was. The infantry had one further advantage as they moved through the morning mist. Horses and wagons would bring up their rations when the time came but no masses of cavalry would be there to get in the way of serious work.

The German infantry, allowed to move to their forming-up places without molestation from British artillery, were ready to move off at the usual time of a little after 6 am. At 6.45 their batteries opened fire, first on the left-hand brigade of the 55th Division and then on the 12th, 'a certain proportion of gas shell being used'. A quarter of an hour later British guns replied, firing on SOS lines, but the targets had gone. By the time the first shell exploded the Germans were bombing the Royal Berkshires of 36th Brigade back towards Gonnelieu. Before the fight had really warmed up the Berkshires ran out of bombs; nevertheless 'blocks were formed and the enemy's advance stopped at about 9 am.' Even this only delayed them. By noon, or a little after, the remnant of the Division was spread thinly over a very wavy line from La Vacquerie to somewhere north of Gouzeaucourt.

The scene was one of complete disorganization of the kind now familiar to the British Army. All communications had been cut since the barrage opened; no commander, from Major-General to Lance-Corporal, knew more than he could see for himself nor could give orders outside the same limited area. Since many of the shells were of phosgene, respirators were needed in order to stay alive and the view became even more restricted. By breakfast-time, however, the word was circulating of Germans being in Villers-Guislain and, an hour later, in Gouzeaucourt itself. Only the scattered bands of dogged men who had been only hours ago the 12th Division and a part of the 55th stood between General von der Marwitz and a tremendous, undreamt of victory. Against them were advancing five complete divisions plus elements of two others, starting from a line between Masnières and Vendhuille, heading west with a little north in it. Substantial though this force was it did not constitute the main German effort. That was to begin two hours later, at the northern or Bourlon

Wood end. Their respective outcomes were very different and must be treated separately. First it seems as well to continue the account of events in the southern part.

The 20th Division's turn came half an hour after the 12th and 55th. At 7.30 three separate barrages, mostly made up of smoke and mustard gas shells, fell simultaneously between the outpost line and the sunken road running between Masnières and La Vacquerie. At 8 o'clock, under additional cover from a thick mist, German infantry advanced along the entire divisional front. The right-hand end of the Division, around the dead ground mentioned before, did not last long. Hardly had the defenders realized that they were being attacked in front than other assailants came from behind their right shoulders: 'The German infantry advanced in a succession of from eight to twelve waves, preceded by a great number of low-flying aircraft which rained machine-gun fire on the troops and dropped smoke-bombs to screen the assaulting lines.' This was something new, newer even than the tank — and equally effective against troops in the open.

The attack on the 29th Division arrived punctually at 8 o'clock when Sir Beauvoir de Lisle was eating his breakfast in the Quentin Quarry, a mile east of Gouzeaucourt. It came as something of a surprise. His South African experience of rifle fire warned him from what direction it was coming but for a moment he refused to believe what his ears told him. His divisional front was four miles to the north, yet he was being attacked from the south-east. 'At once I ordered my HQ to evacuate the quarry and to run for it. For 20 years I have ignored the published story that the general who had to run away in his pyjamas was myself. I knew who it was and did not want to give him away. As a matter of fact I had finished breakfast and was just about to start to visit my front line with my ADC.'

The 29th Division was a tough nut to crack, even when it had been nearly a fortnight in the line. Every German local success was met with immediate counter-attack and after two full days of fighting the General was able to signal to Corps HQ that '29th Division still holds original line'. Though war had brought it some fine, if unexpected, additions — such as the Newfoundlanders and the Royal Guernsey Light Infantry — the 29th was still, in the main, old army. One of its VCs, won near Masnières on that day, proclaims all the old army virtues. Robert Gee had been for 22 years in the ranks of the Royal Fusiliers. In 1915 he was commissioned, sent to the Dardanelles and wounded in the leg. This ended his marching days — he was 40 at the time — and for ever after he walked with a stick shod with what the trade calls an Alpine spike. On 30 November, as Staff Captain to one of de Lisle's brigades, Gee was walking down the street of Masnières when a group of Germans shot at him from the south. His front, of course, faced north. For a start Gee rolled some bales of clothing out of his store, manned this odd barricade with a couple of storemen and kept the enemy at a respectful distance. Being anxious about an ammunition dump in the next street, he jumped over a garden wall into the arms of two more Germans. One he slew with his stick whilst his orderly killed the second. Then, with materials from the dump, they blocked the other of the streets which, in the shape of an inverted V, met at the bridge. At that point Gee remembered a draft of 100 Guernseymen, arrived the night before and still in the cellars of Les Rues Vertes. He and his orderly routed them out, put them into some semblance of order and with them drove the Germans from all but one house in a garden from which machine-gun fire was coming. Covered by some Guernseymen, Gee and his orderly worked round to a flank and rushed the gun. The orderly was shot. Gee, having killed the last of the crew with his revolver, swung the gun round just in time to annihilate a German battalion coming up in close order. De Lisle affirms that the two men saved the village and, with it, the brigade. This was the stuff of the old regular linesman.

It was not, however, the most glorious of days for the infantry of the line when taken as a whole. The German infantry made little progress against the 29th Division and the 55th fought off all assaults during the day around Vendhuille. West of Gouzeaucourt, however, there was something uncomfortably like panic. The slopes were black with fugitives, by no means all of them combatant troops, and for a moment it looked as if Rupprecht's throw might succeed, leaving the entire Third Army in a sack. That it did not happen in this way is due, once more, to the ancient virtues of the British regular army.

The Guards Division was set into motion at 10 am, when IVth Corps passed back news of the enemy being in Gonnelieu and Villers-Guislain. Next, and soon afterwards, came orders that the 1st Guards Brigade should move on Gouzeaucourt and retake the Quentin Ridge, east of the village; the other two brigades were to keep pace on the right. At almost exactly the same time orders reached Colonel Courage that every tank of his 2nd Brigade that could be made to move should be activated without delay and sent to the Guards' assistance.

Those machines that had not left already were undergoing running repairs, most of them extensive after all that they had been through. 'Many of the engines were in process of being tinkered with and not a single tank was filled up or contained its battle equipment. Those whom some emergency has obliged to get out an ordinary car on a cold winter's morning when it has neither petrol, oil, nor water in it and has half its engine strewn about the garage will understand the difficulties that faced the Tank Corps.' The Corps had lost 188 officers and 965 other ranks in dead, wounded or missing during the last ten days; about 200 tanks had been destroyed and most of the survivors were damaged in one way or another. It was not quite the moment at which to ask for some supreme effort. If the Guards could do it, however, so could the Tank Corps. By half past noon 'B' Battalion had made twenty-two machines more or less fit for duty and they were racing towards the battle at their top speed of 4 mph. Shortly afterwards 'A' Battalion had fourteen more running and by 2 o'clock the last twenty, from 'H' Battalion, were on their way to join them. Of all the crews in the other brigades which had been railed back earlier the majority were resting or on leave. Only Courage's fifty-six remained of the great Cambrai Day armada. They were enough — just.

It was also the opportunity that the more sensible men in cavalry regiments had been waiting for — no Balaklava or Mars-la-Tour but hard pounding in unsuitable leather bandoliers with short Lee Enfield and Hotchkiss light machine gun. So far their contribution to the battle had made them a laughing stock, the Ha Ha amongst the trumpets. Now, deadly serious, they were going to serve what should have been their true vocation. Out of the saddle the cavalry ceased to be anything of a joke but became a useful fighting force. It did not seem likely that they would be mounted again in the immediate future. Corporal Dawson of the Tank Corps, who had so carefully noted the German battery at Flesquières, included in his account of the battle one observation relating to 30 November: 'Other evidence of the serious situation was the number of horses which had been stampeded back across country loose.' The Germans may have found a use for them.

It was the arrival of the Guards, however, that turned the tide. To use, positively for the last time, Mr Churchill's bucket of water simile, this was the solid object on the floor that stopped any further progress. There was far more to it than the spectacle of fresh, if that be the word, troops taking over the battle. One who was there wrote that 'The last of them had only recently left Fontaine and the Bourlon positions, caked with mud and having that air of neglect and exhaustion that follows hard fighting. When they counter-attacked at Gouzeaucourt with all the dash of fresh troops, it was noticeable that every man was brushed and polished as if for a march up the Mall. The stream of fugitives from the lost positions, seeing this, forgot their haste. Already three wildly cheering batteries had passed them going into action; these were the 235 Brigade RFA whose guns were to cover the Guards' attack.'

The eleven tanks detailed for the attack on Gouzeaucourt did not arrive until 3.50, more than two hours after the Guards had taken possession of the village and ridge. As soon as they appeared, every German gun, including some captured English ones, opened up on them. Four were knocked out almost at once. Their crews, in accordance with what was becoming Tank Corps tradition, abandoned ship along with their Lewis guns and made a valuable reinforcement for the 2nd Coldstream. Those tanks which survived were pushed forward in order to screen the Guards at their work of consolidation.

The other two Guards brigades, one attacking Gauche Wood and the other Gonnelieu, each had some tank help. Opinions differed about its effectiveness. The account given by Colonel Headlam is that the tanks were late in arriving, compelling at least one battalion to go in without them and suffer many casualties; when they did arrive they were all ditched or put out of action by artillery fire. The left attack, however, by the 3rd Coldstream, 'preceded by four tanks, captured their objective without much difficulty, although it is doubtful whether its task would have been a possible one without the cooperation of the tanks which proved of the greatest assistance to the infantry'. Rare praise, and worth having. Colonel Boraston went further: 'Tanks were in great measure responsible for the capture of the wood.' It was still not possible with the resources available to eject the Germans from Gonnelieu. Nevertheless enough had been accomplished to stop the southern assault in its tracks. General von der Marwitz, in his turn, had reached the tide-mark.

Lieutenant St Leger of the 2nd Coldstream, 21 years old and with less than four months to live, learned here another of the eternal truths. As his company marched forward, watching the hasty retreat of some others, his CSM expressed a point of view. He had never expected to see British soldiers behave like that. St Leger replied, 'If only the whole of the British army was as good as the Guards Division. I wonder why some British divisions are so good and a few so bad.' 'Oh, better led, sir. If all the army were like the Guards Division we'd go right through.'

There were a few others not to be disdained: 'We had seen the cavalry do a most gallant attack during the afternoon. Some hundreds of them had galloped hell-for-leather from the right in a direction half-left across our front about 600 yards away. We were left in peace for a moment as the Huns turned all their machine guns on to the cavalry ... emptying about a quarter of their saddles. They galloped back into a hollow, dismounted and attacked on foot, turning the Huns out of a sunken road.' Nor did they finish there. On the right of the 1st Guards Brigade, between Gauche Wood and Revelon Ridge with its far flank in the air, lay a Kitchener battalion. The nearest company commander, not unreasonably, declined to leave his wretched position without orders from his own CO. Major Little of the cavalry had a better grasp of the situation and for all practical purposes assumed command. The battalion shifted its front and made some effort to dig in. When the cavalry Colonel arrived 'both [he and Little] seemed to be thoroughly enjoying the war ... an air of "we are the Cavalry, you are the Guards, we know and trust each other, but these Mudshire civilians, we must bear with them and make the best of a bad job".' All of which was admirable, save only for one thing. Much of the cavalry was Indian Army, regiments with famous if half-forgotten names like Hodson's and Gardiner's Horse. Every sowar was a fine soldier, in France only out of duty to the King-Emperor and braver men never crossed saddle. The pathetic fact was that they seemed to have wandered into the wrong play, a ruder and noisier affair than any they had known and one which lacked parts for them. European winters, cold, wet and snowy, were enemies enough and inevitably they had been kept behind for long periods in the hope that some opportunity for employment might turn up. This was all that could be offered. It was their misfortune to be in the wrong continent and the wrong century.

Not all the British officers present shared the superior philosophy of Major Lamb. St Leger told how 'We passed our Brigadier [Champion de Crespigny] standing by the side of the road, smoking a cigarette, notebook in hand. We found afterwards that he was taking the names of everyone of the 12th Division going back and heard that he had put 1500 men under arrest.'

Complimentary messages flowed into General Feilding. From the Corps Commander came, to all ranks of the Guards Division, 'his high appreciation of the prompt manner in which they turned out on 30 November, counter-attacked through a disorganized rabble and retook Gouzeaucourt. The very fine attack which they subsequently carried out against Quentin Ridge and Gauche Wood, resulting in the capture of these important positions was worthy of the highest traditions of the Guards.' Which was true; it may be worth adding that one of the officers was to see the place again before his military career closed. Lieutenant-Colonel Viscount Gort, not yet VC*, commanding the 4th Grenadiers, decided to make a reconnaissance on his own and was severely wounded for his pains.

After so many years it is possible to be a little more just to General Pulteney's Corps than he himself felt able to be at the time. That there were fugitives in large numbers cannot be gainsaid. Nor is it necessary to point the obvious, that a lot of these were little more than uniformed navvies whom nobody expected to fight; others were gunners, who behaved honourably, bringing back with them their optical sights and, sometimes, breech-blocks for use another day. Lord Cavan, Lieutenant-General then, Field-Marshal in due course, was everything the imagination conjures up as a Guards General. Three years after Cambrai he was invited to write an Introduction to the History of the 20th (Light) Division. It deserves to be set out in full: 'When one feels a personal affection for a Division such as I do for the 20th, it is the pleasantest task to record it publicly. The 20th Division never failed me, and never failed its neighbours, during the time that I had the honour of commanding the XIVth Corps. How can one say more?' The Division's

* Lord Gort won the Cross nine months later in almost exactly the same spot.

finest hours were on the Somme and in the Ypres Salient but nothing in its part during the Cambrai operations needs to be cried down.

The 55th Division received something more like justice from Sir Frederick Maurice. When writing of the events of 9 April, 1918, and how 'Bethune was saved by the splendid defence of the 55th West Lancashire Division,' he added that 'Not many months before the same Division under the same commander, Sir H. Jeudwine, had given way before the German counter-attack at Cambrai, when weary, weak in numbers, and holding a very extended front. It had then been subjected to a great deal of ill-founded criticism, but in this battle it sent a proud answer to its critics and told them that the simple process of judging by results, which has so often been commended, is rarely applicable in war, and that the popular cry for victims when things are not going well is wrong in nine cases out of ten.' The 12th Division, no less deserving, went unchronicled though Sir Archibald Montgomery, in his *Story of the Fourth Army*, had appreciative things to say about it. The two Victoria Crosses won on 30 November speak for themselves.

So much for the south end of the battle. It is time to go back to Bourlon Wood on the morning of 30 November. Here, in a more defensible position and far less exhausted before the battle began, lay three fine divisions. The 2nd, regulars for the most part, had been through almost everything and still had a year's fighting ahead of it. Yet when Sir Douglas Haig came to write his Foreword to its History he concentrated on one affair only: 'The holding of the line at Bourlon Wood on 30 November, 1917, when the Second Division, in the centre of the German Northern Attack on that day, with the stout-hearted London Divisions on either side of them, prevented a local reverse on another part of the line from developing consequences far more serious.' The 2nd and its right-hand neighbour the 47th were, of course, the divisions ear-marked for Italy but given back in order to stop any possible rot. Far more rot set in than anybody had bargained for and they were never to see the Alps.

The 'stout-hearted London divisions', 47th and 56th, were only a half of the capital's contribution to the Army. In Territorial battalions with such good Victorian secondary titles (since 1908 they had all been absorbed into the new London Regiment) as The Civil Service Rifles, the Kensingtons, The London Rifle Brigade, The Queen's Westminsters, Tower Hamlets' Rifles, London Scottish and Post Office Rifles, they had flocked to the colours more swiftly than most. Two more divisions of them were in the field, the 58th in France since January and the 60th about to take Jerusalem. These were the non-regulars with the longest history, directly in line with the Trained Bands of the first Elizabeth by way of all the various Volunteer Corps to the City Imperial Volunteers that had done so well in South Africa.

Such were the men, genuine or honorary Cockneys, who faced down the strongest German attack since Second Ypres.

It began with a very heavy bombardment of the kind that everybody had now come to expect. Germany still had a monopoly of mustard gas and great stocks of it. Saturation by this weapon seemed, reasonably enough, to be the best way in which to make the English divisions ready to receive their assailants. Choked for a certainty; with luck, blinded also. It worked quite well. German shells doused the wood with dichloroethyl sulphate, known since 1854 but its potentialities only recently appreciated by the Teutonic mind, and poisoned the undergrowth. On the right was the 1/19th London Regiment, still better known as the Poplar and Stepney Rifles, commanded by Lieutenant-Colonel R.S.I. Friend of the The Buffs. When the gas shells began to fall it counted some 600 effectives. By the time the gassing was over about seventy were on their feet. The rest were blinded. All this did little enough for the Kaiser's regiments. The guns, rifles and machine guns of London tore into the attackers, fifty-six Vickers guns to each division. The methods of the British army on 1 July, 1916, have been fairly criticized. One hears less fault-finding with the Germans, though they were, at this point in the war, little or no better. Brigadier-General Coke, commanding a brigade in 56th Division, wrote to his old friend General Snow: 'From a bank just above my battle HQ we had an excellent view of Bourlon Wood and the surrounding country. At 9 am on the 30th we could see at least three battalions of Germans coming over the open at us and with his field guns being brought into position by horse teams. Needless to say, not a moment was lost in getting our own artillery on to them and their columns were severely cut up. However, their attack was by no means stopped and my men had a long and bitter bombing fight on the trenches. The Boches nearly turned us out but we counter-attacked and succeeded in keeping our positions. The fight continued until about 4 pm.'

There was no question of infantry dribbling forward and carrying positions by skilful infiltration. The batteries which had supported the Guards in Bourlon Wood remained to harass the enemy. It was a field day for them. 'They could fire into the brown, it was not necessary to select targets, the enemy formations being so dense; in fact it was like the early days of the war when they attacked arm in arm.' The divisions from Russia would need to do better when the heaviest blow of them all would be struck.

Thus it was all along the line. To pick out a single company of a New Army battalion is hardly fair to the rest, but this is its story. The Essex Regiment, now no more, never claimed glamour. Its 13th, New Army, battalion had nothing to distinguish it from some hundreds of others. It was mere chance that placed it squarely in front of the German tide. As the 2nd Divisional report put it: 'The situation of all the troops in the Bourlon Salient was critical, and should the line break between Bourlon and Moeuvres the prospect of a big reverse would have to be faced.' At 8 pm, long after dark, one NCO, Sergeant Legg, and a runner reached battalion HQ with news of 'D' Company's predicament — isolated and surrounded since morning by great numbers of German troops. Captain Jessop, the Company Commander, was wounded but still living. Of three German machine-guns enfilading a platoon position from the bridge east of Lock 5 one had been knocked out and the others driven off. Hundreds of the attackers had fallen to rifle and Lewis-gun fire but ammunition was running low. Captain Jessop was confident of relief, or so he bravely said, but the possibility that one last rush might overwhelm them was very real. In good 18th century fashion he called a council of war. Present were Lieutenant J.D. Robinson, 2nd Lieutenant E.L. Corps, CSM A.H. Edwards, and Sergeants Phillips, Parsons, Fairbrass, Lodge and Legg. 'It was unanimously determined to fight to the last and have no surrender.' Sergeant Legg and his companion took four hours to get through to the CO. By that time 'D' Company no longer existed. Mounds of German dead concealed the mud-stained khaki. The line held. 'New Army discipline' came in more than one form. During the next Two Minutes' Silence you might spare a thought for 'D' Coy, 13th Essex.

By nightfall von der Marwitz could see that his gallant attempt at a mighty victory was not going to succeed. Seven German divisions had failed to shake the three British; every piece of ground gained had been retaken by instant counter-attack. By the same token it was at last equally plain to Sir Douglas and Sir Julian that Moeuvres and Bourlon Wood were not for them. The noise of battle died away; the burial parties went about their business. Activity transferred itself upwards. Sir Thomas D'Oyly Snow, in his last days of command, noted on 2 December that 'The activity in the air now is terrific and we must build aeroplanes as hard as we can'. Clearly the tank was far less important; certainly the Germans thought so.

There were, obviously, lessons here for everybody. On the British side, tanks had won their spurs but they were not virtuosi of the battlefield. Until they could move much faster and keep out more than small-arms fire they needed escorting by infantry, protection by artillery barrages, smoke of their own producing, air support where possible and at least half-decent communications. In the defensive battle there was no place for them; nor would there be until a stronger tank with its guns in a turret rather than a sponson could crouch behind an *épaulement* and become an artillery weapon. For the time being the fighting tank was, like the tin-opener whose function it shared, a one-purpose product.

Supply tanks were another matter. There would always be a place for them from now onwards. Artillery had learned that it was now possible to bombard something without giving the target considerable advance warning. The dominance of the heavy gun was beginning to fade as the aircraft, their engines and their bombs, waxed in power. If an aeroplane coming from 50 miles away could deliver an equal weight of explosive with fair accuracy there could be no future for the road movements of heavy and unwieldy objects capable only of hitting a target relatively close by.

The infantry was changing. Colonel Lewis's gun and Sir Wilfrid Stokes's mortar had made all the difference in point of fire power. A platoon could now bring down as much in the way of musketry as the company of 1914. Another invaluable club had just been added to its bag. The hand grenade had been used in the English Civil War but then allowed to languish forgotten. The Germans had revived it at the beginning of this war. After various shifts and expedients the army had settled upon the pineapple-shaped Mills 36 — invaluable in trench warfare but hard to throw very far, except under range conditions. Now, late in 1917, came the discharger cup — a steel pot, slightly longer and wider than a Mills bomb, with a pair of hinged lugs that screwed behind the foresight protector of the short rifle. Put a grenade in it, having pulled out the pin but left the lever to be held in place, load the rifle with an unbulleted ballistite cartridge, put the butt on the ground between your feet with the whole thing at an angle of about 45° and press the trigger. The bomb will then go as a lobbed tennis ball goes for about 100 yards and explode damagingly when its four seconds are up. Not Bisley accurate but practice makes it reasonably so. The rifle bomber and the Lewis gunner made the infantry platoon a division in miniature. It only remained to exhort the less experienced to keep strictly to their advancing formations — extended file, arrowhead and the rest — and to avoid bunching. Every sociable instinct tells a man to seek the company of his fellows, especially in times of stress, but to do so spells death or wounds. The Guards, rigid in this as in everything else, suffered far fewer casualties than most when crossing the open. Bunching around tanks, in particular, was a form of suicide. There was little enough time left for these lessons to be digested.

The German army also had to go back to school. Although one is constantly told that the infiltration tactics, so successful in March, 1918, were rehearsed at Cambrai it does not seem to be true; report after report tells of grey-clad infantry coming on in waves as it had done at First Ypres. Now that Germany had the initiative and every need to employ its superior strength before the coming of the Americans, this must be put right. It was.

While these matters were occupying men's minds Sir Douglas accepted the inevitable; many people thought he might have done so earlier, with advantage. The advanced positions were impossible against the day, probably soon, when the next German attack would come. On 4 December withdrawal began to a far better defensible line centred on the Flesquières ridge, leaving the chemically soused wood and villages for anyone to occupy. Even in that operation something miscarried. For the last time it is Baker-Carr's story: 'By a miraculous piece of luck I happened to visit the Third Army Headquarters on the morning of the 4th of December. After discussing my business with Major-General (now Sir Louis) Vaughan, I got up to take my leave. "This withdrawal is rather disappointing," he said, as he wished me goodbye. "But you'll get all your tanks out all right, I hope." "What do you mean?" I asked. "I haven't heard anything about a withdrawal." "What!" he exclaimed. "Orders were sent to Elles this morning telling him that the line was being withdrawn to the original position tonight, and that all tanks must be clear by 11 o'clock." Elles went into GHQ early this morning. I saw Fuller, but he knew nothing about it. "How was the envelope addressed?" [asked Vaughan] "To Elles personally, by name. That probably accounts for it. You'd better rush back to Tank Headquarters and see that orders are issued immediately." Hastily I dashed off to Albert, where I told Fuller what had happened, and we found the orders lying unopened on Elles' table. In a few minutes urgent messages were despatched to all tank units warning them of the coming move. Many valuable hours had already been lost, and it looked as though a large number of tanks, which had been dismantled for the purpose of repairs, would have to be abandoned. Feverish activity prevailed throughout the afternoon and evening until the last possible moment. Many of the tanks were put into condition to enable them to move but many also, alas, had to be left, although attempts were made to render them useless to the enemy by blowing them up.' The 'G' staff work of Third Army maintained its incorrigible amateurishness up to the very end.

The withdrawal was carried out during the days between 4 and 7 December. The Tank Corps, though furious at having to leave machines fit for use behind them, were not ill-satisfied. Their contribution to the battles of the last fortnight, especially the practical demonstration of their ability to cross any trench, crush or uproot any wire and kill any machine-gun post, had brought a host of new friends. Infantry commanders, whether participants in the Cambrai battle or anxious to add to their professional knowledge, sought out Erin and Wailly in order to learn the ways of the Corps. Not everybody found this necessary. Months later, between the March Retreat and the Battle of Amiens, Baker-Carr was addressed on the subject. ' "I know far more about tanks than anybody else, Baker, and this is what you are to do." He then proceeded to outline a scheme which was utterly impossible to carry out. Such trivialities as time and space were completely ignored and the tanks were ordered to dash about a battlefield like a terrier in a cornfield chasing rabbits.' Until he was run over and killed by a car five years later Lieutenant-General Sir George Montague

Harper remained honestly persuaded that only he had a perfect understanding of the future shape of war.

The Staff at GHQ deserves credit. Whether from motives that were educational, historical or merely morale-boosting they wrote down the whole thing: *The Story Of A Great Fight. An account of the operations of the 47th, 2nd and 56th Divisions in the neighbourhood of Bourlon Wood on the 30th November 1917* reads like *The Ballad of The Revenge*, with a dozen Sir Richard Grenvilles — and deserves the same immortality.

CHAPTER ELEVEN

'NOW TELL US ALL ABOUT THE WAR, AND WHAT THEY FOUGHT EACH OTHER FOR.'

The Battle of Blenheim

Robert Southey

THEN, WITH ALL PASSION SPENT, a greater power took over. General Snow, his time in command nearly up, wrote of it in his diary: 'Deep snow and blizzard. Cold is not the word for it. All roads back from us quite blocked.' Even blocked was not the word for it. Snow had been threatening for some while; showers of it had indeed fallen at various times during the fortnight-long battle. Now it had come in earnest, with the whole of north-eastern France looking like the inside of a Victorian paper-weight. Movement of any kind, movement designed not with hostile intent but simply to keep men alive, became nearly impossible to wheeled traffic. Had the Deity sent it a week earlier the consequences would have been even more interesting and the idiocy of Christian men exposed. Whether in those places where their lines were separated by so little, English and German private soldiers surreptitiously helped each other is nowhere recorded. It would not be surprising. In an almost equally awful mountain winter in Spain a century earlier simple soldiers had momentarily buried their hatchets and shared their miseries. Something like it had come again, for a mighty blizzard was sweeping over most of northern Europe.

Their betters had far more important things to occupy them. Once again, as after the Dardanelles, there needed to be an enquiry charged with finding out why the German Second Army was not fleeing through the snow pursued by five divisions of cavalry. Sir Douglas, instructed by Sir Julian, made his own report without loss of time. It was in the War Office before the year ended. The faults, it posited, were those of junior officers and soldiers of the 12th and 55th Divisions. No officer of field rank or above was to blame for anything. It was polished up and submitted to the Secretary of State, Lord Derby, on New Year's Day with the approval of Robertson, the DMO (Maurice) and that admirable dugout − his words − Major-General Callwell. One passage is more pointed than the rest: 'No report has been received from

171

Lieut.-General Sir W. Pulteney … and therefore we desire it to be understood that we may have further observations to make on receipt of his report, which has been called for.' Anyone is at liberty to guess at 'Putty's' thoughts. He was himself a Guardsman and no doubt thought as the other Guardsmen involved had done. All the same, it was his soldiers who were being calumniated. Especially when it came to para 6: 'We have considered the reports of his Divisional Generals. This Corps had gained a considerable amount of ground during the offensive of ten days earlier, but the Divisional Commanders seem [mark that word] to have been satisfied that they could hold their new positions if attacked, and these positions had already been placed in a state of defence.' One question that would have caused the ex-Corps Commander some difficulty was not put. On the evening of the 29th Jeudwine, rightly persuaded that the German attack was imminent, had asked his Corps Commander, Snow, to arrange with Pulteney for the heavy guns of IIIrd Corps to be turned on to the Banteux and 22 Ravines. General Snow was of the same mind. It remained uncertain whether Pulteney had been asked and had refused or whether no request had been made. The former was by far the more likely. In any event, nothing was done and the masses of German infantry forming up under the noses of Pulteney's and Snow's divisions were allowed to do so at their ease. Something had gone wrong somewhere. All three Generals were Old Etonians and behaved properly in keeping the matter to themselves. Pulteney was given a command at home which he relinquished eventually on promotion, if such it be, to Black Rod. The others had mixed fortunes. Jeudwine saw the war through to its end, his stature increasing all the time. Scott lasted only until April, 1918. Sir Douglas had never been a wholehearted admirer. Among Sir Launcelot Kiggell's papers is a letter from the C-in-C, written shortly after the Monchy-Le-Preux battle, in which he calls both Scott and his Division 'not very clever'.

'Wully' Robertson, though putting his name to the report, had not the remotest interest in the subject. In his autobiography the Battle of Cambrai gets two lines. Of the other investigators, Callwell was an amiable sexagenarian, vastly experienced in Victorian wars but observing this one from Whitehall. Major-General Frederick Maurice had all his time taken up with the crisis over manpower, leading to his denunciation of Mr Lloyd George, the Maurice Debate and the end of his own military career. One cannot avoid the feeling that loyalty, a proper consciousness of the enquirers' own inexperience in 1917-style warfare and the need to support an endangered Chief all made contributions to the rhetorical questions they posed. Was Sir Douglas justified in undertaking the attack on 20 November with the forces then at his disposal? Yes. 'From the information in [his] possession he was justified in considering that he would be able to secure and hold the high ground about Bourlon Wood.' Sir Douglas might indeed have done so had the Commander of his IVth Corps been able to see that his orders to one divisional General were obeyed. The Report finds that: 'If this high ground had been left in the enemy's possession at this stage of the battle, our troops would have been badly placed for defensive purposes, and some withdrawal from the ground won would have been necessary. The extent of the success gained in the first 48 hours therefore appears to us to justify Sir Douglas Haig's decision to continue the battle with the object of gaining complete possession of this high ground, and the fact that the enemy's main [mark that word again] attack on 30 November was delivered against this sector of the front and was successfully repulsed shows, in our opinion, that this decision was correct.' No mention of cavalry sweeps, beating-up of rear areas or anything else; nor does the word 'tank' appear anywhere. The whole operation, it seems, was 'to gain possession of this high ground'. Much like the saucer's rim around Ypres.

There is a deal of faint praise in it. The German attack 'fell mainly upon the left of the 55th Division and the right of the 12th Division, i.e. about the locality where old and new line met and where the two Corps met. This could not fail to have been an advantage to the enemy.' And, by inference, some uninspired planning to allow such a joint to be so weak. 'The 20th and 29th Divisions on the left of the 12th Division may be said to have fairly well held their ground' is hardly flattering. The best was reserved for Scott and Jeudwine: 'Our infantry and machine-gunners did not at certain points offer so determined an opposition to the enemy's onset as the Generals commanding were entitled to expect, and that there was a certain lack of efficiency in subordinate leadership.' There is much more on the same note: 'The 55th Division was holding 11,000 yards of front, which is not an excessive length for a Division at normal strength occupying a carefully prepared defensive position.' This observation, questionable in any event, is rather spoilt by the sequitur: 'This particular Division had, however, been heavily engaged in Flanders in August and September and had suffered great losses during those two months; it therefore necessarily contained an inordinate proportion of newly joined drafts. It furthermore was considerably below strength.' None of which irrelevances, apparently, made any difference to the fact that it ought to have held a front 'not excessive for a Division at normal strength'. One cannot wonder at the contempt this document excited once its contents became known. Colonel Oldfield probably spoke for everybody, certainly for all Captains and less: 'The result of the Cambrai enquiry is very misleading and discreditable. Someone ought to be kicked.'

One must pose some further questions after the fashion of little

Peterkin. Was the battle worth while, what were its consequences and lessons and ought it to have been fought at all?

'We are of opinion that the attack on November 20th was justifiable in view of the information in Sir Douglas Haig's possession of the enemy's strength at the point of attack, and that the operations were well planned and executed.' Not everybody adhered to this. Sir Douglas's own Director of Military Operations, General Davidson, for one: 'With the knowledge we possessed in November of the almost inevitable trial of strength which would take place in the spring when the Germans would have brought over the heavy reinforcement of divisions released from the Russian front, and before the arrival of the Americans, I believe our wisest course would have been to cancel the Cambrai operations, conserve the tank force, and settle down to the necessary and urgent measures to meet the German onslaught.' It would be unjust to the General's memory to suggest that the advice he gave at the time was other than that. Brigadier-General Charteris gives another point of view: 'It is a tremendous responsibility for DH and for the first time in the war 'I' has been for holding back and 'G' has been all for going on. DH gives us his final and conclusive reason for going on — that "success here will greatly help the situation in Italy, where the last Italian retreat, to the Piave, is serious". He intends to stop short after 48 hours, unless by that time the situation is so promising that we can take further risks.' That was a few hours before Zero.

Davidson was only the second man in 'G' Branch. At its head sat the quaintly named Sir Launcelot Kiggell, addressed in correspondence by Sir Douglas as 'My dear old Kigge'. Somehow Sir Launcelot never seemed to be the right man in the right place. He was Irish by birth and education, an infantryman who had seldom if ever commanded infantry. For the past 30 years, or very nearly so, he had held one Staff appointment after another, mostly in 'A' branch, including a spell in South Africa as a member of the military family of Sir Redvers Buller. It does not appear that he had ever been under fire. Certainly he had had no overseas service in this war until he arrived during the last days of December, 1915, to be the new Chief of the General Staff to the new C-in-C. As a theoretical ʳoldier he had credentials; the 6th edition of Hamley's *Operations of War* ʰs his work. Though such talents should never be wasted, it is ˢstionable whether they were the ones needed for his vitally important Kiggell, though he never visited the Salient, had put his money on ᵛres offensive and would not hedge his bets. By mid-October, when Cambrai plan was sanctioned, the situation had changed for the The reserves that should have been hurried in once the tanks had ʰe crust were either in their soggy graves or dressed in hospital ᵉll appears to have accepted that Bourlon Wood should be the first objective, followed by a lateral expansion northwards. *The Book of Proverbs* avers that 'In the multitude of counsellors there is safety'. It can hardly have seemed like that to the Commander-in-Chief.

Equally important, possibly more so, is the second question. Why, at the end of the 48 hours, did Sir Douglas decide to transform his successful raid into yet another bare-knuckle fight? 'From the information in [his] possession he was justified in considering that he would be able to secure and hold the high ground about Bourlon Wood.' No question now of some great exploitation. It was merely a matter of driving Germans from the high ground and improving the line. Nowhere is there any mention of the fact that General Harper's failure to obey orders had wrecked the timetable and brought the whole edifice down. Williams-Ellis probably put his finger on the reason: 'When desirable posts of vantage were actually in our hands, we had fallen a prey to "land hunger" and had still fought on and continued to advance in order to consolidate these new and delightful possessions.' The verdict must surely go in favour of Major-General 'Tavish' Davidson. Politicians demanded a further inquest. General Smuts was coroner. It added nothing.

The balance sheet shows no advantage; possibly the reverse. The Third Army losses were, in round figures, 44,000 men (6,000 of them taken prisoner on 30 November), 55 medium and heavy guns plus 103 field pieces. Enemy losses are estimated (no exact figure will ever be known) at about 50,000 including 10,500 prisoners. The tally of captured weapons is near enough the same. The land hunger was not satisfactory. A good stretch of the Hindenburg Line remained in British hands, possibly giving some men a more comfortable winter than they would otherwise have had. There were no further benefits. When the greatest German attack of all came in March the entire right of Byng's army was driven back for something like 10 miles across the zone devastated by the Germans in their withdrawal of a year before and in whose ruined villages men had been trying to live ever since.

The battle had demonstrated serious faults. In all probability some parts of the lower reaches of the Army were not of the Somme quality any more; it could hardly have been otherwise. At the other end matters were almost worse. No Corps Commander had distinguished himself. The Londoners were furious with Woollcombe because he had, in defiance of custom, ordered the cramming of Bourlon Wood by both relievers and relieved when under gas bombardment. Casualties were as heavy as they were needless. 'Putty' was much criticized for his failure to set his artillery on the beginnings of the German counter-attack. In any event, he had earned a rest. Snow was, quite genuinely, a sick man. All were sent home with the thanks of the county.

Their replacements caused some surprise. IIIrd Corps went to Butler, 47 years old (which many people reckoned far too young) another officer who had spent nearly all his working life on the Staff, the last two years of it at GHQ. The VIIth was given to Walter Congreve, and the choice was widely approved. A Rifleman, a Boer War VC and an officer who knew what it was like to go over the bags tired, cold, hungry thirsty and with insufficient orders. The last choice has to be called inspired. The IVth Corps had not always been given talented commanders.* For a time it had suffered under the worst of them all, Henry Wilson. Woollcombe had commanded what was now the 51st Division up to the outbreak of war. He bowed out in favour of the present incumbent. 'Uncle' Harper, Henry Wilson's great friend, who knew more about tanks than anybody, was rewarded for Flesquières by promotion. Private soldiers who flagrantly disobeyed orders risked being spread-eagled across a gun-wheel and left in the sun. The General, however, became a knight and a Corps Commander. There is no space to treat of his future *faites et gestes*. Suffice it that Sir Hubert Gough spoke bitterly of how, during the March Retreat, IVth Corps inexplicably left a gap four miles wide which the German eagerly filled. Charteris had to go. His sin, at any rate the most recent one, was not so much the over-optimistic view of the hammering that the Germans had taken in Flanders as misunderstanding the extent of the threat posed by the disappearance of another front in the east. 'Dear Old Kigge' was also finally shunted off. Sir Douglas, who appears to have felt as he would on ordering the putting down of a favourite dog, was successful in obtaining for him an appointment that his talents fully justified: command of all the troops in Jersey. Charteris's successor, a saturnine Indian Army Brigadier named Cox, accidentally drowned himself off Le Touquet before making his presence much felt. Sir Herbert Lawrence, having taken his place, soon moved higher still as the new Chief of Haig's General Staff. All this was to the good. One has to thank both Generals Byng and von der Marwitz for the better quality of Staff work when the greatest test of all presented itself in 1918. Even allowing for this, the pity was that Montreuil still housed nobody capable of laying down the law on the subject of tanks. Every Branch of the Army, from farms to laundries, seemed to have its well-staffed Directorate. Not so much as a Tank Corps Captain was there to advise what his machines could or could not do.

imberley says that 'I know the (51st) Division was glad to leave IVth Corps as during the everything seemed to go wrong in the 'Q' Department.'

176

CHAPTER TWELVE

THE SHAPE OF THINGS TO COME

NONE OF THE FOREGOING alters in the smallest degree the hard lesson of Sir Julian Byng's foray. The German Army, with unlimited time and all the labour, voluntary or otherwise, that it needed had constructed a defence system as inexpugnable as the Great Wall of China had once been. The British Army, with a rudimentary mechanical device, had ridden through it wherever it pleased and that with contemptuous ease. The last time that Army had attempted the same thing, at Third Ypres, the cost of the 107,000 tons of shells used for wire cutting had been about £22,000,000, about the same as the Army Estimates for a complete year before the war. Of course the new method was a long way from being perfect. Nobody knew that better than Stern, Swinton, Wilson and Tritton. The story of their frustrations was not new. When the monk Roger Bacon had described how to make gunpowder he had been confined to his cell, denied food and refused permission to see friends. One could make a book — somebody probably has made one — about the fates of the inventors of weapons in advance of their time.

Even before Fuller had first obtained Byng's ear the work had been going on. The Mk IV Tank, with its clumsy transmission and steering, was already obsolete. Much better tanks were on the drawing-board and ones better still were in the pencil-stub-and-back-of-envelope stage. Wilson's new epicyclic gear, one of the century's great inventions, would enable the driver to steer unhelped and would do away with secondary gears and gearsmen. That was a long stride towards a superior machine. It would still not satisfy its champions, however, until it could travel a lot faster. Four mph, though about the best that a lozenge-shaped, unsprung, machine could do, was not nearly enough. The search for a 20 mph tank began. The Mk V, though better by far than the Mk IV, save in the matter of ventilation, would never approach this. The Medium A, or Whippet, was coming closer and probably represented the next generation. The French, after their disastrous experiences, were following another path. With no Hindenburg Line to be stormed they could concentrate on making great numbers of tiny tanks, crewed by two and carrying a light weapon of some kind in a revolving turret. M. Louis Renault, maker and designer of most of London's taxis, obliged. His FT 17, unkindly though not inaccurately described as 'a Paris pissoir on tracks' was just what Marshal Foch had in mind. When Stern took him to see a Mk V a week before Cambrai, 'He congratulated me on the wonderful improvements and said, "You must make quantities and quantities. We must fight mechanically. Men can no longer attack with a chance of success without armoured protection".' Not everybody took the same view. Stern had expected it from General Butler when, before his elevation, he announced that there were only 18,500 men available for tanks and that nothing more than a few Whippets would be needed. It was more painful to be told by Mr Churchill, of all people, that instead of thousands and thousands all the Army wanted was 1350 Mk Vs. A quarrel of Homeric proportions followed. Stern was sacked and an Admiral, uncontaminated by ever having seen a tank, replaced him. This was no way to treat a banker. Stern, whose business had brought him many contacts in the States, sought out the Americans. In this he carried with him Mr. Churchill's blessing and a personal letter to General Pershing. On 23 November, while the battle for Fontaine-Notre-Dame was at its height, Stern was calling on the Prime Minister to tell him that along with Pershing, Admiral Sims and other mechanically-minded men he had reached an agreement. Resources were to be pooled, a factory set up near Paris and a fine new tank, to be called the Liberty or Mk VIII, would win the war before civilization finally collapsed. GHQ was firmly of opinion that the tank had shot its bolt. Elles was told so flatly. 'A splendid show,' observed Sir Launcelot Kiggell, still just Chief of the General Staff, 'seated in a Mahatma-like atmosphere of isolation and contemplation in his office at Montreuil, but one that cannot be repeated.' Their reward for success was to be the disbandment of half the Corps — some 2,500 men — in order to fill up some small gaps in the infantry. And this at a time when a far better machine, the Mk V, was beginning to appear in numbers. Elles told Baker-Carr, who demanded three days' Paris leave with no questions asked. There he visited a friend he called 'W'. Subsequent events suggest it to have been Henry Wilson; both were Greenjackets and even in 1917 the power of the Black Mafia was known even if the name was not. In any event, the message reached Marshal Foch himself and led to a request by him for 'every effort to be made to introduce as many tanks as possible', losing not an hour in the process. It was not the moment to deny the Marshal anything. Mk Vs and Whippets began to pour in.

What happened in the enemy camp was very different. The Germans, uncaptivated by the tank, built a few of their own for the sake of public opinion. They were not particularly good. When the great German attacks began in March they were made without benefit of either armour or cavalry but variations on an old theme. The Hundred Days Battle that began on 8 August showed the experience gained at Cambrai to have been invaluable. Sir Henry Rawlinson, who bore the greatest burden, had been well disposed to the tanks since they had first appeared in 1916. He had watched their fumbling performance, had not been over-impressed but saw plainly that here was something worth developing. The Mk V, he noted, was 'a very different proposition from those we have yet had', and, jointly with John Monash, he convinced the Australians. The little Hamel battle of 4 July, 1918, showed how the business should be done. Nobody would assert that tanks alone carried out the advance to victory; nor would any reasonably well-informed person assert that it could have been done without them. Action generates reaction. The German army turned a large proportion of its artillery into anti-tank guns; it would be fair to assert that the mighty 88 was Prince Rupprecht's child. On the 21st, says the Official History, 'he ordered the canal crossings from Crevecoeur to Banteux to be held at all costs. Anti-aircraft guns, mounted on lorries, were said to have done extremely well against the tanks, and the Sixth and Fourth Armies were consequently ordered to send all such weapons to the battle front.' Here was another shape of things to come. Before the war Krupps had advertised for sale their 'balloon gun'. Very early in the war the French had refined it into the 'auto canon', a 75 with a high-angle mounting clamped on the back of a De Dion lorry. A number of them had been procured to help out with the defence of London against Zeppelins. The German version, almost identical, having proved its effectiveness as a tank-buster, was taken into service and continued to grow. The British army, with no money to spare for anything worth having, waited until Hitler's war was well advanced before producing much the same thing in the shape of the Archer self-propelled gun. No use was made of the good 3″ AA gun until 1943 when a number were captured in Tunisia. They had been sent to Russia, hastily remounted on wheels, turned into quite good anti-tank weapons and were then captured by the Germans. The Cambrai battles were responsible for all of them.

In the old Third Army sector some of the original players remained whilst others joined them. When his division stormed and seized Havrincourt again General Braithwaite suggested that in the event of their having to do it for a third time the Yorkshiremen ought to be allowed to keep the place for good. One corner of France did indeed change its sovereignty. Bourlon Wood, taken by Sir Arthur Currie's men in the last days of September, 1918, became along with Vimy Ridge for ever Canada, the gift of Madame la Republique during one of her more amiable moments. And every New

Zealand child knows, or ought to know, of the great feats of arms performed by his forefathers at Masnières and Crevecoeur at about the same time.

Then, greatly to the surprise of almost everybody except Sir Douglas Haig, the war ended before a fifth dreadful winter could be inflicted upon an exhausted world. The dress rehearsal had shown up all the faults. But it had been all right on the night. The speech after the final curtain, by Williams-Ellis, ends with 'every other factor being cancelled out, the fact that the French and English possessed tanks and the Germans did not was just enough to win the last war for the Allies'. And to give the vanquished furiously to think about the next production.

SPECIAL ORDER, NO. 6

1. To-morrow the Tank Corps will have the chance for which it has been waiting for many months, to operate on good going in the van of the battle.
2. All that hard work and ingenuity can achieve has been done in the way of preparation.
3. It remains for unit commanders and for Tank crews to complete the work by judgment and pluck in the battle itself.
4. In the light of past experience I leave the good name of the Corps with great confidence in your hands.
5. I propose leading the attack of the Centre Division. November 19, 1917

HUGH ELLES,
B-G, Commanding Tank Corps.

It was not Elles' fault that the newspapers invented the sub-Nelson passage about every Tank doing its damndest. Mention of it made him very angry indeed. The man may be measured by the contents of his telegram to Swinton: 'Colonel Swinton Committee of Imperial Defence London G618 26 AAA all ranks thank you AAA your show Elles.'

THIRD ARMY ORDER OF BATTLE
(Formations only)

Guards Division (Major-General G. P. T. Feilding):
  1 Gds., 2 Gds., 3 Gds. Brigades.
2nd Division (Major-General C. E. Pereira):
  5, 6, 99 Brigades.
6th Division (Major-General T. O. Marden):
  16, 18, 71 Brigades.
12th (Eastern) Division (Major-General A. B. Scott):
  35, 36, 37 Brigades.
20th (Light) Division (Major-General W. Douglas Smith):
  59, 60, 61 Brigades.
29th Division (Major-General Sir B. de Lisle):
  86, 87, 88 Brigades.
36th (Ulster) Division (Major-General O. S. W. Nugent):
  107, 108, 109 Brigades.
40th Division (Major-General J. Ponsonby):
  119, 120, 121 Brigades.
47th (2nd London) Division (Major-General Sir G. F. Gorringe):
  140, 141, 142 Brigades.
51st (Highland) Division (Major-General G. M. Harper):
  152, 153, 154 Brigades.
55th (1st West Lancashire) Division (Major-General H. S. Jeudwine):
  164, 165, 166 Brigades.
56th (1st London) Division (Major-General F. A. Dudgeon):
  167, 168, 169 Brigades.
59th (2nd North Midland) Division (Major-General C. F. Romer):
  176, 177, 178 Brigades.
61st (2nd South Midland) Division (Major-General C. J. Mackenzie):
  182, 183, 184 Brigades.

62nd (2nd West Riding) Division (Major-General W. P. Braithwaite):
 185, 186, 187 Brigades.
1st Cavalry Division (Major-General R. L. Mullens):
 1, 2, 9 Cavalry Brigades.
2nd Cavalry Division (Major-General W. H. Greenly):
 3, 4, 5 Cavalry Brigades.
4th Cavalry Division (Major-General A. A. Kennedy):
 Sialkot, Mhow, Lucknow Brigades.
5th Cavalry Division (Major-General H. J. M. Macandrew):
 Secunderabad, Ambala, Canadian Brigades.
Tank Corps (Br.-General H. J. Elles):
 I. II. III. Brigades.

A NOTE ON SOURCES

IN DESCENDING ORDER OF VALUE I hold the sequence to be something like this. A few printed books — Official Histories and the like — diaries, letters and manuscript accounts written by participants, official documents such as War Diaries, more printed books and finally Personal Knowledge and Private Information. The books, both kinds of them, are listed in the Bibliography. The second category is surprisingly extensive and to list all that I have consulted would be mere showing off. Those set out below seem to me of the greatest value. I have not repeated those included in General Hobert's *A Narrative of Cambrai*, mentioned at the beginning of the text. They are still of the greatest value; along with these:-

In the Library of The Tank Museum, Bovington Camp.
Papers of Captain (later Brigadier) T R Price, DSO, MC
Action Report by 2/Lieut. W P Whyte
Papers of the late W T Dawson, once Corporal, Tank Corps.
Letter of Captain T A Crouch, DSO
Letter dated 22 March, 1968, from Capt. L N Johnson, late B Bn. Tank Corps.
1st Tank Brigade Summary of Operations
Report on Action No. 1 Coy., A Battalion 25 November, 1917
History 1st Bn. Tank Corps
War History 2nd Bn. Tank Corps
History D Battalion, Tank Corps
History 6th Bn. Tank Corps

At the Imperial War Museum, Department of Manuscripts
Letters of Major E. F. Churchill
      〃   Captain Sir George Clark
      〃   Captain G. Dent, MC
      〃   Lieut.-Col. P. N. Dingley
      〃   Brigadier R. D. Foot
      〃   Brigadier A. E. Hodgkin
      〃   Lieutenant W. B. St Leger
      〃   Lieut.-General Sir Thomas D'Oyly Snow
Miss R. Whitaker, VAD, (letters from the then Col. Oldfield)
      〃   Major-General D. N. Wimberley
      〃   Captain J. K. Wilson
      〃   Lieut.-Colonel J. D. Wyatt

At the Intelligence Corps Museum, Templer Barracks, Ashford, Kent
The Papers of Major-General F. E. Hotblack

At the Liddell Hart Centre for Military Archives, King's College, London
The Papers of Lieutenant-General Sir Launcelot Kiggell
      〃   Brigadier-General Sir James Edmonds
PRO WO/106/314 'Report On The Battle of Cambrai'
Service Periodicals 95/357-380 War Diary Third Army
Royal Engineers Journal June, 1964 – Obituary of Capt. W. H. Livens
Royal Engineers Journal August, 1988 – Article by the late Bryan Frayling on Livens and the Messines Tunnels.
Royal Tank Corps Journal March, 1933 – 'Cambrai Myth', by F. E. Hotblack
RAOC Journal November, 1935 – Article by Capt. S. G. Grant on The Ostend Landing
Two newspaper entries deserve mention. *The Times* for 12 December, 1986 includes a long article by Captain Donald Marendaz, RFC. *The Daily Telegraph* for 8 June, 1991, treats of the 18″ Elswick guns.

Then come those stalwarts Personal Knowledge and Private Information. Few, if any, men writing now can have first-hand experience of these events. In all humility, I regard myself as a kind of connecting-file. Like most men of my generation, I was born to parents who saw it all. My father, badly wounded at Bullecourt, most of his friends, masters at prep and public school (both of them in garrison towns) and many others whom I knew in boyhood had 'been there', though they talked less about it than we who only did Hitler's war. As a young, between-wars, Territorial machine-gun officer my mentors – and revered friends – were both ex-MGC officers, each a holder of the MC, Majors G. D. Bacon and T. R. Reid. My first CO, Colonel D.

J. Dean, VC, had been at Cambrai with the 24th Division; my next, Colonel (later Brigadier) Eric Foster Hall, MC, was there as Adjutant of the 1st Buffs in the 6th Division, and about every twelfth man in the battalion wore at least, the ribbons of what we called Squeak and Wilfred. In later years my knowledge was enriched by many conversations with the late Charles Carrington, perhaps the most gifted memorialist of all. Something, surely, must have rubbed off over so many years.

PRINTED BOOKS

First amongst these must come, of course, that volume of the Official History treating of the last months of 1917. This is something of a curiosity of its kind. It did not appear until the year 1948, having been set aside during a period of stringent economy in order that the greater events of 1918 might be finished first. Sir James Edmonds was 87 when he initialled the Preface; his feelings are understandable. The actual work was done, for the most part, by a stripling of 61, Captain Wilfrid Miles. Even after so many years one can feel the animus against Sir Julian Byng. "[The Battle] had little effect upon the general situation,' as the book begins, proclaims its tone. There is abundant criticism of the way in which the German counter-offensive was allowed to come about but nothing approaching Fuller's panegyric when writing of the tanks and their crews. The delay did at least mean that the German archives were available and used. Edmonds seems to share the view of General Davidson that it were better not to have fought a November battle at all. Here there may be room for more than one opinion, but the Official History is the only mine from which can be dug exact information of the hour-to-hour doings of every unit, formation or ad hoc band. A time capsule indeed, when one remembers that other war that was being waged when all this was being pieced together. Where it is factual one may accept it as the nearest we shall ever get to Holy Writ. In matters of opinion it is less so.

The other Official work that repays inspection is *Services of Military Officers*, published in 1920.

Then come the unofficial histories, the books written by private gentlemen, most of whom had seen service themselves. Those by C.R.M.F. Cruttwell, *A History of the Great War*, (Oxford, 1934) Carey & Scott, *The Great War*, (Cambridge, 1929) and *The First World War* by Cyril Falls (Longmans, 1960) are all valuable for, among other things, showing Cambrai in perspective. The last is particularly interesting. Captain Falls, aged 34, wrote in his *History of the 36th Division*, published in 1922 in Belfast, that 'Whatever chances of success it might have had were extinguished by the failure to take Flesquières.' A little further on, however, he remarks that 'It appears probable today that had 2 fresh Divisions been passed through after the troops had reached their objectives — disregarding Flesquières which actually did very little harm — they could have been firmly consolidated on the Bourlon Ridge by next morning and possibly reached the outskirts of Cambrai.' The Chichele Professor of Military History, nearly 40 years on, looks back with less feeling of chances thrown away: 'It (the Flesquières failure) had a serious effect on the time-table.... it was too late to put the cavalry through. Had this been a summer battle the shortcomings might perhaps have been remedied that evening, but soon after 4 pm darkness was gathering.' On one point he is enthusiastic: 'The tanks were magnificent. They accomplished all that their commander had promised.' And anyone wishing to learn more about the 'blizzard of snow that may almost be called historic' which followed the battle need look no further than the *History of the 36th Division*. Cyril Falls' books, whether written as Captain or Professor, are always a joy to the reader. Only Sir Edward Spears can be reckoned in the same class. His *Prelude to Victory*, published in 1939, is essential reading. The General once told me that he had intended to write further volumes but Hitler got in first. A great loss, for nobody now living can know what Spears knew. The books of personal reminiscence must inevitably vary in quality. Baker-Carr's *From Chauffeur to Brigadier*, Bertie Stern's *Tanks: The Log-Book of a Pioneer* and Swinton's *Eyewitness* are all admirable. The book *Tank Warfare*, by Lieut. Frank Mitchell (Nelson, 1934) has much to commend it.

In point of straight history, there is no substitute for the works of the divisional writers. These were, of course, unofficial and it was almost a matter of luck whether a formation possessed somebody with the will and means to chronicle its doings. There are no histories of any of the Cavalry Divisions. The others vary from such 2-volume works as the *Histories of the Second and Sixty Second Divisions*, both by the author Everard Wyrall, to the little paperback affair by General Marden telling of his own 6th Division. Most were reviewed knowledgeably by Cyril Falls in his *War Books*, Peter Davies, 1930. They all contain information not to be found anywhere else.

Regimental Histories, since they have to deal with many battalions, are not usually fruitful of information. There is one exception. Lieut.-Col. M. M. Haldane's *History of the 4th Battalion the Seaforth Highlanders* (Witherby, 1930) gives an admirable account of the great fight at Fontaine-Notre-Dame. The earlier general histories consulted are *The Battle of Cambrai* by Major-General H. D. de Pree and *Langemarck and Cambrai* by Captain G. Dugdale.

Then come memoirs by the grandees of the Tank Corps. Fuller and Martel both wrote a number of books. For the purposes of this one of the most important are Fuller's *Tanks in the Great War*, (John Murray, 1920) followed by Martel's *In the Wake of the Tank* and, much later *An Outspoken*

Soldier, (Sifton Praed 1949). Though not a tank man himself, Captain Liddell Hart was entrusted with setting down the tale of armoured warfare; it appeared in his magistral *The Tanks*, (Cassell, 1959). Fuller has his biography, by Major-General A. J. Trythall, published by the same firm in 1977. Then comes the interesting part. Hugh Elles remains in the shadows. He wrote nothing himself, nor did anybody reckon it worth while to write about him. In some armoured circles his name is nearly a hissing — it lends itself to that activity — because after the war Elles abandoned the armoured dream. His subsequent career was that usual to an officer of his standing. When invited, after Hitler was becoming rather a worry, to design a new tank he came up with the A 11. It was funny without being vulgar. The fact of the matter was that Hugh Elles had become disenchanted, firmly believing the tank to be finished now that so many antidotes had appeared. Though heresy, I suggest that Elles may have had the right of it. By 1939 there were quite good tanks about the place in every country save this. The German Pz. 2, the French Char B and the Russian BT and T28 were far better than anything seen in 1918. More to the point, the War Office had even then a blueprint for the 6-pdr anti-tank gun which would have effortlessly killed any of them. And from 6-pdr to 17-pdr is only a step. Had Elles been less backward in persuading the Milnes, Montgomery-Massingberds and others that he possessed greater foresight than most history might have been different. Chamberlain's England would never have forked out for masses of tanks; for modest sums it could have made the BEF of Lord Gort capable of slaughtering every panzer that dared to show its nose, air forces permitting, rather than being almost helpless against them.

Memoirs of senior men have to include those of Sir James Marshall-Cornwall, *Wars & Rumours of Wars*, (Leo Cooper, 1984) which includes the interesting information that, at Rugby, the General shared a study with Rupert Brooke. Charteris' contribution comes in his *At GHQ*, (Cassell, 1931). Sir Beauvoir de Lisle's *Reminiscences of Sport and War*, (Eyre & Spottiswoode, 1939) is an admirable specimen of its kind. *Adventure*, by Lord Mottistone, alias Brigadier Seely, (Heinemann, 1929) adds something, in the same way as do Brigadier-General Crozier's *A Brass Hat in No Man's Land* (Cape, 1929) and *Years of Combat* by Sholto Douglas, (Collins, 1963). Baroness de la Grange tells her tale of General Pulteney, along with others of his peers, in *Open House in Flanders*, (John Murray, 1929).

A sufficiency of personal accounts by junior officers and soldiers is still to be had. Captain D. E. Hickey's *Rolling into Action* (Hutchinson), Captain D. G. Brown's *The Tank in Action* and *The First Battle of the Tanks* by J. H. Everest all deserve their places: the Guardsmen Carroll Carstairs' *A Generation Missing* (Heinemann) and Wilfred Ewart's *Scots Guard* (Rich & Cowan, 1934) are both eloquent in their own fashion. David Rorie, ADMS to the 51st Division, wrote *A Medico's Luck in the War* (Milne & Hutchinson, Aberdeen, 1929). On the opposing side there is Ernst Junger's *The Storm of Steels*, published, in translation, by Chatto & Windus in 1929. The cavalry is particularly fortunate, though none of its Divisions found a chronicler. You may remember the distinguished officer of the XIth Hussars who was denied his nice hard canter to Berlin. Captain Robert Hartman, in *The Remainder Biscuit* (Andre Deutsch, 1964) has far more than that to pass on to us who come later. Consider, for example, his story of 'two figures who came into collision in a communication trench on a pitch dark night. "Who are you?", angrily asked one voice. "And who may you be?", demanded the other. "I am Major Sir Frank Swynnerton-Dyer, Coldstream Guards," replied the first. "Oh, are you indeed," said the second. "Well, I am Lieutenant-Colonel Lord Henry Seymour, Grenadier Guards. I beat you on all three points. Get out of my way".'

There are good modern histories, brought out to mark the half-century of the battle: *The Ironclads of Cambrai* by Bryan Cooper and *The First Tank Battle* by R. Woollcombe (son to Sir Charles), the former published by Batsford and the latter by Arthur Barker. Most recent, and covering far more than this series of battles is, *Landships: British Tanks in the First World War*, by the Librarian of the Tank Museum, David Fletcher (HMSO, 1984).

INDEX

(Ranks are usually those held in 1917)